D0786519

SHAKING THE WORLD FOR JESUS

SHAKING THE WORLD FOR JESUS

MEDIA AND CONSERVATIVE EVANGELICAL CULTURE

HEATHER HENDERSHOT

THE UNIVERSITY OF CHICAGO PRESS / CHICAGO AND LONDON

HEATHER HENDERSHOT is associate
professor of media studies at Queens
College, City University of New York. She
is the author of *Saturday Morning Censors:
Television Regulation before the V-Chip* (1998)
and the editor of *Nickelodeon Nation: The History, Politics, and Economics of America's Only
Channel for Kids* (2004).

The University of Chicago Press, Chicago
60637
The University of Chicago Press, Ltd.,
London
© 2004 by The University of Chicago
All rights reserved. Published 2004
Printed in the United States of America
13 12 11 10 09 08 07 06 05 04   1 2 3 4 5
ISBN: 0-226-32679-9(cloth)

Library of Congress Cataloging-in-Publication
Data

Hendershot, Heather.
    Shaking the world for Jesus : media and
conservative evangelical culture / Heather
Hendershot.
        p. cm.
    Includes bibliographical references and index.
    ISBN 0-226-32679-9 (alk. paper)
    1. Mass media—Religious aspects—Christianity.   2. Mass media in religion—United
States—History.   3. Evangelicalism—United
States—History.   I. Title.
    BV652.97.U6 H46 2004
    261.5'2'0973—dc22
                                            2003014235

⊚ The paper used in this publication meets
the minimum requirements of the American
National Standard for Information Sciences—
Permanence of Paper for Printed Library
Materials, ANSI Z39.48-1992.

FOR LEH

CONTENTS

ACKNOWLEDGMENTS

Sincere thanks go to the interviewees who shared their valuable time and insights with me: Scott Brickell, Lisa Carver, Robert Deaton, Eddie DeGarmo, George Flanigan, Cindy Garcia, Barbara Goodwin, David McCollough, Cindy Montano, Ben Pearson, Rev. Michael Piazza, Jonathan Richter, Marty Ruggles, Geoff Stevens, Paul Taylor, Eric Welch, Rev. Dr. Mona West, John Wimberly, and Stephen Yake. Thanks also to Walter Osborn at the Moody Bible Institute. The Queens College Media Studies Department helped fund a research trip to Chicago, and the PSC/CUNY Research Foundation funded my research in Dallas. Womyn pals Anna McCarthy, Laurel George, and Rachael Adams helped out with an early version of chapter 5, and Marie Griffith later provided valuable feedback on chapters 3 and 5. Allison X. Miller provided terrific assistance in editing chapters 5 and 6. Thanks also to Robert Wuthnow and the Center for the Study of Religion at Princeton for inviting me to their workshop to discuss chapter 2; Henry Jenkins, who invited me to MIT several times to present nascent versions of the research; Randall Balmer and the members of the Columbia University Seminar on Religion in America, who invited me to speak on the subject of chapter 6; the Columbia University Seminars, for their help in publication, and Mike Errico, who went to a Carman concert with me. Rock on! Leyla Ezdinli invited me to Smith College when the broadest outlines of this book were finally taking shape. Much later in the life of the project, Tom Streeter listened to ideas and provided encouragement. While Sarah Michelle never actually listened, she did inspire me at a few crucial junctures; spirit fingers to Myrtle, who often facilitated on this front. Likewise, double features with Kevin Maher sustained me through the final months of revisions. It is no exaggeration to say that this book might not exist were it not for Lynn Love, who first encouraged me to write up my early research. David Murray, Peter Gose, Susanna Elm, Aditya Behl, Julia Smith, Valerie Flint, Tony Grafton, Peter Brown, Dirk Hartog, and other Davis

Center seminar attendees read several chapters and offered wonderful feedback. Ken Mills, a smart book guy, provided friendship and support at Princeton. Special thanks to my editor at Chicago, Alan Thomas, and to the anonymous reviewers who offered truly exceptional feedback on several versions of the manuscript. My brilliant in-house editor and idea man, John Palattella, generously gave precious assistance at the eleventh hour. Finally, I owe my deepest gratitude to the Shelby Cullom Davis Center for Historical Studies at Princeton University. A fellowship at the center provided the priceless luxury of time for reading, writing, and thinking.

Nonbelievers often respond to evangelical Christians with fear or ridicule. When conservative Christian candidates dominated the elections in 1994, many Americans panicked. Of the six hundred national, state, and local candidates supported by religious conservatives, 60 percent won.[1] Evangelicals weren't simply marginal "kooks," it seemed; they were voters with political muscle whose policies threatened the separation of church and state. Four years later, when the Reverend Jerry Falwell outed the children's TV character Tinky-Winky as gay, everyone had a good laugh. Evangelicals were in the spotlight again, but this time they were out of touch and feckless. Falwell was instantly targeted by stand-up comedians, and a wag in the *New York Times* not only postulated that the Teletubbies were "operating in league with a global cabal of gay television executives and purse manufacturers, bent on nothing less than world domination," but also raised questions about the sexual orientation of Rocky and Bullwinkle, Bert and Ernie, and Yogi Bear and Booboo.[2] Rather than simply laughing at Falwell, we might have wondered what the whole brouhaha revealed about the culture's overwrought anxieties about children and sexuality (or why many of the anti-Falwell jokes were no less homophobic than Falwell himself).[3] Laughter, however, was the easy response.

Reducing evangelicals to caricatures does not help us understand their spiritual, political, or cultural agendas. Many historians and sociologists, of course, have avoided caricature, producing a substantial literature on evangelical history, politics, and theology. Scholars such as Colleen McDannell, David Morgan, Diane Winston, and Leigh Schmidt also transcend caricature in their studies of the material culture of Christianity.[4] Rather than critiquing religious commodities as evidence of how commercialism dilutes faith, these researchers explore "the subtle ways that people create and maintain spiritual ideals through the exchange of goods and the construction of spaces."[5] Research on

1

material culture takes seriously the artifacts (mass-produced pictures of Jesus, religious trinkets, etc.) that many nonevangelicals laughingly dismiss as kitsch.

Admittedly, "evangelical" is a broad, somewhat amorphous category. Who exactly are evangelicals? Often referred to as born-agains, evangelicals are hard to pin down as a discrete subculture. They don't go to conventions. They don't have membership cards. Most don't see themselves as part of a political movement, although many do believe that there is a spiritual revival occurring in the United States and that God's power is driving it. At the most basic level, the evangelicals targeted by the Christian cultural products industry are Protestants who have been transformed by accepting the Lord Jesus Christ into their hearts as their personal savior. They emphasize "the role of human volition in the salvation process," as Randall Balmer puts it, exalting "the individual's ability to 'choose God' and thereby take control of his or her spiritual destiny."[6] They believe that it is important to share the "good news" of the Gospel with others, often through giving testimony of their own personal conversion experience; they understand the Bible to be the true, infallible word of God; and they are frequently morally and politically conservative, distancing themselves from any kind of liberal thinking, whether political or spiritual. Asked about liberalism, one evangelical cited in Smith declares, "Absolutely not, I am not a liberal. A liberal is someone who takes the Word of God loosely, takes the Bible loosely. He says that it may not be inerrant, that it may be fallible."[7] Evangelicals are more likely to call themselves "Bible-believing Christians" or simply "Christians" than "evangelicals." Many see "fundamentalist" as an insult. Although nonbelievers often call conservative Christians "fundamentalists," the group that this book looks at is more accurately described as evangelical; fundamentalists are, strictly speaking, more separatist than evangelicals and tend to emphasize more adamantly the differences between believers and nonbelievers. Like fundamentalists, though, evangelicals tend to see themselves not as a *type* of Christian but as the only true Christians; they have found the one true path to heaven. Throughout this book, I use "evangelical," "Christian," and "born-again" as synonyms unless otherwise noted. Although there are obviously many types of Christians, both evangelical and nonevangelical, I have opted to echo my subjects' appropriation of "Christian" to refer only to conservative evangelicals.[8]

Shaking the World for Jesus examines the vast industry of books, films, videos, and magazines that have targeted the conservative evangelical American middle class since the seventies. While a sizable number of studies have examined the growth of televangelism,[9] few have paid attention to the Christian cultural products industry—the thousands of films, videos, CDs, and magazines sold to millions of evangelicals via mail order, the World Wide Web, Christian bookstores, and increasingly, in secular bookstores and national chains such as Wal-Mart and K-Mart. The growth of evangelical media also has been virtually ignored by film and media studies researchers, with the notable exception of Julia Lesage and Linda Kintz's *Media, Culture, and the Religious Right*,[10] and even this impressive collection focuses mostly on overtly activist media, largely bypassing the huge, rapidly growing market in less politically oriented entertainment media.[11] More often, it is not evangelical media products but evangelical politics—evangelicalism as a "social movement"—that are subjected to scholarly investigation. Researchers such as Chip Berlet, Sara Diamond, Russ Bellant, David Bennet, Didi Herman, Clyde Wilcox, and Rebecca Klatch have examined fundamentalism as a right-wing political force,[12] often emphasizing the dangers of Christian activism. If such researchers consider evangelical media at all, they view it as propaganda—overtly political, painfully unsubtle, and inherently dangerous.

In my experience, however, most evangelical media are not propaganda designed to induce a political or spiritual conversion. Of course, when a TV preacher invites viewers to be saved, even to put their hands on the monitor to "touch" the preacher's hand, media are intended as a conversion tool. But outside of the televangelical context, Christian music, videos, films, and magazines are not uniformly designed to convert consumers. More often, consumers are assumed to already be saved, or it is hoped that this media might soften the unsaved consumer's heart so that a one-on-one encounter with a saved friend, family member, or coworker might be more effective. Media such as Christian videos are not considered as powerful as personal testimony, but they might plant the proverbial mustard seed, an idea about salvation that might someday take root if properly nourished. This is hardly the hard sell approach that one would expect from "propaganda."

Shaking the World for Jesus moves beyond the propaganda paradigm to take a closer look at Christian media, examining that media's industrial history, the subtleties of the products themselves, and their success in the religious and, increasingly, the secular marketplace. In other words, this book brings together industrial and textual analysis in order to understand how Christian media are produced and what they try to communicate to consumers. *Shaking the World for Jesus* thus seeks to begin to fill an enormous gap in our understanding of both media history and contemporary culture. Serious study of exploitation films, home movies, industrial films, and other previously ignored genres by film and media studies researchers is recent. This book strives to contribute to this growing body of research on previously undervalued media artifacts.

In addition to books, CDs, and videos, religious bookstores are now packed with Christian tchotchkes, jewelry, and even junk food. To nonevangelicals, products such as Scripture Candy and Testamints may seem profane. But to dismiss such products is to ignore how they figure in the daily lives of evangelicals. Born-agains place religion at the center of daily life, believing that one can serve the Lord through the most mundane acts—being on time to class, playing ball with your son, even picking up your husband's dirty socks. Similarly, when young Christians produce a five hundred gallon milkshake in honor of the Teen Missionaries International theme, "Shake the World for Jesus" (from Ezekiel 38:20: "All the men that are upon the face of the earth shall shake at my presence"), they do not see themselves as belittling the Lord. Rather, the milkshake is taken as a potent symbol of missionary commitment to the Gospel. Everyday cultural products such as Christian music and magazines can also help trigger and maintain this kind of commitment. Chastity, too, can be sustained with the help of products such as "True Love Waits" gold pendants and psychedelic "Virtuous Reality" posters. Thanks to such Christian lifestyle products, the consumption of mass-produced goods can now be justified as serving a holy purpose (figs. 1–2).

While the "Christianization" of secular media such as heavy metal music and science fiction films is new to American culture, the existence of a highly permeable boundary between the sacred and the secular is not. Evangelicals, and their more separatist fundamentalist cousins, have always had a complicated relationship with the secular world. One result of the 1925 Scopes trial—in which a Tennessee schoolteacher was put on trial for teaching the theory of evolution—was that evangelicals acquired an "antimodern" reputation; supposedly, these were people opposed to scientific progress, mass media, and new technologies. But in fact, evangelicals have embraced—although often not without debate—any "modern" means that could be used to spread the Gospel. As Quentin J. Schulze has observed, American evangelicals have made use of

every imaginable form and medium of communication, from Bible and tract printing to tent revivals, gospel billboards, books, religious drama troupes, radio and television broadcasts, parade floats, motorcycle evangelism, periodicals, and even Rollen Stewart . . . who holds up Scripture signs ["John 3:16"] in front of the TV network cameras during sports events. American evangelicals were often leery of new media, especially those that provided "worldly en-

FIG. 1 CHRISTIAN PRODUCTS HELP ORGANIZE DAILY LIFE, INFUSING FAITH IN EVERY ACTIVITY. PHOTO
BY THE AUTHOR.

tertainment," such as the stage and, later, film. But they also pioneered one
form of mass communication after another.[13]

In the 1920s, some Christians had reservations about creating radio
programming, since sending messages through the air seemed almost
supernatural. The Bible, after all, refers to Satan as the "prince of the
power of the air." Such doubts were short-lived. "Modern times," Joel
Carpenter has explained, "demanded modern technology, so what the
church needed was to adapt to the automobile age and then 'step on
the gas.'"[14] Thus, Christians quickly became major players in early radio broadcasting.

In its simplest form, secularization theory would have us believe
that religion inevitably fades in modern societies. But if modern life dilutes religious belief, how can we explain not only the continued presence of evangelicals in America but also the fact that their ranks seem
to be growing? Evangelicals have clearly not been stamped out by the
"secularizing" influence of the modern world. For all their reputation
as intransigent Bible-thumpers, evangelicals have survived by being
flexible and making accommodations to modernity.[15] As Carpenter argues, "rather than viewing evangelicalism as a throwback, as a religion
of consolation for those who cannot accept the dominant humanist,

FIG. 2 MASS-PRODUCED GOODS SUCH
AS BUMPER STICKERS HELP SPREAD THE
GOOD NEWS. PHOTO BY THE AUTHOR.

modernist, liberal, and secular thrust of mainstream society, perhaps it is more accurate to see evangelicalism as a religious persuasion that has repeatedly adapted to the changing tone and rhythms of modernity."[16] American evangelicals are, as Christian Smith explains, both "embattled and thriving." If today's thriving Christian cultural products industry illustrates anything, it is that evangelicals continue to spread their messages using "the newest thing," be it film, video, or the Web. The growing Christian market in films, videos, and Web sites, then, is not evidence of the "secularization" of evangelical culture but rather of the complicated osmosis occurring between the "secular" and the "religious."

This book strives to complicate the by-now familiar narrative of evangelical adaptation to the "rhythms of modernity." The story I tell is new on several fronts. First and most obviously, as stated above, many Christian films, books, videos, magazines, and other cultural products have until now received only scant scholarly attention, and so my study serves as a corrective. Secondly, and perhaps more importantly, I believe that examination of the contemporary Christian media industry reveals a new development in the way that evangelicals have made accommodations to secular culture. To the untrained eye, it might seem as though evangelical media have simply become "more secular"

FIG. 3 *WILLIE AMES'S POPULAR STRAIGHT-TO-VIDEO BIBLEMAN SUPERHERO SERIES.*

FIG. 4 *BIBLEMAN QUOTES SCRIPTURE WHILE HE FIGHTS BAD GUYS.*

as they have grown. This would account for the recent Top Forty success of "Christian" songs like Sixpence None the Richer's "Kiss Me," which doesn't mention God, Jesus, or, for that matter, anything overtly religious. I would argue, however, that over the course of the past thirty years Christian media have become not more secular but more ambiguous, and that a wide variety of products must be examined to formulate an accurate picture of the different levels of evangelical intensity in today's Christian media. Some products seem deliberately fuzzy about their religious intentions, whereas other products remain overtly, even dogmatically, evangelical, such as Willie Ames's popular straight-to-video *Bibleman* superhero series for children (figs. 3–4). Still other products, such as *VeggieTales* children's videos, are produced by evangelicals but are only gently "religious," promoting an ecumenical belief in God. In sum, contemporary Christian media are incredibly uneven in the degree to which they overtly proclaim their faith.

Of course, Christians and their media have always come in all shapes and sizes. Listening to a right-wing, redbaiting fundamentalist radio broadcast by Carl McIntire in the fifties would have been different from listening to the evangelical Rev. Billy Graham deliver a radio sermon in that same decade. But at some point both men would have spoken of salvation through Jesus, and it is unlikely that a listener would have mistakenly assumed that he or she was listening to a secular broadcast or that the speakers were Roman Catholic or Jewish. Today a wide range of products, all produced by evangelicals, convey different levels of evangelical intensity and ambiguity, and they all coexist on the shelves of Christian bookstores. Moreover, some of them (usually the least overtly evangelical ones) have been stocked by Wal-Mart and the now-bankrupt K-Mart. Importantly, Christian products have made it into the secular marketplace not only because their religious messages are ambiguous, diluted, or absent but also because they are increasingly distributed by huge, non-Christian companies. A third contribution that this book makes, then, is to reveal the new economics of the production and distribution of Christian cultural products.

I spend less time addressing how Christians interpret their media. Although the book does not take audiences as its central focus, it does assume that evangelical media are designed to provide something of spiritual value to believers. At the very least, by virtue of not promoting certain "dangerous" liberal values, these media are designed not to harm consumers. If you are an evangelical who doesn't like secular sitcoms or cartoons and you think they might be bad for your kids, all you have to do is call the country's biggest producer and distributor of Christian media, Focus on the Family, and, with credit card in hand, purchase a Christian alternative. From this perspective, consumers use Christian media not as tools of salvation but as safeguards against secular contamination.

Beyond providing clean-cut entertainment, such media can also help people deal with emotional crises, teach them political lessons, instruct them in chastity and other Christian modes of behavior, or provide inspirational models for praise and worship. In short, such media both reflect and construct evangelical understandings of the sacred and the profane, of the saved individual and his or her place in the wider world. The idea that media and other cultural goods might help to create or sustain faith may be ridiculous to evangelical readers, since from their perspective it is the supernatural power of the Holy Spirit, in interrelationship with the individual believer, that creates and sustains belief, and to contend otherwise is to misunderstand what evangelical Christianity is all about. A chastity ring or T-shirt, thus, does not *bring about* a commitment to sexual abstinence. Rather, as David Morgan found in his study of attitudes toward popular religious images, such objects *remind* the wearer of the spiritual commitment that has been made.[17]

This, at least, is how things should work in principle. In practice, the symbolic object can sometimes take on a more active, performative role. But many evangelicals would disagree with this analysis, preferring to deemphasize the spiritual importance of chastity rings and other lifestyle products such as magazines and videos. In not toeing the evangelical line, as it were, my approach is clearly that of an outsider, and I sometimes draw conclusions about how Christian cultural products might be used or interpreted that are at odds with the conclusions that evangelicals themselves would draw. At the same time, my conclusions may challenge the assumptions of nonevangelicals, many of whom perceive Christian culture first and foremost as a political culture and reduce evangelicalism to a synonym for the Christian Right. Although some Christian media are designed for overtly political and sometimes incendiary purposes—Christian Coalition training tapes or antigay videos like *Gay Rights/Special Rights*[18]—the majority of Christian media does not have overt political intentions, and most everyday evangelicals aren't activists or substantially more politically engaged than the average American Episcopalian, Unitarian, agnostic, atheist, or even Satanist. Christian Smith has found that many evangelicals define activism not as protesting, picketing, boycotting, or even voting, but rather as witnessing.[19] Indeed, a common perception among the people Smith surveyed was that political change would only come as people's individual hearts changed. In the long run, spreading the Word would be more effective than political organizing. Evangelical media sometimes help spread the Word to potential converts. Often, though, they speak to people who are already within the evangelical fold. Although I remain outside that fold, I have tried to balance my analysis, considering what such media might mean to evangelicals while also analytically dissecting that media.

Contrary to popular stereotypes, not all evangelicals are militant Bible-thumpers. Those whom I met in the course of my research typically gently gave their testimony and didn't expect me instantly to fall on my knees and accept the Lord. They hoped to plant a seed, and the best way to do that was by positive example, just by showing that the Lord had made a positive change in their own lives. Whether they had been supernaturally transformed, or in the secular formulation, merely thought they had been, the people I encountered saw themselves as better, happier people since they accepted the Lord into their hearts. These may seem like naive observations to some readers, but they are worth stating for people who come to this book identifying themselves as opponents of the Christian Right. The Christian Right is not any more central to the identity of the average evangelical than the Democratic Party is to most political liberals.[20]

Shaking the World for Jesus looks at the "center" of conservative evangelical culture, the middle-class, mostly white Christians who can afford to buy into the "Christian lifestyle" market. The Christian market includes a number of popular African American authors, and certainly many successful African American (and some Latino) musicians; African American recording artists CeCe Winans and Kirk Franklin are notably successful. Yet the vast majority of the goods produced for the Christian lifestyle market are targeted to white consumers, and it is this market that this book will focus on. People of color are largely absent from Christian media, and when they do appear, it is not unusual for them to be marked as "the other," as in an episode of the straight-to-video cartoon series *VeggieTales* when Junior Asparagus does not want to invite a "different" vegetable (with a Latino-sounding last name) to his birthday party. All of the *VeggieTales* characters appear to be white (although most are technically green) except for Mr. Lunt, a Mexican gourd with greasy hair and a gold-capped tooth. African Americans appear as token sidekicks in several Christian movies, cartoons, and sitcoms, but they are never protagonists. Such tokenism indicates an attempt to "reach out" to people of color, as when the Promise Keepers, a predominantly white men's ministry, made racial reconciliation a major goal. Their pamphlets featured a handshake between white and brown muscular hands, but their membership remained mostly white.[21] Like the Promise Keepers, some Christian media may attempt to speak to nonwhite consumers, but for the most part, evangelical media are made by whites and for whites.[22]

Many evangelicals are nondenominational, while others come from Pentecostal, Charismatic, Southern Baptist or other traditions.[23] Christian cultural goods are marketed to conservative evangelicals from a variety of backgrounds, as long as they have disposable income.[24] These are the evangelicals who, if they see themselves as "political" at all, might identify as Republicans, or possibly as members of the Christian Coalition, but certainly not as members of the Ku Klux Klan. They are distanced from the far right of militias and other Christian extremists. Ralph Reed, the former head of the Christian Coalition, tried to project the image of this kind of Christian. Reed portrayed conservative Christians as just one element of a pluralistic, democratic society.[25] These Christians are, according to Reed, completely average people who just want to have their say. They are not old-fashioned, separatist fundamentalists. Rather, they are modern evangelicals, attempting to be "in the world but not of the world."

To be "in" but not "of" the world is to engage with people outside of the evangelical belief system, and hopefully to lead them into that system, without becoming more like the outsiders yourself. Today's conservative evangelicals want to engage with the wider culture because they think their belief system is the truth—indeed, the only hope for humankind—and they want to share this reality with others. Media can help accomplish this task. Yet in interacting with the world, there is always the chance (indeed, the probability) that you yourself will be changed. This is, in fact, exactly what has happened to contemporary evangelicals. Examination of evangelical media reveals the complex ways that today's evangelicals are *both* in and of the world. This is not a negative value judgment; evangelicals have not simply "sold out" or been "secularized." Rather, evangelicals have used media to simultaneously struggle against, engage with, and acquiesce to the secular world.

Chapter 1 lays the historical and theoretical groundwork for the book. First, I briefly explain how fundamentalist culture changed in response to the Scopes trial in 1925, went into hiding (all the while building separatist institutions of education and culture), reemerged via the "new evangelical" movement of the late 40s, and reentered the wider public consciousness in the 70s. It was at this time that the Christian lifestyles industry began to emerge. Chapter 1 looks at some of today's typical products, youth-targeted straight-to-video series that take secular media genres (the cartoon, the sitcom) and respin them to suit evangelical purposes. These videos have made numerous accommodations to secular culture, ranging from toning down their salvation message to adapting themselves to nonevangelical attitudes toward child rearing.

It should not be surprising that evangelicals know how to manipulate the conventions of popular media. After all, a completely isolated culture could not be evangelical, could not reach out to share "the good news" of the Bible with others. This is as true today as it was a hundred years ago when evangelist Dwight L. Moody took out advertisements for revivals in secular newspapers, and when Moody's musical accompanist, Ira Sankey, caused a scandal by introducing modern hymns. On one level, using sitcom formulas or computer animation is simply the twenty-first-century equivalent. But there is also more to the evangelical appropriation of media: these products help forge a place for contemporary, middle-class, white evangelicals in modern American consumer culture. Intentionally or not, the products stake a claim for evangelicals as a viable demographic of savvy, up-to-date consumers. The biggest success story for this demographic has surely been the Christian music industry, which grew by leaps and bounds at the end of the twentieth century. Chapter 2 examines that industry's growth and increasing inroads into the wider secular marketplace. Christian music and music video provide an excellent illustration of how evangelicals have created cultural products of uneven and ambiguous spiritual intensity.

Having drawn a picture in the first two chapters of how evangelicals have created their own culture industry, in chapters 3 and 4 I shift from industrial issues to issues of sexuality. Chapter 3 examines how chastity media conceptualize teenage bodies. Through their construction of sexual abstinence, food consumption, eating disorders, and weightlifting, therapeutic evangelical youth media define bodily control differently for girls and boys. Chastity media clearly echo secular media in the ways they understand teen bodies, even as they put an evangelical spin on that understanding. In the mid-1990s, the chastity movement was aggressively and overtly evangelical. Like Christian music, however, the chastity movement has recently changed in ways that make its religious foundations more ambiguous. Just as "God" has become "He" in many Christian songs, chastity has been repackaged for secular audiences with a more religiously neutral name: abstinence.

Chapter 4 examines the Cathedral of Hope, the world's largest gay and lesbian church. This case study takes a step away from conservative evangelical culture, showing that we can learn much about what evangelicalism is by examining a culture that identifies so strongly as *not* being evangelical, or as the members of that congregation are more likely to put it, "fundamentalist." Just as evangelicals see themselves as different from "the world" yet use worldly media forms to their own ends, the Cathedral defines itself, in large part, as a response against fundamentalism, while also incorporating elements of that culture into itself. Undertaking political, religious, and cultural analysis, this chapter is a case study in how a community finds cohesion in its interpretative strategies for understanding the Bible, the Christian Right, televangelism, and its own countermedia. This chapter is, admittedly, the book's odd man out in that it is not focused on evangelical media *per se* but rather on ex-fundamentalists and their understandings of their sexual identity. My research on the Cathedral is included here as a counterbalance to the preceding chapter. As chapter 3 shows, evangelical media portray chastity as fraught; it is, theoretically, challenging and empowering, painful and liberating. Chapter 4 turns to the group for whom evangelical sexual prohibitions are perhaps most fraught, gays and lesbians, who are pathologized and, sometimes, demonized by evangelical media. The Cathedral of Hope offers sanctuary for those who realize the futility of the "cure" promoted in Christian videos, books, and magazines.

The final third of the book examines Christian film production, distribution, and exhibition, focusing particularly on scientific and apocalyptic films. What these media have in common is an emphasis on facts, rationality, and logic. Both types of media strive to construct an aggressively *nonfiction* Christian picture of the world. The evangelical science films examined in chapter 5 rely on the "facts" of science to prove that our world could only be the product of an intelligent Creator. The apocalyptic films discussed in chapter 6 draw on science fiction and horror film conventions, but their producers contend that they are simply using drama to show something that will *really* happen: the rise of the Antichrist and the end of the world. Both Christian scientific films and apocalyptic films have sought out wide audiences beyond the evangelical market. With both kinds of films, as with other kinds of Christian media, we see that the wider the desired audience, the more carefully tempered the evangelical message will be.

Evangelical negotiation of mainstream culture is in some ways a textbook example of how scholars such as Michel de Certeau, Henry Jenkins, John Fiske, and Dick Hebdige have described the mechanics of popular culture: as a process of appropriation, of poaching on the terrain of the mass-culture industry.[26] To produce their own countermedia, evangelicals have repeatedly drawn on previously existing forms, often turning them completely on their ear, as in antimarijuana reggae songs or rock tunes advocating submission to parents. On the other hand, evangelicals would prefer not to poach on mass culture; their preference would be to transform mass culture, making it entirely evangelical. In other words, if evangelical media producers and consumers constitute a "subculture," it is one that aspires to lose its "sub" status.

Since evangelical media express different levels of evangelical fervor, one might say that some evangelical media products are more subcultural than others. To put it simply, Scripture-quoting music videos about the Last Judgment are more on the edge of mass culture than videos of happy Christians dancing in fields as mellow elevator music plays in the background, and given such differing levels of spiritual fervor, it is unlikely that Christian media as a whole will be absorbed into the mainstream any time soon. The primetime TV sitcom *Touched by an Angel* is one thing, but advertisers would certainly be wary of a music video or television show preaching an overt message of salvation. The mass culture industry is "conservative," then, insofar as it preserves the status quo by rejecting didactic Christian media out of hand. Not surprisingly, of course, evangelicals are likely to describe mass culture not as conservative but rather liberal, left-wing, or even satanic.

Television and cultural studies scholars, conversely, are more likely to describe mass culture as ideologically conservative. Mass culture, in one formulation, is "hegemonic," and resistance to that culture is "counterhegemonic." But evangelical responses to mass culture provide a picture of "resistance" very different from that described by most academic researchers. In my examination of a conservative culture, I look at resistance that has been invisible to many of the researchers interested in the progressive potential of popular culture. Although the celebratory nature of much early cultural studies work has already been criticized (often by its very practitioners), the question of what it would mean to "resist" mainstream culture from a conservative political position has been asked all too infrequently.[27]

FOR-PROFIT PROPHETS: CHRISTIAN CULTURAL PRODUCTS AND THE SELLING OF JESUS

Strolling in a mall in Birmingham, Alabama, a few years ago, I saw a pimply, lanky teenage boy wearing what appeared to be a Gold's Gym T-shirt. As he walked past me, however, I saw that the T-shirt actually said "Lord's Gym." The back of the shirt featured a bloody, muscular Jesus lying on the ground, struggling beneath the weight of a cross on his back. On the cross was written "the sin of the world," and the slogan beneath this sweaty, Rambo-like Jesus read "Bench press this!"

This was my first encounter with "witness wear," evangelical clothing, mostly T-shirts, targeting teenagers (figs. 5–6). The Lord's Gym shirt is a perennial bestseller, purchased by hundreds of thousands of people. Other obviously boy-targeted shirts favor heavy metal style skulls and gothic script; they even picture Christ vomiting blood. A Hell's Angels shirt, on closer examination, is actually a "Heavenly Divine Son" T-shirt. One outrageous T-shirt offers this take on the Crucifixion: "Body piercing saved my life." Girl-targeted shirts take a gentler tack. "Sonseeker" is the delicate tag line beneath a picture of a sunflower; a nautical-themed pastel shirt reads "my anchor holds." Some less gender-specific shirts appropriate secular logos and slogans. "Reebok" becomes "Reborn." Nike's "Life Is Short, Play Hard" becomes "Life Is Short, Pray Hard." And one shirt even pictures a fried Energizer Bunny, still pounding his drum, with the tag line "Hell keeps on burning, and burning, and burning." With such appropriations of logos and brand names, evangelicals attempt to use humor to bridge the apparent divide between believers and nonbelievers. Saved and unsaved may disagree about school prayer, but anyone can make fun of the Energizer Bunny.

The marketers of these products claim they are not shallow ads for Jesus but rather useful evangelizing tools. A major retailer of witness wear, Living Epistles, tells visitors to its Web site that "a message will actually be read 9,600 times in the life of the average witnessing shirt. And that's actually a conservative estimate! So don't forget to pray every

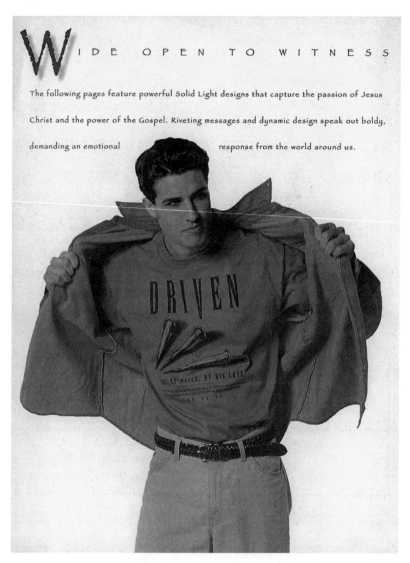

W I D E   O P E N   T O   W I T N E S S

The following pages feature powerful Solid Light designs that capture the passion of Jesus

Christ and the power of the Gospel. Riveting messages and dynamic design speak out boldy,

demanding an emotional   response from the world around us.

FIGS. 5–6 WITNESS WEAR AS AN EVANGELIZING TOOL.

time you put on that witnessing shirt!"[1] The company has been very successful, especially with its famous Lord's Gym T-shirt. Living Epistles and other marketers would have us believe that thanks to witness wear and other Christian lifestyle products, purchases can have a justified, holy purpose. Christian cultural products seem to promise evangelicals that they can consume without being tainted by "worldliness."

It is unlikely, however, that many evangelicals honestly expect a T-shirt to provoke a profound spiritual transformation. A person already receptive to religious questions might stop and talk to the T-shirt wearer, or a lapsed person might be spurred to start going to church again. Of course, some evangelicals object to the commercialism of religious products, complaining that they trivialize faith. A participant in a Christian Internet discussion group, for example, attacks witness wear:

When I want to make a statement about my faith I no longer have to worry with uncomfortable things like killing my flesh, feeding the hungry, clothing the poor, comforting the afflicted, and wearing poly-blends. Nope, now all I need to do to witness is grab one of my 100 % cotton Living Epistles [brand] witness wear t-shirts from my wardrobe and "Put on the Lord Jesus Christ."[2]

Living Epistles's motto—"Put on the Lord Jesus Christ"—clearly represents a "worldly," commercialized approach to evangelism. The question is, how did a culture that fifty years ago was nervous about make-up, Hollywood movies, and rock-and-roll make such an about-face and embrace worldliness? How did evangelicals become such prolific producers and consumers of popular culture?

This about-face didn't happen over night. As Colleen McDannell has shown, Christian retailing goes back to the second half of the nineteenth century, when religious goods were sold alongside nonreligious merchandise. A company selling artistic prints for the home would offer not only landscapes but also pictures of Jesus. Noah's Ark toys, drinking glasses etched with "Rock of Ages," and even saws inscribed with the Lord's Prayer were among the religious objects common in Victorian homes. "Victorian producers assumed a homogeneous buying public that saw Christian art and objects as an integral part of domesticity."[3] McDannell argues that by the early twentieth century, and certainly by the end of World War I, streamlined, "modern" styles displaced the cluttered Victorian domestic aesthetic. "Religious goods disappeared from ordinary stores and catalogs not because Christians rejected the commercialization of their beliefs but because religious art was no longer fashionable. The figurative image, whether sentimental or religious, was being replaced by the abstract form."[4]

McDannell does not account for changes in American religious life that might be tied in with such aesthetic changes. The forces of industrialization and the continuing shift away from an agrarian economy, the growth of cities, the continuing influence of mass culture and particularly the new medium of film, the massive influx of European immigrants, many of them Roman Catholic—all of these factors, among others, changed American religious culture in dramatic ways. As a fundamentalist of the time might have put it, creeping modernism (and Darwinism) seemed to be winning the war for American souls. Evangelicals were losing their grasp on American culture. If taste in décor changed from old-fashioned to modern, it should not be surprising that "modern" meant, in part, a reduction in the amount of religious iconography found in the home.

As secular companies stopped selling religious goods, McDannell explains, they "left a vacuum that would be filled by explicitly religious companies with specific Christian commitments."[5] For the first time, Christian companies began creating Christian goods. Like today's Christian businesses, the companies used modern manufacturing and advertising techniques. These businesses were unlike today's in several ways, however. First, there were no Christian bookstores at the time, so sales came mostly from catalog orders and the door-to-door circuit. Second, there was no room for ambiguity in terms of the spiritual messages of these products. "Spread-the-light" reading lamps sold in 1935 featured pictures of Jesus on their shades. Wall plaques said "Jesus Christ the Same Yesterday Today and Forever." One 1937 advertisement noted that "pencils are considered one of the best commercial advertising mediums. Why not spread the Gospel through the use of Scripture-text pencils?"[6] If it was clear that these products were using commercial techniques, it was equally clear that they were designed to spread an overt Gospel message. Finally, unlike many of today's goods, the products were for the most part cheap and cheaply made.

Christian bookstores only began to appear in the years following World War II, as the door-to-door salesman became increasingly obsolete. McDannell reports that "between 1965 and 1975 the number [of Christian bookstores] more than doubled from 725 to 1850. Average store sales grew at an annual rate of 16 percent between 1975 and 1979, well above the national retail growth of 9.7 percent."[7] The stores were small mom-and-pop endeavors, but a national trade association, the Christian Booksellers Association (CBA), was formed in 1950. The Jesus movement of the 1960s and 70s created a new demographic—hippie Christians (or "Jesus freaks")—and T-shirts, key chains, bumper stickers, jewelry, and Bibles were all specially marketed to this crowd. Specialty Bibles were nothing new, but this era saw the first denim Bible (fig. 7). Further, "producers and bookstore owners proclaimed that a new era in Christian merchandising had begun. They disparaged previous generations of goods they felt were cheap, shoddy, and old-fashioned."[8] One successful Christian jewelry maker complained in 1979, "'Christian junk' makes me sick." Distancing himself from low-class aesthetics, he added, "I'm determined our jewelry will never be classified as cheap or gaudy. We hope to establish a standard that cannot be surpassed."[9]

As the quality and diversity of goods increased, the market in Christian products grew. By the late 1990s and the early twenty-first century, "cheap" and "gaudy" goods were not completely eliminated, but the hugely expanded market in high-end Christian goods seemed to confirm that evangelicals were respectable middle-class consumers. McDannell reports that in the early 1990s Christian bookstore sales exceeded $3 billion. By 2000, sales had reached $4 billion (figs. 8–11).[10]

FIG. 7 FROM THE EARLY DAYS OF CHRIST-
IAN BOOKSTORES: A DENIM BIBLE PUB-
LISHED IN 1972 TARGETS HIPPIE
CHRISTIANS. PHOTO BY THE AUTHOR.

The industry has come a long way since it first started increasing the production of T-shirts and bumper stickers to tap into the Jesus freak market. Notably, however, many of the early Jesus freak musicians were themselves quite cynical about the power of commodities to get people closer to God. In fact, in 1968 musician Larry Norman attempted to release an album entitled *We Need a Whole Lot More Jesus and a Lot Less Rock-and-Roll*. (The record company changed the title to *I Love You*.)[11] In the early days of Christian roll-and-roll, musicians who had a crisis of conscience about selling salvation actually gave their music away. Keith Green had released two successful albums when he decided in the late seventies that his third album would be free. He explained,

I think it's wrong to put a price on an item that contains a spiritual message that came free from God. If I was doing a disco album or an instrumental album, or even if I was an entertainer who happened to be a Christian . . . then it would be a *product*. It would be my skill, my trade. But since I'm foremost a minister, my music is just a tool to present the ministry.[12]

In the current boom market of Christian commodities, this philosophy has pretty much disappeared. Musical entrepreneur Carman may offer

FIGS. 8–11 TODAY'S CHRISTIAN BOOKSTORE CHAINS SELL PRODUCTS TARGETING A WIDE RANGE OF AGES AND SPECIAL INTERESTS. PHOTOS BY THE AUTHOR.

free concerts, but his albums, videos, and T-shirts are not free. As Christian musician and industry executive Eddie DeGarmo notes, "you've got people . . . sworn to poverty . . . [and] you've also got some people who wear so much gold on their hands that it's hard to believe that they can pick their knuckles off the floor."[13] Dan Harrell, a wealthy Christian talent manager (and brother-in-law of Christian pop star Amy Grant), takes a pragmatic stance. "A lot of the other industry leaders view [Christian music] as church work, not as the music business. A lot of them struggle with, 'What are we doing? Are we selling Jesus?' Absolutely. That's our product."[14]

If the numbers of sales are any indication, contemporary born-agains—at least those with disposable income—have certainly developed an "appetite for worldly ideas and practices—sports, therapy, sex manuals, politics, glossy magazines, television, Disney special effects— which they [have] appropriated selectively and Christianized with great skill and zeal."[15] This chapter explains how such Christian cultural products have developed, succeeded, and finally, been influenced to varying degrees by the secular world. After providing a historical overview of the growth of evangelical engagement in American culture since World War II, I chart the growth of evangelicals as a middle-class consumer demographic, finally culminating the chapter with three short case studies of evangelical youth videos that illustrate the fluctuation between evangelical and secular ideas in today's Christian media products. The issue is not that evangelical Christians are tainted by interaction with secular culture, but rather that the boundary between "secular" and "evangelical" has become ever more permeable as evangelical media have grown over the past twenty years. Of the wide variety of products now produced, some, like a Lord's Gym T-shirt, wear their evangelical message clearly on their sleeve. Others promote God but not Jesus, or make other concessions to the secular market. And some products are only vaguely "religious" or "spiritual." Angel knick-knacks, for example, became very popular in the late nineties; the same angel products might turn up at Wal-Mart, a Hallmark store, a New Age bookstore, or a Christian bookstore.

Interestingly, by the end of the 1990s the small Christian booksellers were encountering the same problems experienced by nonreligious independent bookstores in trying to compete with Amazon.com, Borders, and Barnes & Noble. Many of the same neighborhoods whose local bookstores were replaced by a Barnes & Noble (with a Starbucks café included in the package, of course) also had their local Christian bookstore supplanted by a Lifeway national Christian bookstore chain. Furthermore, in the Bible Belt the "secular" chain bookstores were increasingly packed with many of the same books one would find in a national Christian chain. While most of us would not think of Barnes & Noble as a "Christian bookstore," it is also problematic to simply label it "secular" when the branches in the most religious regions of the country have enormous Christian sections. If some Christian products seem "less Christian" by virtue of their diluted content and presence on the shelves at Kmart, Kmart, conversely, becomes "more religious" by virtue of the presence of the same products. And as inspirational, self-help, spiritual, and religious book categories begin to melt into each other, it becomes even more difficult to keep "secular" and "religious" straight. After all, Gwen Shamblin's evangelical dieting book, *The Weigh-Down Diet*, is now shelved in the same area of mainstream bookstores as the Dalai Lama's *The Art of Happiness* and the "Chicken Soup" series of inspirational books.

Like Ira Sankey's hymns a century ago, today's evangelical cultural products are symptomatic of both engagement with and distance from the secular world. American evangelicalism has remained strong "not because it is shielded against, but because it is—or at least it perceives itself to be—embattled with forces that seem to oppose or threaten it . . . the evangelical movement's vitality is not a product of its protected isolation from, but of its vigorous engagement with pluralistic modernity."[16] In other words, American evangelicalism is not weakened by its differences from and conflicts with the wider culture. In fact, one might say that evangelical identity is shored up by such conflicts. Of course, evangelicalism is more than a reactive posture against modernity. Yet it is true that American evangelicals know what they are, at least in part, because they know what they are *not*—members of the secular, morally bankrupt world.[17]

FUNDAMENTALIST WITHDRAWAL AND NEOEVANGELICAL ENGAGEMENT

To understand the nature of evangelical engagement with the modern world, we need to return to a pivotal moment in the 1920s. In 1925, John Thomas Scopes, a public school teacher, was put on trial in Tennessee for teaching evolution in his classroom. Clarence Darrow, a Yankee lawyer, represented Scopes. "Darrow spent a lifetime ridiculing traditional beliefs. He called himself an agnostic, but in fact he was effectively an atheist."[18] William Jennings Bryan, a deeply religious Southern lawyer, represented the state of Tennessee. Scopes was convicted, but it was in many ways a Pyrrhic victory for old-fashioned Christians. The Scopes trial received wide newspaper coverage, and conservative Christians (and Southerners) were portrayed as stupid, irrational, and backward. Yet rumors of the death of fundamentalism were greatly exaggerated. Fundamentalists chose to withdraw from the wider culture in the 1930s and 1940s, yet their culture nonetheless continued to thrive as they built their own separate networks of Bible schools, radio programs, churches, and publishers.[19]

In the post–World War II years, a constituency arose that hoped to forge a new place for evangelical cultural engagement. These "neoevangelicals" were frustrated by fundamentalist alienation from mainstream society, and many were particularly frustrated at the paucity of evangelical scholarship. They wanted to see less "doctrinal hairsplitting" and more intellectual rigor.[20] Carl Henry, the movement's "chief theological advocate,"[21] envisioned evangelicals engaged in the world not only intellectually but also as a force that could make a political, social, and of course, spiritual impact. As Joel Carpenter explains, "Christianity is a 'world-and-life view,' Henry insisted, not just an individual rescue. A Christian community living out that conviction would have a profound influence as 'salt and light' throughout society, and the world might well see, as a result, 'a new reformation.'"[22] In 1956, Henry became the founding editor of the magazine *Christianity Today*, which provided a place for the new evangelical reformers to promote their perspective.[23]

Although not an intellectual like Henry, Billy Graham was another key figure of the evangelical reemergence. He got his start as a Youth for Christ worker. A movement with a national following, Youth for Christ "was the first sign that the revival of revivalism, which had been percolating deep within the fundamentalist movement, was finally breaking out into public view."[24] Youth for Christ rallies were nothing if not modern. They featured updated Gospel music, and they were preceded by extensive advance publicity. "From a fundamentalist perspective, the rally leaders were borrowing from the very dens of the Devil—Hollywood and Radio City—to accomplish the Lord's purposes."[25] Later on his own, Graham similarly broke with tradition by inviting different congregations—some of them liberal—to work together in producing his crusades.[26] He would also become the unofficial spiritual advisor for the postwar generation of U.S. presidents. Evangelicals like Graham and Henry were not intransigent separatists, like the old-fashioned fundamentalists, but they were not like Jerry Falwell, either. They started a national "prayer breakfast movement" for preachers to get together with members of Congress, but they were not militant politicos. Intense and public evangelical political engagement would not come until later.

Many historians cite the election of President Jimmy Carter as pivotal to the reemergence of conservative Christian politicking in the 1970s. Incensed about the sexual revolution, pro-ERA activism, rising divorce rates, the legalization of abortion, the elimination of school prayer, and the teaching of evolution, many evangelicals hoped Carter would make some changes. Carter was an avowed born-again, but to the disappointment of his conservative Christian supporters, he turned out to be something of a liberal in sheep's clothing. Just having a born-again in the White House, however, helped to get evangelicals onto the popular culture map. *Newsweek* boldly declared 1976 to be the "Year of the Evangelical," and that same year Chuck Colson's *Born Again* became a bestseller. Anita Bryant began her Christian crusade against gay rights in 1977, the Moral Majority was founded by Falwell in 1979, and another professed born-again, Ronald Reagan, was elected president in 1980. By then, evangelicals were in the public eye in a way they hadn't been since the Scopes trial.

Anthropologist Susan Harding points to the founding of the Moral Majority and, specifically, to the rhetorical prowess of its founder, Jerry Falwell, as the linchpin of the fundamentalist shift back into aggressive political involvement. Falwell was a key engineer of a truce between evangelicals and fundamentalists, and according to Harding, this truce was "essential to the formation of the core constituency of the New Christian Right, to the realignment of evangelicalism and fundamentalism, and to their ultimate overturning of the cultural verdict of the Scopes trial."[27] By 1980 there had been, Harding explains, a "major realignment of public religiosity"; born-agains and non–born-agains no longer agreed that "the public arena was off-limits to openly Bible-believing voices."[28] Harding may seem to give a little too much credit to Falwell, but importantly, she notes that Falwell could not have succeeded in transforming the status of Bible-believers, especially in terms of speaking to and encouraging their professional middle-class aspirations, if an enormous institutional and cultural infrastructure had not already been in place.[29]

Some old-school fundamentalists continued to resist Falwell's call for involvement in worldly politics, especially when he went so far as to suggest forging alliances with conservative Roman Catholics who opposed abortion. But those who accepted Falwell's invitation to action were, in effect, transforming themselves from separatist fundamentalists into engaged evangelicals. And cultural goods such as videotapes, music, and books may have helped to ease and maintain this engagement. Like evangelicals themselves, these cultural products were staging a new dialogue with the wider culture. They drew on the genres and styles of the mainstream mass-culture industry, using pre-existing forms ranging from soap opera and sitcom to hip-hop and heavy metal. Today, Christian rockers star in MTV-style videos, and Christian girls' magazines look like *Seventeen* and *YM*. Kids can even find "a superhero who lives up to his calling" when they play Joshua:

The Battle for Jericho, a video game that is Sega-, Nintendo-, Game-boy-, and PC-compatible. Evangelicals have appropriated conventions of horror, science fiction, and melodrama in what may be the most popular evangelical films of all time, the Prophecy Series, four films that dramatize Biblical predictions about the Apocalypse. Bar codes, scanners, and computers figure as enemies in the Prophecy Series be-cause all of these technologies will be used by the Antichrist when he forces everyone to take "the Mark of the Beast" on his or her forehead or right hand. The mark will be either 666, or a bar code, which will be read by grocery store scanners. As in many secular horror and science fiction films, one finds that Christian media express both technophilic and technophobic tendencies; technologies are both useful evangeliz-ing tools and potential tools of the Antichrist.[30]

In their appropriation of secular forms such as science fiction, heavy metal, or hip-hop, evangelicals seem to say that these forms are not in-herently secular but, rather, neutral forms that can be used to meet evangelical needs. Such appropriation elides the historical specificity of popular forms. Rap is dissociated from black culture and becomes a style that can be used to promote any message. Reggae promotes drug-free submission to authority. Rock-and-roll does not resist parental norms but rather secular culture's pressure to have premarital sex. Even a sexy pop song can become a chastity song. In the 1980s, one band ripped off George Michael's "I Want Your Sex," but their song was called "I Don't Want It." Evangelical media producers often take styles and genres that nonevangelical youth might use to articulate "resistant identities" (themselves heavily commodified) and respin that resis-tance in previously unimagined ways. Christian hip-hop might be a means, for example, of resisting the "dangers" of secular hip-hop.[31]

To distribute their alternative versions of secular commodities, evangelicals have created a network of Christian bookstores, and in-creasingly, these goods are also found in secular bookstores and even movie theaters. Evangelicals, in other words, have created an alterna-tive culture but as "respectable" middle-class consumers are also in-creasingly themselves becoming part of the mass culture industry.

THE RELIGIOUS MARKETPLACE AND THE SEARCH
FOR MIDDLE-CLASS RESPECTABILITY

As the market in evangelical cultural goods grows, it is tempting to see the explosion of Christian novels, T-shirts, CDs, videos, and video games as evidence of diluted evangelical faith. Obviously, if evangeli-cals are actually more interested in diversifying the colors, shapes, and sizes of Bibles than they are in the content of the Good Book, something is awry. But there is no evidence that this is the case. The assumption that the market in evangelical goods is a sign of shallow faith is simplistic. After all, American religions have always been players, in one way or another, in the marketplace of culture. National Christian bookstore chains may not have existed when the Republic was founded, but the First Amendment's declaration of "disestablishment"—that the United States will have no government-sanctioned official religion—guaranteed that the number of religions would multiply and compete with each other to win over the nation's souls and wallets. Religions have proliferated in America in part because the First Amendment established what one might call a "free market of religion."[32] Televangelists like Oral Roberts and Jimmy Swaggart may take fundraising to new heights, but in the absence of a state religion and taxpayer support, American churches have always had to convince people to provide financial support. As R. Laurence Moore has observed,

Religion's role "in the marketplace of culture" began in the nineteenth century as an effort to influence and in some cases to ban altogether the commodities being offered for sale . . . Rather than remaining aloof, [religious groups] entered their own inventive contributions into the market. Initially these were restricted to the market for reading material, but their cultural production diversified . . . By degrees, religion itself took on the shape of a commodity . . . [and] looked for ways to appeal to all consumers, using the techniques of advertising and publicity employed by other merchants.[33]

Moore recounts eighteenth- and nineteenth-century debates over how entertaining sermons should be, whether sermons should borrow theatrical techniques, whether religious books could use novelistic dramatic devices, and whether tracts could use advertising techniques. In virtually every case where believers have been nervous about whether pleasure in religion was legitimate, the advocates of theatrical revivals and advertising-like tracts have won out in the end.

Moore further argues that no religious faith is entirely immune to the lure of the marketplace. This is an important point to keep in mind when we critique evangelicals, who with their TV fundraising and burgeoning media industry may mistakenly seem like the only folks competing for believers.

Once churches began to do something other than tending the faithful, once they started beating the bushes in search of new members, once they took on the holy mission of converting the world, they were in the business of selling. Selling breeds entrepreneurs who will do whatever the law allows and will press the limits. The religious proselytizing generated by free markets and competition will always in someone's opinion be hucksterism. Those who cry "hucksterism" with respect to someone else's religion are usually no less engaged in selling. They only imagine that their selling is *more professional, more tasteful.*[34]

Evangelicals are not the only people "beating the bushes" for converts and contributors; they are simply, currently, the ones doing the best job.[35]

Moore's phrase, "more tasteful," is interesting because it points to class issues at stake in the different ways religion sells itself. Televangelist Tammy Faye Bakker, with her tarantula-like eyelashes, big hair, and bright clothing was an easy butt for the cruel jokes of middle-class viewers. Former Christian Coalition leader Ralph Reed, conversely, appeared on respectable network news shows wearing fashionable, "tasteful" sweaters. Bakker evoked "low-class" fundamentalism, while Reed sported the style of the up-to-date evangelical. This was an upscale boyish patriarch selling the image of bourgeois respectability. In his introduction to the Christian Coalition's 1995 book promoting the "Contract with the American Family," Reed argued that

while the media has frequently caricatured people of faith active in the political process as "fire-breathing radicals" or "poor, uneducated, and easy to command," the reality is very different. People of faith in this country want for their families, for their communities, and for their country what almost everyone else wants. We want a nation of safe neighborhoods, strong families, limited government, lower taxes, term limits, and schools that work.[36]

Reed portrayed himself and his organization as the representatives of a new version of Richard Nixon's "silent majority"; he was just the average Christian, a middle-class American, not "poor, uneducated, and easy to command."

It is this mythical average American evangelical that the Christian media industry targets. Christian books, CDs, films, and videos function as markers of status, like Reed in his expensive sweaters. To purchase Christian products is to declare one's *respectability* in a country in which people are most often addressed by mass culture not as citizens but as consumers. In America, to buy is to be, yet while other minorities have been singled out by marketers, evangelicals have been largely ignored. Gays and lesbians, for example, have started to appear occasionally in ads, and they are beginning to turn up more frequently on television shows. As one journalist explained in 2000, "after decades of being marginalized, demonized, or completely ignored, gays have finally found their way onto mainstream TV by becoming that most powerful of special interest groups: an audience demographic."[37] Many evangelicals are stunned by the increased media presence of gays and lesbians, not only because they consider homosexuality to be sinful but also because they wonder why this minority has surpassed them in demographic respectability.[38] Depending on whose figures you accept, 60–95 million Americans are evangelicals. That's a stunning 25–40 percent of the population. Where is *their* recognition as a demographic? Notwithstanding the success of *Touched by an Angel,* evangelicals are rarely directly targeted as desirable consumers by the mass culture industry. Advertisements may sometimes be conservative and speak to old-fashioned values, but they rarely risk alienating non–born-agains by using overtly Christian discourse. Faced with a lack of options on the secular culture menu, evangelicals have forged their own media industry, thus staking a claim for themselves as modern consumers.

The 1991 premiere episode of the straight-to-video Focus on the Family cartoon series *Adventures in Odyssey* contains an exchange of dialogue that pointedly illustrates an evangelical perception that the world sees Christians as backward, the antithesis of all that is modern. Faustus, an evil used car salesman trying to manipulate people into caring only about worldly possessions, tells the kindly old inventor Mr. Whittaker, "Your ideas are old-fashioned and outdated . . . part of another age. In fact, you really don't belong in the modern world at all." Whittaker retorts, "You're wrong . . . there are those of us who know what's truly important. Our hope isn't in wealth and power. Our hope lies in something you can never control or conquer: our faith." Bear in mind that this idea is being expressed in a wildly successful home-video cartoon series created by one of the most successful distributors of Christian cultural goods in the United States.[39] These cartoons are filled with prayers and Biblical lessons, and they sell extremely well because they offer an alternative to secular cartoons that evangelicals appreciate.[40] But they are also important in and of themselves as *objects,* as best-selling cultural products that illustrate that evangelicals *do* "belong in the modern world."

Statistically, evangelicals cover the economic gamut, yet many non–born-agains still imagine evangelicals as low-class. Smith's study, however, did not find enormous differences between the income or education levels of evangelicals and nonevangelicals. In fact, overall, the evangelicals he studied tended to earn more and had completed more higher education than secular people.[41] Perhaps the misperception that born-agains are poor and uneducated explains why Christians literally don't count in terms of calculating book sales; until recently,

Christians have not been perceived by secular publishers as big readers, so Christian bookstores have not been charted in the secular bestseller lists. Many people would have been surprised to hear that *The Living Bible*, which paraphrased the Bible in contemporary language, was the highest-selling book in the United States in both 1971 and 1972. By 1982 it had sold over twenty-five million copies.[42] In 1982, Francis Schaeffer's *A Christian Manifesto*, a conservative evangelical call to political action, outsold *Jane Fonda's Workout Book* two to one.[43] Yet the secular market didn't notice evangelicals in the early 1980s, even though by this time they seemed to have proven themselves as a powerful consumer group.

Evangelicals had spent money, but they hadn't changed their image. Conducting a training session for Moral Majority activists in 1982, Cal Thomas warned his listeners that reporters would often be hostile or condescending. To combat this, it was crucial to project the right image.

If you don't look the way they think you ought to look, then you're dumb [in the reporter's opinion] . . . I don't care how much you may love those polyester pantsuits, don't wear them. That's not an option. Don't do it. No white shoes and socks—especially in winter. No matter how much you like them. I'm serious. Take stock of your wardrobe. Some of you guys look like you got dressed in a closet with the lights off. . . . The way you look can speak volumes.[44]

Thomas was clearly forging a strategic response to the mainstream media, which he correctly assumed would be likely to condescend to evangelicals whose taste in clothing coded them as low-class. In retrospect, it may be hard to feel sympathy for the white shoes and pantsuits crowd, since the Moral Majority made a huge political splash and was, for a short period in the eighties, a daunting, frightening force of the political Right. But setting aside the politics of Falwell's group, what is interesting here is how clearly Thomas articulates the importance of style, that only a middle-class wardrobe will gain respect for the wearer and that evangelicals interacting with the secular world are at a disadvantage because they are automatically assumed to be low-class and, by extension, ignorant.[45] Christian novelists, musicians, and filmmakers may be genuine in their fervent desire to affect people's hearts and souls through their art, but the rise of Christian media is symptomatic of more than spiritual outreach. Whether consciously intended or not, the creation of such products is in a way like trading in the old white pantsuit for khakis from the Gap. These products help create a place at the table of middle-class consumer culture for American evangelicals.[46]

For people who remember the Moral Majority's heyday, the idea of Christians who enjoy shopping may seem a bit odd. The Moral Majority, as well as Rev. Donald Wildmon's Coalition for Better Television, were widely understood as censorious boycotters. Both groups favored the targeting of advertisers as a means of removing "objectionable" programming, and they achieved some success: *Soap*'s gay character eventually went straight, the *Maude* abortion episode was picked up by few local affiliates.[47] Rather than point to specific instances of TV censorship, however, it might be more accurate to say that the conservative Christian attack on television in the eighties created an environment of fear in the television industry that provoked self-censorship. It was easier for the television networks to pretend that abortion and homosexuality did not exist than to risk provoking boycotts and endangering relationships with advertisers.

The story of Christian attacks on the entertainment industry in the 1980s usually focuses on outcomes, on the extent to which Christian activists succeeded. But what if we approach this era of activism from a different angle? How did these censorship attempts affect not the images seen on prime-time television but rather the image of evangelicals themselves? The obvious answer is that conservative evangelical activists were perceived as a danger to the separation of church and state, to civil rights, and to freedom of speech. But evangelicals were also *outsiders*, not only because of their censorious politics but also because of their threatened boycotts. They professed to be willing to not buy cars, food, clothing, whatever it took to get objectionable shows off of television. They were willing to be nonconsumers with a vengeance.

The TV industry's response is interesting. Alerted to the possibility of losing advertising money, the networks and advertisers became nervous about alienating evangelical viewers. But if evangelicals constituted such a large market, and if losing their patronage would be so devastating, why not actually target them? If as many as sixty million people in the United States are evangelicals, why not add evangelical characters to sitcoms and soap operas? Maybe this felt dangerous. Why risk alienating liberal and moderate viewers? It seems more likely that the thought of adding evangelical characters never even occurred to the networks. Followers of Wildmon and Falwell were not seen as consumers so much as people you didn't want *not* to consume. Boycotts aside, they existed as a public relations crisis, a problem to be resolved as quickly as possible.

No longer the backward fundamentalist of the 1980s who threatened to not buy, the contemporary evangelical (at least as envisioned by today's growing Christian media industry) is a buyer. As a manager of an Indianapolis Christian radio station explains, when a typical listener hears an ad on the radio, "she takes it to the bank: 'That car dealer must be a Christian, because he advertises on my radio station.'"[48] Dr. James C. Dobson, founder of the Christian organization Focus on the Family, may be appalled by contemporary culture, but his primary solution is not to organize boycotts but rather to offer up his own products. He has, in fact, become a millionaire through the therapeutic Christian lifestyle products—videos, books, and audio cassettes—that are distributed by Focus on the Family.[49] The sheer magnitude of the products sold by Focus is astounding. Focus had an estimated income of $78 million in 1992; in 1995, the figure had risen to $101 million.[50] In 1999, Focus rolled their twenty millionth mail order cassette off the duplication line. "If all that tape was spliced together and stretched out, it would circle the earth fifty-two times," they proudly announced.[51] Dobson's industry clearly targets bourgeois consumers, not Bible-thumping boycotters.

TARGETING CHRISTIAN KIDS

Much of the media created by Dobson and other Christian producers is directed at youth. This demographic is the one most heavily targeted by evangelical media because youth are considered the group most vulnerable to the lure of secular culture's pleasures, pleasures ranging from cigarettes and liquor to occult-themed music and sexually explicit Hollywood movies. A wide range of products are sold to kids, and the products are all of varying—or ambiguous—evangelical intensity. What these products have in common, however, is, first, their dependence on evangelical ideas about the effects of media on children and, second, their status as cool commodities that make kids feel less alienated from American consumer culture. Evangelicals use music in particular to construct a hip, alternative youth identity. A virginity rally spokesperson observes that by mimicking mainstream styles, evangelical music shows youngsters that "Christians can be as cool as, say, the Rolling Stones."[52] The remainder of this chapter will examine the youth market for Christian media, observing the ways that such media reflect evangelical ideas about the nature of the sinful child but also include elements that clearly reflect accommodations to the secular world. Obviously, such accommodations are made to make these media more appealing to young Christian consumers.

Carol Flake, who was raised as a Southern Baptist, explains that she had to change her beliefs when she left home for college. "Taking my religion with me to the campus and the big city would have been like traveling with a rube relative in a loud plaid jacket who'd try to order a hamburger at a French restaurant."[53] Flake's feeling that her religion made her "out of it" at college is one shared by many evangelical teens who pursue secular higher education, and Christian media, parents hope, can serve as a kind of counterbalance against "big city" pressures. If secular culture encourages teens to be independent and resist parental authority, Christian culture also offers resistance to young consumers. Not having sex, for example, can be presented as a way to radically resist the norms of mainstream culture. In this way, not having sex is made hip, and teens can revolt, but not against their parents. This is an idealized picture, of course, of how evangelical adults would like to see their children behave, and it may not always work. Regardless of efficacy, what is particularly interesting here is that underpinning this approach to shaping how kids think about sex is an implicit theory of subjectivity: children can be shaped to think the way that their parents (or God) would like them to think.

Of course, most nonevangelical parents would also like to shape their children's beliefs, and both born-again and non–born-again parents are nervous that music, video games, and television may misshape their children. But there are some crucial differences between how the two groups approach the perceived problem of the effects of media on youth. Whereas mainstream secular culture most commonly portrays youth as inherently innocent yet infinitely corruptible when exposed to the wrong media (excessive cartoon violence, Internet pornography), Focus on the Family and other evangelical media producers conceive of children as inherently corrupted by sin yet capable of innocence. Dr. Dobson, who is not only the founder of Focus but also a child psychologist who has written several popular books advocating authoritarian child rearing, argues that certain kinds of behavior can be ingrained in children at an early age. He explains that, like baby geese, who can be biologically imprinted to follow their mother or, in her absence, any other animal or moving object, children can be imprinted (or "indoctrinated") in certain irreversible ways.[54]

Although Dobson never goes so far as to suggest fighting thumbsucking or binding children while they sleep to prevent masturbation, his approach in a number of ways resembles the behaviorist child rearing methods of the early twentieth century. As Martha Wolfenstein explained in 1951,

The conception of the child's basic impulses has undergone an extreme transformation from 1914 to the 1940s. At the earlier date, the infant appeared to be endowed with strong and dangerous impulses . . . The impulses "easily grow beyond control" and are harmful in the extreme . . . The mother must be ceaselessly vigilant; she must wage a relentless battle against the child's sinful nature.[55]

By the postwar years, fun was supposed to infuse all of the mother's activities with the child; allowing the child to gratify impulses was no longer seen as encouraging "wickedness." Wolfenstein does not overtly discuss religion, yet she speaks of "puritanical" ideas in the past tense and even goes so far as to ask, "Is it because we have come to realize that the Devil does not exist that we are able to fuse play and fun with business, child care, and so on?"[56] Seeing pleasure as sinful is old-fashioned, like believing in the Devil. Dr. Dobson shows us, however, that neither perceiving children as wicked nor believing in the Devil, are ways of thinking that have disappeared. According to Dobson, though, pleasure can be properly managed so that it is not sinful.

A youth properly indoctrinated with Christian beliefs does not need to be told what media is verboten. Instead, a properly raised child instinctively knows how to censor his or her media consumption. Focus's 1992 *Learn to Discern* video opens with children viewing sexy MTV videos and scenes from violent movies. Since the kids are educated in media "discernment," the looks on their faces range from confused to appalled. Later in the video, children who have not been taught proper close-reading skills explain what they like about slasher movies; their faces are digitally scrambled. Although the intention is, presumably, to maintain the anonymity of the young horror movie fans, the effect is a pathologizing criminalization of these "corrupted" children. Ironically, it is the instinctively *knowing* children shown at the beginning of the video who are *innocent*, since their knowledge of what is corrupting is what enables abstinence from that dangerous media. Their properly frightened and appalled faces are not scrambled; instead, they are offered as proof that, in the Focus on the Family universe, Christian children do not want to see sex and violence. So what do they watch? Since sex and violence—not to mention swearing—permeate the media, Christian kids would not have many options were it not for the growing market in evangelical media that mirrors secular culture's styles.

As the Christian media industry has grown, it is the music industry that has developed most quickly. Christian music targets all age groups, but teens are a particularly coveted demographic. This should not be surprising, insofar as much of the secular music industry also targets teens. Simply put, teenagers like music, and middle-class adolescents are a lucrative market. The Christian music industry makes money off of teens, but there is much more to the proliferation of youth-targeted Christian music than the profit motive. Teenagers tend to be alienated, rebellious, and horny. Secular teen culture cashes in on these feelings by providing music and music videos that portray teens as alienated, rebellious, and horny. Evangelicals worry that their kids will accept the invitations that secular culture offers, invitations to resist parental authority, drink alcohol, engage in sex outside of marriage, use profane language, and in general, not honor the Lord. Christian music acknowledges the problems that teenagers face, but it offers up Jesus as a solution. It also implicitly offers up itself, as a commodity, as a purchasable solution. If many Christian teens already feel like geeks, imagine how much worse it would be if they didn't have their own music and music videos. Manager Dan Harrell pointed to this when he observed that, "What [Amy Grant's Platinum album] 'Heart in Motion' did . . . was give Christian kids something to be proud of. They could say, 'Hey, we're normal.'"[57]

Through their alternative media production, Christian media producers seem to be striving to forge a Christian youth identity that is legible to adults. A number of scholars contend that the thrill of youth culture lies precisely in the fact that adults "don't get it,"[58] yet the goal of Christian youth media products is to somehow provide pleasure (since kids won't consume media they find dull) while eliminating the very generation gap crucial to that pleasure in the first place. The angry youth response to Rev. Jimmy Swaggart's infamous condemnation of contemporary Christian music (CCM) shows that the generation gap that some adults hope will be mended by CCM still exists. From the adult perspective, CCM works either as a placebo for secular pop culture (according to Focus on the Family) or as a wolf in sheep's clothing (according to Swaggart). Focus literature directed to parents persistently makes statements like, "If your kids like Megadeath, this is a good substitute." Or, "Sounds like Nine Inch Nails, but with a better message." Swaggart rejected this substitution approach, and he created quite an uproar when he attacked CCM in a 1985 interview:

I think that the attitude, the atmosphere of trying to make a group *look* like a rock group . . . I don't know why anyone would want to do that. Yes, it's popular: I know a lot of young people fall for it. Most all of them do . . . It's like giving a drug addict methadone. [The teen rock-and-roll fan is] on drugs, so you give him methadone. You give this to the kids to appease that lust for rock 'n' roll and the energy, and it has great appeal to it . . . I don't feel that's leading kids to the Lord.[59]

Although CCM *is* sometimes designed to "appease lust," it is condescending and unfair to its youthful fans to imply that they merely consume a lust substitute. Swaggart argued that any conversion that took place through CCM was not true conversion, and artists and fans went wild disagreeing with him. It seems that neither Focus's placebo endorsement of CCM nor Swaggart's blanket rejection is sensitive to the social and spiritual demands CCM may aid young fans in negotiating.

In particular, CCM may serve a useful function in helping kids negotiate their relationship with authoritarian parents. While some kids are not allowed to purchase secular music at all, others are allowed to consume any "safe" secular music. Having been taught how to censor secular music's dangerous messages without parental guidance, Christian kids are under pressure to properly choose their own music. Teen girls sometimes write to Focus's girls' magazine *Brio* asking for advice, because they've found secular music that they think is OK, but they're worried they may be wrong, that they may have accidentally disobeyed God and their parents in making their musical choice. One teen thinks that two songs on a Boyz II Men CD promote Christian values and asks if she's right. *Brio* says yes, but she should program out the other songs on her CD player. Another teen has heard a rumor that a performer she likes is New Age. *Brio* says the group is OK, but reassures the girl that she is justified in being nervous, since New Age is "a movement with a spiritual agenda that clearly contradicts the teaching of Jesus."[60] Modern evangelical kids have been taught to carefully weed through secular music, but what if they mess up? CCM helps take such pressures off kids. As teens in a *New York Times* article explain, CCM is "something that doesn't influence us negatively . . . If you listen to secular music, you have to think about what they're saying. Here the message is simple. It's put in simple terms. You can understand it and you don't have to worry about the influences you get in secular music."[61] CCM seems to offer entertainment without anxiety about disobeying one's parents. And there is an added bonus, one teenager explains: "it makes it not so nerdy to be a Christian."[62]

As teen anxieties about secular music demonstrate, parents and groups like Focus on the Family are correct in realizing that music is an important battleground for managing youthful desires. Evangelical advocates of CCM have sought to make youth faith in music sacred rather than secular, and in doing so, they have distanced themselves from the stereotypical fundamentalist Christian who, like Swaggart, condemns rock music as satanic. Laughing at the old-fashioned, ignorant, and implicitly, uneducated and low-class approach to music ("It's hard to play a CD backward" to hear the Devil's messages, quips Bob DeMoss), the avowedly middle-class Focus argues that inspirational lyrics will be palatable to youth if accompanied by a spoonful of sugar, a rock or heavy metal beat.

This foot-stomping beat may actually be a weak link in the Focus scheme. By changing the lyrics while replicating secular music in style, evangelicals may leave unchanged the bodily or carnal relationships that their teens have with music. The experiences of time, energy, emotion, desire, and pleasure that music enables cannot be erased as easily as secular lyrics can be.[63] Although it would be specious to argue that rock-and-roll is *inherently* lusty as a musical form, it does seem misguided to claim that music can please the spirit while having no relationship to the body. Indeed, secular reviewers of CCM concerts consistently note a writhing ecstasy among aroused concertgoers that clearly defies any dualistic conception of body and spirit where music is concerned. In sum, directing teenagers to Christian music is a risky gambit. If these young consumers were imprintable geese, as in the Dobson formulation, the operation would be guaranteed success, but the realities of the use and experience of music are more complex than either Dobson or Swaggart imagines. Today's evangelicals clearly take a risk when they embrace secular forms imbued with Christian messages. Separatist fundamentalists were never fully sheltered from secular forms of entertainment, for even as they attacked worldly mass culture as dangerous they selectively drew from that culture when it suited their needs. Contemporary evangelicals, on the other hand, have become less selective. They have wholeheartedly made use of secular forms, and as we will see shortly, these forms can sometimes be a Trojan horse for "worldly" content.

SHIFTING TOWARD THE SECULAR WORLD: MCGEE AND ME AND VEGGIETALES

McGee and Me and *VeggieTales* are two very successful straight-to-video Christian series for kids. While both emphasize the power of prayer and the importance of belief in God, *VeggieTales* softens its message to reach a wider crossover (not strictly evangelical) audience. Both series, however, maintain the importance of adult authority—even if the adults happen to be asparagus spears! Both *McGee and Me* and *VeggieTales* have sold millions of copies, but *VeggieTales* will ultimately sell more, having made it onto the shelves of Target and Kmart. And while *McGee and Me* ceased production in the mid-nineties, *VeggieTales* is still going strong. The series ranked number one in Christian video sales in 2001, and in 2002 its production company, Big Idea, released a *VeggieTales* feature film, *Jonah*, in secular theaters. Released on video and DVD in 2003, *Jonah* sold 1 million copies in just three weeks. The number of VeggieTales products in mainstream toy stores will continue to increase, since *VeggieTales* characters have been licensed to Fisher-Price (fig. 12). The differences between this series and *McGee and Me* point to the multiple ways that evangelicals have increased their worldly presence since the early 1990s. Created by Focus on the

FIG. 12 AN ELABORATE DISPLAY OF VEGGIETALES PRODUCTS AT A CHRISTIAN BOOKSTORE. PHOTO BY
THE AUTHOR.

Family, *McGee and Me* represents a transitional moment for evangelicals,
where they dove into video production, drawing on secular forms (in this
case, the sitcom) but hung onto explicitly evangelical messages. *Veggie-
Tales,* conversely, seeks a wider market and thus has a tempered, ambigu-
ously "religious" message.

    McGee and Me is a live-action and animated show about Nick, an
eleven-year-old Christian boy. The series began production in 1991,
and according to Focus, by 1993, 600,000 copies had been sold; by
1996, Focus had sold 15 million. *McGee and Me* episodes often illustrate
the importance of obeying adult authority, a central tenet of evangelical child rearing literature. In the episode "The Not-So-Great Escape,"
Nick defies his parents by sneaking out of the house to see an R-rated
horror film. As in the *Learn to Discern* video, Nick and the other kids in
the movie theater are shown as repulsed and terrified (figs. 13–15).
When Nick comes home his parents coldly ask him how the movie
was. He tells them it was awful.

    One can imagine a similar scenario on a family sitcom like *Roseanne*
or *Everybody Loves Raymond.* In fact, most family sitcoms are pretty
moralistic; kids disobey their parents, and then they suffer the consequences. If Nick were on most shows, his parents would notice his fear,
ask him if he was OK, explain why it is important not to see TV or
movies until you are old enough to handle them, give him a big hug,

FIG. 13 IN FOCUS ON THE FAMILY'S SITCOM MCGEE AND ME, NICK SNEAKS INTO A SCARY MOVIE THAT HIS PARENTS HAVE FORBIDDEN HIM TO SEE.

FIGS. 14–15 SINCE NICK IS A PROPERLY RAISED CHRISTIAN CHILD, HE REALIZES INSTINCTIVELY THAT WHAT HE IS WATCHING IS WRONG.

and then probably punish him by grounding him. In "The Not-So-Great Escape," however, Nick's parents tell him that it really doesn't matter whether he enjoyed the film or not. The problem is that he now has horrible images in his brain, injected there by the film, and he will never be able to rid himself of them. (In Dobson's terms, he has been negatively imprinted.) Nick's parents send him to his room to think about how he has harmed himself, and his dad says he will come up soon to talk over his punishment. Nick says, in voice-over, "Let's just say that we did more than talk about my punishment," implying that corporal punishment was administered. In the video's final scene, Nick happily tells his animated friend McGee that doing endless extra chores as punishment is infinitely better than having to see another R-rated film.

McGee and Me targets a young demographic. Unlike Christian rock music, then, which targets and is purchased by teenagers, it is parents who buy these videos, which makes it difficult to gauge how much kids like *McGee and Me*. It is clear, however, that these videos advocate an approach to child rearing that is radically different than that which is found in most of popular culture. The sassy kids from *Roseanne* wouldn't last five minutes in the *McGee and Me* world. In fact, shows like *Roseanne* are seen as a problem by many evangelical parents. In her ethnographic study of Christian child caregivers, for example, Ellen Seiter found that "the portrayal of permissive parent/child relationships on television, especially situation comedies, is often used [by Christians] to explain the lack of regard for childhood obedience that pervades the culture."[64] Since *McGee and Me* promotes Dobson's authoritarian child rearing theories, it might seem like a safe haven for parents anxious about secular TV. Yet the video series has ceded to secular culture insofar as it uses the sitcom format and avoids the extensive Biblical exegesis and long preachy scenes that were typical in earlier Christian media. Focus on the Family videos want to teach a lesson, but they also work hard to entertain, which means using classic sitcom gags and narrative structures. Since sitcoms quite often end with a moral lesson, the genre is quite compatible with Focus's evangelical goals.

VeggieTales is "more secular" than *McGee and Me* insofar as the depiction of parental authority is less severe in the *VeggieTales* world. The computer-animated series, which is touted as containing "Sunday morning values and Saturday morning fun," stars Bob the Tomato and Larry the Cucumber, adult-coded vegetables who teach lessons like "God is bigger than scary monsters you see on TV, so don't be afraid" (figs. 16–17). Targeting children from roughly three to ten years old and appealing to kids much younger and older,[65] the videos often in-

FIGS. 16–17 VEGGIETALES'S
LARRY THE CUCUMBER AND BOB
THE TOMATO TEACH CHILDREN
BIBLICAL VALUES WITHOUT INVOK-
ING JESUS.

clude a "silly song" about, say, Larry's desire for his lost comb, and they often, but not always, include a Bible story. They promote respect for parental authority, and so, unlike most secular children's television shows and advertisements, they do not portray an "appealing vision of a world where 'kids rule.'"[66] In "Where Is God When I'm Scared?" Junior Asparagus disobeys his parents by watching a scary movie on TV. His mother sends him to bed, but he is not in trouble, and he doesn't get a spanking. Naturally, his parents were right that he was too young for the movie: he is too scared to go to sleep. Soon Larry and Bob arrive and teach him that God will keep him safe. What we have here is a modified—or partly secularized, if you will—version of "The Not-So-Great Escape." Both Nick and Junior Asparagus learn a valuable lesson, but Nick has to suffer to become a better person. Junior Asparagus, conversely, engages in adventures that teach him about God, and the parental authority issue is soft-peddled.

But it's not only its authoritarianism-lite approach that moves

VeggieTales closer to the world of secular media than to the world of *McGee and Me*. The fact that *VeggieTales* videos are pro-God but lack a message about Jesus increases their potential viewer base to Jews or to Christians in denominations that don't emphasize salvation as the linchpin of religious identity. When Bible stories appear, they are drawn from the Old Testament. And the silly songs are for the most part areligious, which means some parents may opt to buy the silly song compilation videos, not the original videos that only contained one silly song surrounded by Bible stories. Thanks to the silly song videos, even atheists can find a version of *VeggieTales* suitable for their children.

Launched by Big Idea Productions in 1993, this series was originally marketed only in Christian stores, selling three million videos. An additional eight million were sold after the first twelve titles were introduced at Target, Wal-Mart, Walgreen's, and Kmart in March of 1998. The overall sales of Christian videos rose 41 percent in 1998, and most of this growth was due to *VeggieTales*. In fact, *VeggieTales* held eight out of the ten slots on the Christian Bookseller Association's 1998 list of bestselling videos.[67] As its audience widens, it is clear that *VeggieTales* appeals beyond the evangelical market. In fact, in December 1999 *VeggieTales* advertised in *TV Guide*, a publication that has one of the largest subscription bases in America. With their 2000 release of *Queen Esther*, Big Idea positioned itself to get into the feature business. *Queen Esther* abandons the old *VeggieTales* format and opening song; the narrative of the forty-minute mini-feature is in the formulaic Disney mold and features Disney-like songs. Queen Esther, a green onion, even has the pretty, bouncy hair that is required of all contemporary Disney animated heroines. Like many *VeggieTales* narratives, this one is firmly ensconced in the Old Testament, although at one point we do see a taxi company advertisement that reads "Why wait for A.D.?" This is literally the only reference to Jesus in any *VeggieTales* cartoon.

So, is *VeggieTales* evangelical? As media produced and distributed by evangelicals succeeds in the mainstream marketplace, we need to ask what exactly the "secular market" is and what a "Christian video" is. The boundaries are not so clear. *VeggieTales* videos may be produced by evangelicals, but there is no easy consensus among consumers that these videos are fundamentally Christian. Creator Phil Vischer says that "if you want your kids to be more sarcastic, more aggressive, more disrespectful, there are plenty of shows to teach them that . . . But what if you want your kids to be more forgiving or kind? That's what motivated us."[68] There's nothing here that would alienate nonevangelical parents.

But is the absence of a clear salvation message controversial for evangelicals? Cindy Montano, a Christian music video producer who enjoys watching *VeggieTales* with her daughter, has no explanation for the lack of overt evangelism in the series. Nor is she particularly bothered by that absence. Rather, she argues for the value of *VeggieTales* on several counts. First, it is better than most kids' TV, which is violent and teaches bad values. Second, because it doesn't teach the secular values promoted elsewhere, it may actually "soften the hearts" of viewers, which will make them more receptive to a message of salvation later. And third, the videos always quote from the Bible, implanting the idea that Scripture has use value and that it can be applied to daily life.[69] These seem like good arguments for the evangelical value of *Veggie-Tales*. One might legitimately protest that there is something fishy about Christian media that doesn't mention Christ, but on the other hand, why must a Christian message be literal and unsubtle? Messages about love and forgiveness could certainly be interpreted as "Christian." Besides, feel-good "prosocial" messages are standard on children's television. Like the sitcom, the TV cartoon is a secular genre that often includes a clear didactic message. Substituting a religious message for the standard secular lesson is not difficult. Ultimately, even if *VeggieTales* is wholesome and promotes an evangelical attitude about the everyday use of the Bible, one cannot help but read the lack of Jesus as a concession to the secular marketplace. Summing up his selling philosophy, creator Phil Vischer says that "if you can tell a story that improves people's lives *and* cracks them up, you can get people to pay for things that make them better people."[70] *VeggieTales* may indeed promote certain "Sunday morning values," but the idea that purchased objects will make you a better person is certainly a concession to materialism, to the secular world. It is a concession, in sum, to Saturday morning values.

EDGE TV

Christian media for teenagers present a unique set of challenges for producers. Teens are less likely to tolerate the didactic messages of media directed to younger children and, as puberty sets in, are more likely to be struggling with the urge to challenge adult authority. Evangelical teens who have trouble obeying their parents are also going to have trouble obeying an adult authority figure like Dobson. In the 1980s, Dobson, Josh McDowell, and other evangelical media personalities turned out a lot of "Q&A" videos in which teens asked advice about sex, drugs, and peer pressure. By the end of the 1990s, however, evangelical media producers had realized that teens would rather hear advice from other teens. Rather than fighting this, producers made a

major concession to secular culture by making their videos less authoritative and preachy and more fun and kid-centered. Today's teen
videos continue to promote a conservative evangelical worldview in
many respects, but now the visual of the talking head patriarchal authority figure is gone, and there is no longer an authoritative adult
voice-over.

Many of these new videos belong to series that were created specifically for use in youth groups, which are a key means for trying to keep
Christian youth within the fold. Youth groups are an older version of
Sunday school, where teenagers study the Bible but also discuss their
personal problems. Youth-group videos are typically broken into
seven-to-ten-minute topical segments, and they come with discussion
manuals for the pastors who lead the groups. A large evangelical
church will typically have a full-time youth pastor on staff to run
youth group meetings and plan other teen activities. Youth pastors are
among the biggest purchasers of teen media, especially music videos
and issue-oriented discussion videos.

Perhaps the best example of the teen discussion video is *Edge TV*, a
popular series that began production in the early 1990s. Each *Edge TV*
video has a different thematic focus, such as "entertainment," "sexual
choices," or "reconciliation." The magazine-format videos are full of interviews with kids and adults such as youth pastors, musicians, or comic
book artists. The style is hip, and the editing and graphics have changed
over the years to match contemporary styles. The earliest *Edge TV* install-
ments took a more adult-centered approach than later videos would. In
a 1992 episode, an unseen adult asks a teen questions about his drug
use, putting him on the defensive. In the end, the police come, and adult
power prevails. In the early videos, featured musicians offering insights
on life were often fortyish rock-and-rollers, or mellow, soft-rock types.
The music was often stuff kids wouldn't be caught dead listening to. By
1995, it was common to see younger, hipper musicians on the show
singing music most Christian adults would approve of in principle but
which they would probably not want to listen to themselves.

The discussion manuals that come with *Edge TV* videos are designed
to lead viewers in the right direction, and the series's conservative outlook is clearly discernible: abstinence is mandatory, homosexuality is a
sin, abortion is murder. What makes the videos less conservative is that
these messages are revealed through teen testimony, not through an
adult authority figure.[71] Even if many of the messages have a traditional evangelical ring, the videos' privileging of teen testimony invests
teens with an authority that would have been anathema in evangelical
videos in the early eighties. What is particularly remarkable about *Edge
TV* is the extent to which it dares to leave room for doubt and debate.

While *McGee and Me* and *VeggieTales* offer clear didactic messages (and entertainment) to younger viewers, speakers in *Edge TV* videos say things that are provocative and even controversial. In a segment on materialism, a Christian snowboarder does not show much self-aware-ness when he discusses all the free promotional snowboarding supplies he has accepted from sponsors. In a segment on youth in Northern Ire-land, a young woman claims that God sees Roman Catholics and Protestants as exactly the same, an idea that many conservative evan-gelicals would question. The producers must realize that a teenager is less malleable than a ten year old and will expect to think for him- or herself rather than be lectured to. This seems to be a realistic conces-sion to permissive, nonevangelical modes of child rearing, an acknowl-edgment that strictly authoritarian child rearing will inevitably lose its grasp when kids become teenagers who encounter secular TV, go to Hollywood movies, and perhaps end up attending a non-Christian col-lege or university. Ultimately, *Edge TV* illustrates that permissive child rearing, so dominant in mainstream culture, has inevitably leaked into evangelical culture. Separatist fundamentalists might be able to main-tain more strictly traditional child rearing techniques, but evangelicals who create their own culture industry and who selectively partake of secular mainstream culture will not be able to keep permissive ideas about child rearing from intruding into their lives.

When Christian chastity videos first appeared in the eighties, largely in response to AIDS, it was adults who held the microphone and the answers. In an *Edge TV* abstinence public service announce-ment from 1999, conversely, teens are represented as very much in control. Chastity is a directive that comes from adults, as we will see in chapter 3, but *Edge TV* manages to make it seem like an idea that origi-nates with youth themselves. Speaking in unison, the angry teens are emphatic and a bit self-righteous:

Don't hide the truth from us. Show us the way, or get out of the way, and we'll show you. Yeah, we're young. That doesn't mean we're stupid. Just because some of our parents had no self-control doesn't mean we don't. Maybe we're smarter. Maybe we're strong. Maybe we're wiser than they were. Wise up. These are not the good old days. Grow up. Sex is not a game.

This is remarkable, since traditional authoritarian child rearing dictates that kids don't talk back to their parents. Parents are right, kids are wrong, and there is little space for negotiation. Here, however, the kids seem to be telling not just other teen viewers but also their own par-ents who came of age during the sexual revolution of the 1960s and 1970s to "grow up." Their parents had no self-control, but these teenagers will do a better job. After almost a decade of trial and error, the makers of *Edge TV* now seem to take it for granted that straight adult authority will not work with contemporary teens. In making this concession, *Edge TV* has clearly been influenced by nonevangelical ideas about adolescent autonomy.

The series has also clearly been influenced by permissive ideas about teaching through entertainment, embracing what Wolfenstein referred to as "fun morality." Analysis of one *Edge TV* segment, "SK8 Church," will illustrate this point. "SK8 Church" is about a church in Portland, Oregon, that ministers to teen skateboarders. Paul Anderson explains that one day he was studying in the library at his Bible college when some "squirrely punk kids" who were skipping their youth group meeting came in and noticed his skateboard. He lent it to them so they'd leave him alone, and then it occurred to him that he should witness to the kids. Then the Lord sent him a message: "Like, dude, those kids are going to steal your board." He decided to start Skate Church, as a way to minister to kids, and within two months he had 250 kids (boys) skating around the parking lot of a church. They also skated in the basement, bothering the kitchen staff, and some of the kids urinated in the parking lot. Anderson says that the congregation just didn't get it; they wanted the kids "to be good little church people before they were even saved." Anderson's take was "who cares if we have dents in our building and somebody urinates outside of the facilities? If they're getting saved and they learn how to use the bathroom eventually, that's cool." This attitude is completely antithetical to the Dobson approach to raising kids; it is hard to imagine Dobson taking a lackadaisical line on teenagers who still need potty training.

Shows for younger kids such as *McGee and Me, Adventures in Odyssey,* and *VeggieTales* promote the power of prayer and the importance of obeying God and parents. *Edge TV* promotes these same ideas but acknowledges that teenagers will have more trouble obeying their parents. Furthermore, the series also shows kids whose parents *should not* be obeyed because they are abusive, bad parents. One kid in "SK8 Church" notes that he has been taught to honor his mother and father but that his dad is "hard to love." Another kid says that he sees Skate Church as his family. This is territory that Focus videos would not delve into; there is no room for bad parents in that world (unless, of course, they are non-Christian parents). *Edge TV* speaks to kids not only by acknowledging that some of them may have bad parents but also by letting them *talk* about their bad parents. That is to say, the videos make use of the therapeutic discourse that is so prevalent in secular culture; kids seek a cure through speaking endlessly of their feelings, a theme we will revisit in discussing chastity media in chapter 3.

According to the teenage boys' testimonies, Skate Church's anti-authoritarian approach works. One boy explains, "I just got up there, and I told them, dude, I want to accept God as my personal Lord and Savior, and they hooked me up." Another says that "some people told me about the Lord Jesus Christ, that he saved us from our sins, and that's why I love to come here and have fellowship with my Christian brothers and skate." Anderson says that when the congregation heard the saved kids' testimonies, even the adults who initially "weren't stoked" about the project came around. When someone bequeathed a lot of money to the church, Anderson asked to have it to build a skate warehouse, and the church agreed. He is now officially known as the church's Pastor of Skateboard and In-Line Ministries. Anderson's stance is pragmatic: "The program stands or falls on how big the ramps are. If your ramps are bitty, kids aren't going to come, and they aren't going to hear the Gospel." This may be accurate, but it is striking that Anderson does not mention the supernatural power of the Gospel. The Word in and of itself is not enough to bring the kids; big skating ramps lead the way to salvation.

"SK8 Church" is quickly cut and heavily processed with visual effects, and a hip musical backbeat runs throughout. As voice-overs tell us about being saved, we see close-ups of fast skating, not believers kneeling and praying. The message is clear: getting saved is cool, and so is skating. Or, perhaps, skating is cool, and so is getting saved. As one kid explains, "it was just like a perfect fit for me, because I could serve the Lord while skating." Although Anderson and the kids are extremely earnest, the segment *visually* privileges skating first, and then salvation.

For teen viewers of *Edge TV,* the segment constitutes a big ramp; if *Edge TV* isn't entertaining, kids won't watch it and hear its Gospel message. Again, this differs strikingly from the traditional approach, where you don't use games or fun stuff to get your kids to obey you. A permissive advice book tackling the problem of kids who are picky eaters, for example, might counsel parents to make food more fun: try Mickey Mouse shaped pancakes.[72] In his anti–Dr. Spock child rearing manual, *Dare to Discipline,* Dobson advised parents, à la Mommie Dearest, to keep offering picky kids the exact same plate of food until finally, starved, they would eat. *Edge TV* is definitely closer to the Mickey Mouse pancake school of thought.

Toward the end of the segment, the video finally shows kids studying the Bible. This is a half-hour Bible study and testimony period sandwiched between two one-hour skating sessions. To many non–born-agains, this would seem absurd. If they worship God, they do it in temple on Saturdays or in church on Sundays. To worship while performing a mundane activity—skateboarding, scrubbing the tub, taking out the garbage—is laughable. For an evangelical, however, God's presence can be felt in any situation. If you are outside of such a belief system, the mundane seems to impoverish faith; if you are within the system, faith glorifies the mundane. The question is, if a video is to have *evangelical* value, if it is to speak to kids outside of the system in order to convert them, can it succeed by speaking within the system, taking for granted that viewers already accept the idea that skateboarding can be sanctified? In other words, for this video to succeed, do you have to already be open to the idea that the mundane can be holy, that skateboarding could serve the Lord? Kids not brought up in evangelical households are likely to laugh at these videos. In fact, such kids will most likely never even see them, since they are mostly used in organized youth groups. Rather than seeking out new believers, the videos preach to the choir, trying to make sure that viewers remain in that choir. Ironically, the videos have gone secular insofar as they are strongly inflected by permissive attitudes, yet their audience is composed solely of evangelicals.

SOLD OUT?

Evangelicals hope that the Lord will change the world. And that maybe Christian music, videos, and T-shirts will help out. The risk of this kind of evangelical engagement (as opposed to fundamentalist separatism) in the world of material culture is that that world will change you. This seems to have happened to some extent. Evangelicals may not be recognized as a desirable audience by most producers of Hollywood films, but the growth of Christian bookstores and the influx of Christian media in secular chain stores prove that evangelicals truly are a significant and valuable demographic.

While *McGee and Me* and *Adventures in Odyssey* seem unwavering in their attempts to keep secular ideas at bay, they do draw on popular secular television genres, the prime-time sitcom and the Saturday morning cartoon. These series have generated big sales at Christian stores and through Focus on the Family mail order, but to really spread the word, you need to broaden your message to a wider audience. *VeggieTales* widens the message, but the cost seems to be the elimination of Jesus. *Edge TV* speaks to kids already within evangelical culture, but it realizes that they are also within secular culture. In sum, by examining these different video series we can see that evangelicals haven't simply sold out; they've adjusted their tolerance for secular ideas. In so doing, they have produced a wide range of products that are uneven in their evangelical intensity. *VeggieTales* may have secured the top place on the children's video charts, but *Bibleman,* a live-action superhero show starring Willie Ames from *Eight Is Enough* and *Charles in Charge* as a Scripture-quoting superhero, is a serious competitor. In 1998, *Bibleman*'s sales constituted less than 1 percent of the Christian kidvid market, but by 2001 it accounted for 11 percent of Christian kidvid sales. (In 2001, it was number three in sales, behind *VeggieTales* at number one and a new Big Idea series, *3-2-1 Penguins!* at number two.) By 2001, 10 percent of *Bibleman*'s sales were coming from general market retailers like Target and Wal-Mart.[73] This program could not be more evangelical in its hardcore Bible-quoting intensity and its emphasis on Jesus, yet it is holding its own against *VeggieTales.* Rather than simply taking *VeggieTales* and *Edge TV* as proof, then, that evangelicals have gone secular, we need to consider the full spectrum of Christian videos: some, like *Bibleman* and *McGee and Me,* have little hope of appealing to nonevangelicals, while others have made many concessions to increase sales beyond the evangelical market.

Christian music and music videos take such concessions to a whole new level. To the nonevangelical, such music and videos are not so much "Christian" as wholesome, or sometimes just plain square. The Christians involved in the music industry whom I've talked to, however, do not see themselves as sellouts. A Christian music video may not mention Jesus, but it also doesn't mention sex, profanity, violence, or Satan. Christian parents would rather their kids listen to the CCM group Big Tent Revival sing a light, Beatles-sounding song about the charms of the family dog than a Madonna song about hot sex or a Marilyn Manson song with occult overtones.

One Christian music video producer I interviewed actually did describe herself as a "sellout." Cindy Montano always had a personal relationship with God, but she used to be less passionate, less committed. Her music videos didn't contain a lot of spiritual depth because she wasn't herself spiritually deep enough. Now, however, she explains that she has finally "sold out" for the Lord; she's given her whole heart over to him. Montano uses "selling out" to mean complete surrender. You have sold out once you let down the barriers and give everything up for Jesus. This rhetorical twist points to the perils of calling evangelicals sellouts simply because they use secular forms or dilute their Christian messages. This interpretation is tough on evangelical media, reading their most obvious elements and ignoring their subtleties, ignoring the ways that evangelicals can take any pop culture form and make it their own. To dismiss today's evangelical media producers and consumers as sellouts is rigid, fundamentalist even, in the most negative sense of the word.

WHY SHOULD THE DEVIL HAVE ALL THE GOOD MUSIC? CHRISTIAN MUSIC AND THE SECULAR MARKETPLACE

Sex, drugs, and rock-and-roll once seemed to constitute an inviolable triumvirate. In recent years, however, American evangelical Christians have entered the musical marketplace with a vengeance, staking a claim for rock-and-roll's wholesome potential. What is the spiritual value of this music? Does it evangelize listeners? Evangelicals feel that it is their duty to share the Good News of the Gospel with others. By definition, then, evangelicals are out to change the world. As we have already seen, however, the reverse often happens. In the course of interacting with the secular world, evangelicals have themselves been changed. So it is not surprising that the Christian bands succeeding in the secular market are those that have tuned down their evangelical messages. This chapter takes the Christian music industry as a case study for understanding how evangelicals have used their music to simultaneously struggle against, negotiate with, and acquiesce to the secular world.

Chapter 1 showed how videos have, to varying degrees, "gone secular" in order to successfully speak to evangelical kids. The Christian music and music videos examined in this chapter also speak to that evangelical youth audience. But some Christian music producers also actively strive to speak to the wider culture, even more than *Veggie-Tales*, the cartoon series with tempered Christian messages. Many non-evangelicals are unaware that successful bands such as Creed, P.O.D., Jars of Clay, and Sixpence None the Richer have evangelical roots. Carman, on the other hand, unambiguously promotes a clear Gospel message, and will therefore never find success outside of the Christian marketplace. In examining the Christian music industry, then, we will see how uneven today's Christian media products are in their evangelical intensity, and, thus, how uneven their penetration into the secular marketplace has been.

Although the roots of the Christian music industry go back to the late sixties, its greatest growth spurt took place over the course of the nineties, when Christian radio outlets increased and the number of Christian musicians and record companies rose dramatically. As the industry has grown, the varieties of Christian music have increased, too. A large Christian bookstore will typically stock rock, hip-hop, reggae, ska, adult contemporary, alternative, and heavy metal artists. For punk and the heaviest heavy metal, consumers can turn to the classifieds in *Hard Music* (formerly known as *Heaven's Metal*) magazine or to the hundreds of Internet discussion groups where Christian music is bought and sold.

Christian music would not have grown so quickly were it not for evangelicals' increased social and economic visibility. Moreover, secular record companies would not have invested in Christian music if they had no sense of evangelicals as a viable segment of the middle-class market. It is tempting to link the rise of Christian music to the rise in evangelical *political* visibility in the past thirty years, but Christian music's growth cannot simply be explained as a by-product of Christian activism or as propaganda to further Christian politics. In fact, the way that Christian music has grown and changed is in many ways typical of how subcultural forms of music, if they catch on beyond their niche market, become mass cultural forms. When punk caught on as a marketable genre it was hastily sold to the very bourgeois mass audience that the music had originally defined itself against. Many fans accused successful punk musicians of being sellouts, and their "authenticity" came under scrutiny. Hip-hop has also undergone a similar trajectory, where successful African American artists have been accused of losing their edge to reach a wider audience of white suburban teens.[1]

The Christian music industry has run a course that perhaps most closely mirrors that of country music, which similarly began as a small, subcultural, largely Southern phenomenon. Country was seen as backward, "hillbilly" music for years, and it was once rare to find country music played on the radio or for sale in record stores outside of the South. In the early eighties, however, the Nashville-based industry began to grow, country radio outlets expanded across the country, and stations seen as potentially profitable were bought up by big companies. As country music began selling on a wider scale and small record companies were purchased by larger ones, the budgets of both the music and the music videos increased, shooting up to as much as two hundred thousand dollars per video in the late nineties.[2] As the industry has grown, the music has changed to increase its commercial appeal, which often means taking on an adult contemporary or pop sensibility. Icons of country music such as Patsy Cline, Hank Williams, George Jones, Tammy Wynette, Loretta Lynn, and Dolly Parton do not get air play on today's mainstream country stations, which focus on "the consumer-driven, youth-oriented New or Young Country movement of the 1980s and nineties."[3] It seems that the style of these older artists is too close to the old hillbilly roots, roots which do not enhance the increasingly upscale image that country music is striving for. As Cecelia Tichi has observed, "country perennially struggles for status and legitimacy. Its longtime identification with lower-class whites tends continually to raise suspicions that this music belongs to the subliterate, not to the musically discerning."[4]

In this struggle for legitimacy and upward mobility, country music is not unlike Christian music. Both industries have Southern roots, are based in Nashville, have seen their budgets increase over the past decade, have grown as radio outlets have expanded, and have found themselves bought up by conglomerates. And the evolution of both is heavily intertwined with the desire for legitimacy and the desire to escape the "subliterate" stigma. Christian music seems to lag about ten years behind country music in terms of budget, and perhaps even farther behind in terms of gaining mainstream respectability, but like country music, Christian music is changing as it grows. Just as country music has assimilated to wider audiences by going pop and toning down the old-style twang and old-fashioned instruments (banjo, fiddle), Christian music has toned down its didactic salvation messages. The Christian music and videos that make it into the mainstream market are wholesome and clean-cut, often with only muted spiritual references. The members of P.O.D. explain, "If you're religious or not religious, we want to leave you after you listen to our music with a good feeling in your heart . . . If you accept us for what we believe, cool. And if you don't but you love the music, that's cool just the same. As long as you're listening."[5]

One might conclude that Christian musicians and video makers have sold out. It is more accurate, however, to say that people in the Christian music industry are attempting to negotiate between their heartfelt beliefs and a secular marketplace that they realize is wary of both evangelical faith and politics. Many would like to lose the "Christian" label altogether and simply be appreciated as great musicians. When I began this research I assumed that Christian musicians were being lured by the big record companies into abandoning their hard-sell evangelism in order to succeed in the secular marketplace. While this may be true of some artists, I found a more complicated picture when I discussed these issues with people in the business. For many, the Christian message has not been "diminished" but changed. This chapter examines these changes by looking at how evangelicals understand the bands and the music that have succeeded in the secular market. These crossover bands represent a modern version of evangelism that uses a new language, a new evangelical discursive style. This chapter considers the interpretive questions that this successful music raises and also examines the politics (or lack thereof) of contemporary Christian music and music videos. I also examine the economics of production and distribution, since like most media, Christian media are ultimately slaves to Mammon. First, however, we will turn to the history of the Christian music industry.

THE RISE OF THE INDUSTRY

Contemporary Christian music (CCM) owes its greatest debt to the Jesus freaks and musician Larry Norman. Today's Christian musicians often sport goatees, tattoos, blue hair, and body piercings. Likewise, the Jesus freaks of the sixties replicated the youth style of their time. These Christian flower children were "shaggy and unshorn, but resplendent in bandannas, boleros, and Jesus buttons, [and] they looked to John the Baptist as the original Jesus freak. An editorial in a Jesus weekly . . . explained, 'We know he lived in the wilderness, ate grasshoppers and honey, had long hair, and he stank!'"[6] The Jesus movement flourished primarily in California, where born-again surfers were baptized in the Pacific Ocean (and Pat Boone's swimming pool), and where groups of freaks would occasionally invade evangelical churches, flourishing tambourines and proclaiming that the end was near.[7] These Christian hippies included a few folk singers, and therein lies the beginning of CCM.

Musician Larry Norman soon emerged as "the poet laureate of the Jesus revolution."[8] Norman was a longhair whose lyrics didn't pull any punches. He asked how you could keep screwing around, even after catching a sexually transmitted disease; he complained about amoral newsmen covering Vietnam; and he wondered how money could say "In God we trust" when school prayer was outlawed. One of Norman's early songs, "Why Should the Devil Have All the Good Music?" boldly advanced that rock-and-roll was not inherently satanic, a message that did not fly with older fundamentalists of the Jimmy Swaggart ilk. Norman took a lot of flack. Likewise, Mylon Lefevre, an early Christian songwriter and session artist, was expelled from Bob Jones University for "singing Jesus jazz."[9]

By the mid-eighties, however, things were changing. DC Talk, one of the most successful Christian bands of the nineties, started recording and performing hip-hop at Rev. Jerry Falwell's Liberty University in the eighties. ("DC" stands for decent Christian.) In fact, their first public performance was in Falwell's backyard.[10] Bob Jones University remains a sectarian, fundamentalist institution, but it is telling that an evangelical school like Falwell's, an avatar of Christian discipline that banned smoking, drinking, and sex, came around to the possibility that music and dancing could comfortably exist in a conservative Christian setting.[11] It seems that in the eighties many Christian adults finally realized that the problem with rock-and-roll was not that it was the Devil's music but that it was loud. And loudness could be tolerated as long as it had a Christian message. Octogenarian evangelist Billy Graham may not personally enjoy CCM, but he has repeatedly shared the stage with young Christian musicians like DC Talk.[12]

In 1981, "contemporary Gospel" grossed $100 million, and Gospel was the fifth-largest-selling category of music, accounting for 5 percent of the total record and tape market, compared with 2 percent for jazz and 4 percent for classical music.[13] Most of the music was not "Gospel" in the African American tradition, but this label was apparently the only one that the music industry had at that time for white Christian rock music. And it was definitely the *white* Christian music industry that was growing by leaps and bounds. To the consternation of black Gospel musicians, by 1991 the Gospel Music Association wasn't even including black Gospel categories in the televised part of its annual Dove Awards ceremony.[14] In 1978, *CCM* magazine was started, and eventually CCM caught on as a name for the new market in Christian music. Some mainstream record companies started their own Christian labels in the early eighties, and in 1992 EMI bought Sparrow, which was the second largest Christian music label after Word Records.[15] EMI went on to purchase Star Song in 1994 and ForeFront in 1996.[16] Eventually, virtually all of the successful independent Christian labels had been bought up by the larger companies. Former Reunion president Terry Hemmings observes that, "the Christian music market changed from an entrepreneurial environment to a corporate environment. [It] substantially and rapidly changed—it didn't really evolve. It happened almost overnight."[17] In 1998, Christian music outsold jazz and classical music combined, accounting for 6 percent of overall sales in the U.S. music industry.[18] By 2001, Christian music accounted for 7 percent of the market.[19]

Not surprisingly, Christian radio has expanded along with the music. According to the 1995 *Directory of Religious Media,* the number of full-time evangelical radio stations increased from 399 in 1972 to 1,328 in 1995.[20] And *Christianity Today* claims Christian radio to be the third most common programming format after country and adult contemporary, while *Broadcasting and Cable Yearbook* ranks religious radio at number seven.[21] Although much of religious radio programming consists of talk, there is more and more Christian music going out over the airwaves. And the numbers of Christian albums sold are astonishing. By 2001, DC Talk had three gold records, three platinum albums, three Grammies, two gold-certified long-form videos, and numerous Dove Awards. Petra, a rock band that dates back to the Jesus freak days, has sold over five million albums since 1974. The earliest big seller, of course, was pop star Amy Grant. Grant's 1982 album *Age to Age* had no national radio or video exposure, but it went platinum, selling over one million copies in the evangelical market.[22] Her 1991 *Heart in Motion* album sold over five million copies. Grant has sold over fifteen million albums total, and about one third of those sales have come from her later, wholesome-but-secular albums.[23]

Aside from Grant, the only Christian musicians noticed by secular culture in the eighties were the glam-metal rockers Stryper. Stryper derived its name from Isaiah 53:5, which reads (in the King James Version), "But he was wounded for our transgressions, he was bruised for our iniquities: the chastisements of our peace was upon him; and with his stripes we are healed." (The New International Version translates stripes as "wounds.") The band worked a striped motif, wearing black-and-yellow Spandex outfits in concert, and they were well known for tossing miniature New Testaments into the concert audience. Formed in 1983, by 1988 the band was getting played on MTV; they had one platinum and two gold albums. By 1990, they were producing music without overt Christian content, although the lyrics remained clean. "Not That Kind of Guy," for example, is about refusing a one-night stand. When we consider Stryper along with Amy Grant, we can see a pattern emerging: the more performers sold, crossing over into secular markets, the more likely they were to decrease the overt Christian content of their albums.

SEARCHING, WALKING, AND CROSSING OVER

As Christian music becomes bigger business, the conglomerates that have swallowed the small Christian labels hope to continue to cash in with crossover hits. Whereas reggae or bluegrass have certain key tropes that mark them as such, Christian music can be in any style, including reggae and bluegrass. As a genre, then, Christian music is strangely unstable. Once a large company plucks a Christian band from the Christian marketplace, it will often market it according to its actual style, even if the group technically signs with the company's Christian music division. The record companies want to have their cake and eat it too, profiting from the large existing audience for Christian music but not signing anyone whose music is "too Christian." Mark Lusk, Atlantic Records's vice president of Christian music marketing, explains that "Atlantic doesn't want me spending their hard-earned cash on some crusade."[24] This does not mean that the secular industry simply forces Christian artists to veil or eliminate their beliefs from their music, however. Christian band manager Scott Brickell explains that the companies are more subtle.

I know . . . several Christian artists who had an opportunity to get a secular partner, a record label. But they'd go to a meeting and the secular label would go, "You put Jesus all over six of your songs. I just want four that don't say anything about him. You can write about your girlfriend, you can write about your car, you can write about your day, you can write about struggles you're going through in work, or whatever, just don't mention anything spiritual in those songs, and we'll sign you as an artist."[25]

Brickell has no problem with Christians writing songs about their car or their girlfriend but feels that it's wrong to decide to do this specifically "to get a secular partner."

Not surprisingly, artists who accede to the demands of a secular partner in order to make it onto Top Forty radio sometimes take heat from their original Christian fans for selling out. In 1991, Amy Grant outraged many of her fans with the innocuous commercial hit "Baby Baby." This pop song could not have been farther from the earnest poetry that Larry Norman was setting to music twenty years before. Indeed, by 1986 Norman had already concluded that the commercialization of Christian music was a dead end: "We have prostituted ourselves . . . We write three songs on an album for MOR [middle-of-the-road listeners], three avant-garde songs, three traditional songs, and one novelty song. We write for consumption."[26] Other Christian musicians were also concerned that people were losing sight of the fact that "the industry exists to support the ministry,"[27] not the reverse.

Among today's Christian musicians, there is no consensus about how ministry and business should be balanced. Greg Ham, president of ForeFront Records, which markets DC Talk in the Christian market for EMI, says, "It's a real tension—if you cross over, is it Christian anymore? . . . The motto we tell our artists to live by is: Don't cross over unless you plan to take the cross over."[28] DC Talk has toned down the Christianity in their music but still "takes the cross over" by regularly preaching at the end of concerts. Jars of Clay and Sixpence None the Richer are a bit less likely to preach the Gospel, however, and Hansen and Creed have been wishy-washy about their Christian roots. Neither band will allow its music to be classified under the Christian label. The lead singer of Creed says, "No, we are not a Christian band. A Christian band has an agenda to lead others to believe in their specific religious beliefs. We have no agenda!"[29] Creed distances itself from the Christian label because Christian bands are seen as coercive, as spreading propaganda. Another reason that bands distance themselves from the Christian label is that Christian songs have a reputation for being musically lightweight. A member of P.O.D. (Payable on Death) explains how he first joined up with another early member of the band:

I went over to his house, and I said, "Hey, man, what are you into? 'Cause I'm into Slayer and Metallica." And he said, "Me too." And I said, "Well, OK, let's start a rock band that has *beliefs*. Let's do it not cheesy." I'm not saying that all Christian music's cheesy, but every time I was around someone [Christian], it was nice of them, they'd always bring me like a Petra tape or something. And I'd be like, "It's not really my gig, man." We were just two guys that loved God but at the same time loved music.[30]

P.O.D. is much more open about discussing Christianity than Creed, but like Creed and other bands they know that "Christian band" is a stigma.

P.O.D. raps over a heavy metal beat. Describing themselves as heavy, loud, and wild, they represent a growing trend of successful Christian music with a heavier sound. Many Christian musicians who have had crossover hits, however, have done so with "wholesome love songs and not the 'confessional' lyrics that originally qualified as contemporary Christian music."[31] As disgruntled CCM artist Steve Camp has argued, much of the Christian music on the market is "Christ-less, watered-down . . . God-as-my-girlfriend kind of thing."[32] The watered-down music succeeds because it is not recognizable as Christian by nonevangelical listeners. This is a deliberate strategy on the part of Christian artists; if they are overtly religious, they are more likely to be shut out of the mainstream. "It's frustrating," explains Toby McKeehan of DC Talk, "It feels like you sneak into the mainstream, [radio] figures out you're Christian, and then they shut you down.'"[33] The record company executives "have told them flatly that their explicit Christian content is limiting their crossover success."[34] Rey Roldan, a publicist promoting Third Day in the secular market, has had similar experiences. Two high-profile publications actually pulled their reviews of a Third Day album after Roldan sent the reviewers the CD booklet, which mentioned the Bible. "When you brand a band Christian," Roldan explains, "there's a stigma attached to it."[35]

Creed is a popular band that has worked hard to avoid this stigma. Jonathan Richter, an animator at an independent Christian record label, observes that

whenever anyone asks Creed if they're Christian, they say, "No, but we're searching." It's obvious they've either done their homework very well or they have some sort of a Christian foundation in their background. And I think that's great. It's great that they're very careful, with the way the world is today, the way popular culture and the people they're trying to sell records to are. Creed's not ostracizing themselves by communicating that they've found all the answers.[36]

Creed may avoid the Christian label, but they also use the word "searching," a dead giveaway that they actually *are* evangelical Christians. In evangelical parlance, people are either "searching" (for God, for "all the answers"), or they are "walking the walk," meaning they have accepted the Lord as their personal savior. It seems that for many evangelicals, "searching" and "walking the walk" have largely replaced "unsaved" and "saved," especially in conversations with searchers, or, if you will, nonwalkers. This shift in language points to one way that evangelicals have absorbed the therapeutic discourse of the secular world.[37] "Searching" has displaced "unsaved," like "issues" has displaced "problems" in secular therapeutic discourse. ("Searching" also presumptuously assumes that people who aren't walking the walk are actively looking for spiritual meaning; the word does not allow for disinterested parties.) Old-fashioned fundamentalists get saved, while modern evangelicals are walking. The past participle—"saved"—seems to point to a fait accompli. Walking, conversely, references salvation as a process, not an instant supernatural moment. You don't find God in an ecstatic moment of revelation. Rather, you *work on your relationship* with God. The lead singer of Plumb, another band that prefers not to call itself "Christian," says, "I just have a *relationship* that hopefully shows up in my lifestyle and my lyrics."[38] In sum, the therapeutic language of CCM artists reinforces their "worldliness" (an old-fashioned word) and their engagement with the wider secular culture.

This evangelical therapeutic rhetoric is, in part, simply a natural by-product of the fact that evangelicals live in a culture infused with discussion of interpersonal relations. Consciously or not, the shift in language is also a means of interacting with nonwalkers and of avoiding negative reactions from nonevangelical listeners. In softening its spiritual rhetoric, CCM, like the *VeggieTales* videos discussed in chapter 1, performs a kind of euphemistic act that facilitates communication with nonevangelicals. Producer Cindy Montano, who works at Stephen Yake Productions, a company that has produced some of the most overtly hard-sell evangelical media, including many music videos, has no problem with more soft-sell varieties of Christian media. She explains that the more low-key Christian media help to soften people's hearts, which is important, because a hardened heart cannot receive the Lord. Montano says, "Nobody wants a finger waved in their face. But you desensitize that hardness so that when they do encounter somebody who is walking the walk, and they can see it, it's like 'oh!' and there's that moment when the doors open, and there is an opportunity to talk. They won't go running screaming, 'You crazy Bible-thumper, you! Get out of my face!'"[39] In Montano's view, it is the softened, receptive heart that makes the potential convert (an old-fashioned word that she would never use) not run away. But the avoidance of words like "saved" and "unsaved" surely help as well. Explaining the production process for a new Christian youth series she is working on, Montano says that the big question is, "How strong do we make the message? Are we making this for people who are already walking? Are we making it for people who are searching? And the thing is, if you want to reach the people who are searching, you can't come on too strong with the whole Christian-y, spiritual mumbo-jumbo, so to speak. Because it doesn't mean anything to them."[40]

Like crossover musicians, Montano believes that evangelism works best without "Christian-y, spiritual mumbo-jumbo." Indeed, the new-style evangelism can be performed so that the evangelizee doesn't realize what's going on, doesn't think that he or she is hearing someone "giving witness." Montano emphasized in the course of my interview with her that the Lord had really made a difference in her life. She concluded our discussion by explaining that before she was really "sold out on her walk," she was very aggressive in her business dealings. "I would buzz somebody down the middle and just walk right through the falling parts of the body and not bat an eye. I got a rush out of that, of just crushing people. And I don't work that way anymore. I go home at night, and I sleep, and I wake up and look in the mirror, and I don't like the wrinkles I'm seeing now, but I like who I see." This was, I realized later, Montano sharing her Christian testimony with me. She was using a non-Bible-thumping approach, showing me exactly how the Lord had changed her life for the better. Montano was "seed-planting." If my heart was receptive ("soft"), the seed might grow some day: "The way I view what I do through the programming that I do is that I'm planting seeds. The only people I'm going to *save* [her emphasis] or help to learn about salvation are the people I encounter one on one."[41] Interestingly, this was the only point when Montano used the words "saved" and "salvation," and she used them in response to a question in which *I* had repeatedly used the words.

From the seed-planting perspective, crossover music and music videos that seem spiritually diluted actually constitute the best kind of evangelism. To an outsider eager to see all evangelicals as hypocritical Elmer Gantrys, the idea that the best evangelism is the kind that doesn't overtly discuss salvation and avoids the usual "mumbo-jumbo" sounds a bit fishy, but perhaps the best way to understand the new approach is to see it as part and parcel of a modern evangelical style. Today's evangelical is very different from the stereotypical separatist, fire-and-brimstone fundamentalist. The new evangelical quietly "shares" with "searchers" rather than preaching hellfire and damnation from a pulpit. The hoped-for result is the same—that the listener will welcome

Jesus into his or her heart—but the means, the language, is different. Nonetheless, as with old-school fundamentalism, language remains the key tool to provoke a potential change in the listener. Susan Harding argues in her study of fundamentalist language that

> the Holy Spirit brings you under conviction by speaking to your ear. Once you are saved, the Holy Spirit assumes your voice, speaks through you, and begins to rephrase your life. Listening to the Gospel enables you to experience belief, as it were, vicariously. But generative belief, belief that indisputably transfigures you and your reality, belief that becomes you, comes only through speech: speaking is believing.[42]

In Harding's experience, listening to religious language positions you as a "convert."[43] If you are willing to listen, you are already part of the conversion circuit, even if it ultimately disconnects and you are not saved. Crossover Christian music may be soft-sell evangelism, but if you are listening, you may start searching. If you are listening you are implicated in the circuit.

From this perspective, just listening to a crossover band that is walking the walk positions the listener as a searcher. No matter how tepid the spirituality of the music, the band is doing the Lord's work. Of course, some Christian bands may really be after crossover hits because of the money. Elmer Gantry is dead; long live Elmer Gantry! But at least in principle, Montano's theory of conversion—or, less elegantly, walk inducement—works well for explaining what's going on with crossover artists who have tempered their Christian message or are extremely cagey about whether or not they are Christians. They don't want to be called Bible-thumpers, and they don't want people screaming and running away from music that slams religion down their throats. On a practical level, these artists are making a strategic response to a secular world that assumes all evangelicals are Jim Bakker clones. On a spiritual level, such artists are planting seeds, softening hearts, spreading messages that, if not overtly about God, at least are not about Satan, sex, parental disobedience, and other Christian bogeymen. And they are hoping to be an example of what searching and walking are all about. As Montano's boss, Stephen Yake, explains, "Creed is not trying to evangelize the world; I think they're letting the world just see them."[44] See them, that is, as searchers who, as Richter said, are not "ostracizing themselves by communicating that they've found all the answers."

From a business standpoint, the crossover artist who doesn't label him- or herself "Christian" is walking on a tightrope. Until all the Christian-bands-that-don't-call-themselves-Christian are mixed in with everybody else for sale in mainstream music stores, the local Christian bookstores can make or break CCM artists. The mom-and-pop bookstores are particularly tough on artists. If they don't think an artist is Christian enough, he or she will not make it onto the shelves. One band in 2000, for example, had all of their CDs pulled when bookstore owners decided they had used the word "Hell" inappropriately in a song. When crossover artists start to make it in the mainstream, the mom-and-pop stores train an eagle eye on them. Sixpence None the Richer got some flak for their hit love song "Kiss Me," but when they were on *Late Night with David Letterman* they gently explained their spiritual position. This may not have been a deliberate tactic to fix their image, but it didn't hurt, either. As Montano explains, once a crossover band gets to "that platform where they have the opportunity to either speak their heart or not speak their heart, that's where they're going to show their true heart. They're either going to use that platform to spread the message or to be a witness, or they're going to continue watering it down. And then they better really push that secular deal, because the mom-and-pop bookstores are going to say, 'Did you see them on *Letterman?* They didn't even once mention . . . ,' and they'll lose that market."[45]

One problem with accusing Christian artists of selling out is that the accusation assumes all Christians operate from an identical spiritual position and that they all have—or should have—the same goals. The sellout insult presupposes that all musicians working within the Christian market see themselves as preachers out to save souls. In reality, Christian musicians differ widely in their opinions about the spiritual status of Christian music and in their understandings of what they themselves have been "called" to accomplish. Some artists see themselves as evangelists running a "music ministry," while others are "Christian entertainers." At the next level down in terms of evangelical intensity, we find "entertainers who are also Christians."[46] Evangelist musicians are most likely to preach the Gospel, both in their songs and with a Bible in hand during concerts. Christian entertainers like Amy Grant talk about God in some of their music and are widely recognized as Christians but do not preach in concert and turn out some albums that don't reference God at all. Entertainers who are also Christians— such as the hit band Sixpence None the Richer and the up-and-coming Switchfoot—produce clean-cut music with perhaps occasional veiled references to salvation in their songs. Many outside of the Christian music subculture are not even aware that the groups are evangelical.

Finally, there are some people in the Christian music industry who position their work first and foremost as art rather than as evangelism per se. Employees at the hipster production company Squint, the company that Sixpence is signed to, might call themselves entertainers who are also Christians, but they see the company's primary goal as a creative one. As cinematographer Ben Pearson explains, "Squint just wants to create great art. Period. Whether that ministers to the church or brings something new to the world, it really doesn't matter." Pearson adds, however, that "if you're truly after excellence and serving God with everything you have, to obtain excellence, people respond."[47] Pearson sends a telling mixed message here: it doesn't matter if you minister to people, but people *will* respond to your art if you are serving God. Like many people in the business, the Squint employees I talked to hoped that the "Christian" label would simply disappear so that great music could just compete in the marketplace as great music. Yet because they believe in the power of God, they believe that art that serves the Lord will necessarily touch people differently than art that does not serve the Lord. High-quality music and music videos can stand on their own as art, regardless of the beliefs of their creator. But if the artists are inspired by the Creator, the effect will be positive. Hearts will be softened.

INTERPRETATION

"You think of a Christian video, it's a guy and a girl in a field, and they're dancing around, and there's wind and sunshine, and that's a typical Christian video. To me, that gets to be comical. There's no creativity in that." So says Christian band manager Scott Brickell, and it's hard to disagree with him; many Christian music videos, especially those produced only for the Christian market, are bland and offer little spiritual complexity. God is good, and, as the ska band the W's indicates with the title of one of its songs, "The Devil Is Bad." In other words, Christian songs and videos are often painfully literal.

This literal worldview is in many ways in sync with the evangelical approach to the Bible as the inspired, inerrant word of God. Evangelicals debate (within limits) how to understand and use the Bible. They also emphasize the importance of having a personal relationship not only with God and Jesus but also with the Bible itself. They believe that every word of the Bible is true and that even if humans cannot always grasp God's intentions, the Bible remains a vessel of God's black-and-white admonitions to readers. When such literalism, at its worst, translates to video, we end up with Carman's "Satan Bite the Dust," a Western-themed video about demons who end up getting zapped by a gun loaded with the Holy Spirit (figs. 18–20). Other black-and-white videos focus on upbeat spirituality, usually striking out in terms of creativity and artistry.

Eric Welch, widely seen as one of the most creative and interesting

FIG. 18 IN HIS MUSIC VIDEO, "SA-
TAN, BITE THE DUST," CARMAN
TELLS OFF THE DEVIL.

FIG. 19 THE DEVIL AS AN EVIL
COWBOY.

FIG. 20 CARMAN USES A SITAR TO
STRIKE DOWN A TURBANED "DE-
MON OF FALSE RELIGION."

directors in the industry, notes the one-dimensionality of many videos. "Christians often feel the need to be blatant or obvious in order to justify presenting the Gospel. I believe Jesus spoke in parables to intrigue people, yet the modern-day version of Christian art overlooks this." Welch prefers "videos that pique people's interest rather than bang an idea over their heads or shove it down their throats. Very few Christians have a handle on subtleties and symbolism—check out C. S. Lewis folks!" [48]

Welch tries to make videos that are more subtle, videos that are ripe with symbolism and that you have to watch a few times to figure out. I say that he "tries" to do this, because ultimately he is beholden to his employer—the record label—which means that sometimes an interesting idea will get shot down in favor of black-and-white messages and slick images of the artists. "For example," Welch explains, "you develop an idea where you try to visually showcase the lyric in a creative and symbolic way, but the powers that be only want to show the artist singing. Or they want some old-style formula video. In the end, we are hired and paid to create what the labels want. Sure, it stings sometimes, but that really is our job—creating four-minute commercials for performers."[49]

Welch's critique of many videos as lacking subtlety holds water, but there is also a minority of slick videos—usually the ones vying for MTV status—that seem to offer up more possibilities for ambiguity and multiple interpretations. This is a fascinating development; ambiguous videos are being produced by a culture that cherishes literal-reading strategies. Many of the people in the Christian music business admit that Christian songs can be read in radically different ways by different listeners, and that this is not problematic. Specifically, I asked a number of people if it was plausible that crossover songs, and the videos that go with them, would be read as Christian by those in-the-know but as secular by those not familiar with evangelical subculture. Scott Brickell, who manages the successful Audio Adrenaline, as well as the newcomer Switchfoot, explains that

Audio Adrenaline are Christian entertainers. They do what a lot of people would consider the "cheerleading songs" for Christian youth groups. Like "Never Gonna Be as Big as Jesus," "Big House," "Can't Take God Away." All those kinds of songs are cheerleading. Switchfoot's got more of a secular feel. It's more of a [*long pause*] . . . just a good band to listen to. You know, great music, great musicians. Their lyrics, I think, get you thinking more about who you are and what your purpose is and what's God's call on your life. Switchfoot has a lot more interpretations of their songs out there than Audio Adrenaline does. Audio Adrenaline, you can't really have more than one interpretation. "Never

Gonna Be as Big as Jesus" [the title of one of their most popular songs]—where are you going to go with that?![50]

In Brickell's mind, both the cheerleaders and the just-plain-great-music bands serve worthy purposes, but they are very different. Switchfoot songs allow for interpretive ambiguity, while most Audio Adrenaline songs do not. This room for ambiguity points to the contemporary evangelical engagement with the modern world discussed in chapter 1. While an old-fashioned fundamentalist would only (perhaps) tolerate the cheerleading band and be wary of more ambiguous musicians, the evangelical sees room for peaceful coexistence of both types of artists.

Like Switchfoot, Sixpence None the Richer is "a good band to listen to" that creates songs that allow space for multiple interpretations. Some of the tracks on their self-titled 1997 album directly address spiritual issues, but their hit "Kiss Me" is their most secular song. Lacking any reference to God or Jesus, the lyrics of "Kiss Me" sweetly request kisses, without lustful overtones. The music video is similarly sweet in tone; it is a frolicking pastiche of François Truffaut's French New Wave classic *Jules and Jim* (figs. 21–23). Truffaut's film is an odd choice, since, from a conservative perspective, *Jules and Jim* portrays adultery and, ultimately, chic hopelessness. The "Kiss Me" video would thus seem to be a crystal clear example of how a music video can undercut the wholesome message of a Christian song, compromising conservative Christian values.

The video's cinematographer, Ben Pearson of Squint Productions, sees things differently. Pearson explains:

There really wasn't any discussion as far as should we be doing this [using the film] or not. It was more that style of abandon, that wonderful New Wave style that Truffaut was kind of the father of, that appealed to us. It was a bit of that carefree filmmaking style that we responded to. Natural light, handheld cameras or on a tripod, whip pans. And the camera we actually used is from that period of time as well. It was from the early sixties, an Arriflex 2B camera, and the Angenieux lens that we used for the whole thing was a French lens from the same period.[51]

Here, Pearson is less concerned with content than with form and technique. He understands the video as a piece of art and aligns what the Squint production team was doing with the French New Wave, thereby positioning Squint not so much as a part of an outsider religious subculture but rather as part of an outsider artistic subculture.

Unlike the New Wave, however, music videos do not represent a

FIGS. 21–23 THE VIDEO FOR SIX-
PENCE NONE THE RICHER'S "KISS
ME" IS AN HOMAGE TO FRANÇOIS
TRUFFAUT'S JULES AND JIM.

radical new artistic form, and while "Kiss Me" is devoid of violence and overt sex, it does not otherwise stand out as a particularly unique music video. If it is not so much the video itself that is novel, why does Pearson make the analogy to Truffaut? Pearson's identification with Truffaut is about more than aesthetics. "We admired Truffaut an awful lot for what he did," he says, "the whole movement of not being part of a studio system that is personified in the New Wave movement so well, when people just recklessly decided to make films. And that's kind of what was the inspiration. And there's kind of a wistfulness in that too."[52] Here, the parallel between Squint and Truffaut is in part one of style ("wistfulness"), but also a question of economics and economic exclusion.

This brings us back to the fact that Squint is a Christian company, even if they would like to lose the label. Christian videomakers may make stuff that looks a lot like MTV, but crossover hits remain sporadic, and Christian companies remain outside of the business, outside of Los Angeles and New York, outside of the studio system. And as is generally the case, once outsiders become insiders—which may be the future of Christian music and music video—something is lost. For better or for worse, subcultures that become part of the cultural mainstream will inevitably be changed. Pearson points to what happens when subcultures lose their outsider status: "Time usually only gives you those opportunities once or twice. Because due to the success of 'Kiss Me' and the band, I don't know if you can ever go back and reproduce what you've done. Just like, for example, in the later years when Truffaut did *Fahrenheit 451*, he for the first time had a budget, was working with union people, and it was a total flop."[53] The further comparison to Truffaut once again underlines Squint's romantic ethos, while also pointing to anxiety about the artistic costs of making it in the big time.

While the "Kiss Me" video can be interpreted strictly on Pearson's terms as a piece of art made on the fly by New Wave fans, I'd like to return once again to my earlier suggestion that crossover videos tend to be spiritually diluted. When "Kiss Me" was picked up for the soundtrack of *She's All That* (Iscove, 1999), a movie starring teen heartthrob Freddie Prinze, Jr., a new video of the song was made without allusions to Truffaut and with the intention of advertising the film. This was quite different from Jars of Clay's "Flood" video being remade for the secular market to make it less overtly spiritual, since "Kiss Me" was not spiritual in the first place. Or was it? From my own "not walking" perspective, this at first seemed like a patently obvious interpretation. Music video director Eric Welch set me straight, however. To the secular ear and eye, a Christian song or video that doesn't mention Jesus simply doesn't fly as "Christian." Welch contends, however, that "the mainstream needs more artists with a positive Gospel message." From his perspective, a "positive message" *is* "a Gospel message . . . I don't think a song about love is anti-Christian or not Gospel-relatable. Don't Christians kiss, get married? I think Christians need to address such issues."[54] "Kiss Me," then, is not un-Christian by virtue of being a light romantic tune. In fact, it is Christian precisely because it is a light romantic tune: it offers a Christian take on love. Welch contends that Christians can address all kinds of issues and that, in fact, they *need* to address such issues:

People need songs that give positive responses to broken homes, alcoholism, AIDS, homosexuality, the loss of faith, and other such weighty issues. The fact that Christians have not addressed these issues with compassion instead of judgment has made them irrelevant and "unsalty" [not being "light and salt"] in our culture. "Just Jesus" is nice, but people need real, practical and gut level answers. By retreating within their own ranks and preaching to the choir, Christians have left those who need hope to the other voices.[55]

In other words, Christian artists should address all kinds of social issues (issues that clearly also have political dimensions—evangelical attitudes about homosexuality have a history of translating into oppressive policy measures). If artists stick to "just Jesus," Welch argues, they are stuck in the realm of theory, without attending to real people's practical needs.

Just who are the real kids listening to and interpreting Christian music? Are evangelical youth using this music to minister to "searching" friends? William D. Romanowski contends that by the end of the 1980s, the market for CCM was clearly "twelve- to thirty-five-year-old white evangelicals, not the 'unsaved youth' for whom the music was allegedly written."[56] Today, P.O.D., Sixpence None the Richer, Jars of Clay, and Creed reach both evangelical and nonevangelical radio listeners, while the bands that do not achieve crossover success remain available only in Christian bookstores and are therefore, by default, only accessed by evangelicals. While some teens certainly might share their music with searching friends, it is not unreasonable to assume that most evangelical teens listen to their music the same way other teens do, on their Walkmans or alone in their rooms.[57] How do they interpret this music? The question is an ambitious one that can hardly be answered fully here. CCM wants to convey "positive" values, but it is impossible to be sure that teens "get" the intended message. Social scientific studies of music listeners have found that fans frequently "misunderstand" music. While Patricia Marks Greenfield and her coresearchers thought that Bruce Springsteen's "Born in the U.S.A." had a message of "despair, disillusionment, and resentment," few of the fourth-, eighth-, twelfth-grade, and college students they studied saw this message in the song. "Rather, many seemed to simply take the upbeat title and catch phrase of the refrain at face value."[58] Similarly, teenagers in another study read Olivia Newton John's "Physical" as "a call to aerobic exercise," and both prochoice and prolife organizations thought that Madonna's "Papa Don't Preach" supported their cause.[59] It's tricky, of course, to decide what a song "really" means and then test listeners to see if they get it right. For one thing, when seemingly downbeat lyrics are accompanied by an exhilarating beat, who's to say that a listener who is exhilarated is missing the point of the song? If many social scientists see interpretation as being strictly about lyrics, it's no wonder that they find listeners getting music "wrong."

But don't evangelical teens have a special stake in getting the lyrics right? Indeed, one thing that makes CCM unique is that it is *supposedly* all about lyrics. In theory, then, a Christian hard-core band like Oblation can sing a death metal song that is antiabortion, and even though their thrashing beat feels violent, their antideath lyrics will redeem the song. What listeners make of this style/content dissonance is an unresolved question. One study has found that "male undergraduates who heard either sexually violent heavy metal or Christian heavy metal were *both* more likely than those who listened to classical music to express negative attitudes toward women."[60] This single study proves nothing definite. Perhaps undergraduate males in general have negative attitudes toward women, but listening to classical music makes them inexpressive! One thing that is certain, however, is that teens claim that the lyrics of Christian music are very important. It is the lyrics, they claim, that redeem the music, that make it Christian, and that therefore make listening to music a Christian activity. The lyrics ostensibly make even the most seemingly sensual song "really" be about the mind and the spirit, not the body.

Whether or not evangelical youth actually do listen carefully to CCM lyrics and "properly" interpret them remains open to debate, and the rise of increasingly ambiguous Christian crossover music certainly makes these questions of interpretation even more difficult to answer. Creed's number one hit in 2000, "With Arms Wide Open," speaks of a personal transformation, a huge change that the singer says fills him with joy. The video emphasizes the lead singer's sexy hair and muscled chest, and shows him immersing himself in a pool. Is this a moment of baptism or a male wet T-shirt contest? Finally the singer makes the only apparent reference to God, referring to a mysterious "He" who the singer hopes "will understand." What He needs to understand remains unstated. Since neither the song nor the video actually overtly anchors the "change" in this song to Christian salvation, there is nothing to prevent listeners from interpreting "He" as referencing a lover, and the big change as a coming-out narrative. Amazingly, a religious culture that shuns "moral relativism" and favors literal Biblical interpretation is increasingly producing cultural artifacts with messages that are hard to pin down.

Even Christian songs with messages more explicit than Creed's will often be undercut by their videos. The video for Rebecca St. James's song "Pray" is so peppy and over-postproduced that the prayer invective is all but lost, even though St. James is one of the artists who definitely sees her work as "music ministry." Small Town Poets illustrates an anti-idolatry message in a goofy video in which golden cows are represented by a cake that everyone wants to win by playing musical chairs. The Guardian video for "Way Home Back" features dwarves,

Chihuahuas, Elvis impersonators, and smoke machines, attempting to be cool and to send a message about the value of being nice to people, but ultimately evoking a Spinal Tap parody video. Mark Joseph, who leads seminars on expanding into secular markets, argues that subtlety is the key to exiting the "Christian ghetto" and achieving crossover success. He notes that "C. S. Lewis pointed out that what's important is not to write books or songs about Christianity, but books or songs that reflect a Christian worldview."[61] But clearly when a Christian spiritual worldview becomes too subtle, stylized, or subsumed in symbolism, it can be hard to decipher as Christian at all.

Like "With Arms Wide Open," DC Talk's 1998 song "You Consume Me" shows how a video can support—or not support—an already veiled evangelical message. "You Consume Me" is a passionate song re-counting the singers' all-consuming intimate relationship with God. As the trio's de facto leader Toby McKeehan explains, "We view our re-lationship with God as very personal, and some people might get upset because the relationship in 'Consume Me' is so passionate and real . . . We wrote this as a spiritual song because to us, faith is a passionate, personal, committed love relationship with Jesus Christ."[62] While the lyrics explicitly mention heaven and baptism, they also read like a sen-sual love song. "You are like a burning flame that runs through my veins, I drown in you, you flood my soul."[63] The accompanying music is slow and sensual.

But if you listen to the song while watching the video, "You Con-sume Me" is less about rapturous love than trapped obsession. The stylish science fiction-style video shows a dystopian community of people with special breathing masks attached to their faces; the masks are linked to tubes attached to containers (of oxygen?) on their backs. When a minion tries to escape, a cruel guard knocks him over. His mask falls off, and he fumbles to get it back on. At the end of the video, a rebel tears off his mask, as if to attempt suicide. He falls to the ground, but it turns out the masks were a scam. The air is not poisonous after all, and the other people take off their masks too, liberated at last. The video's tone is bleak and pessimistic until this final moment, and the implication seems to be that once the masks are removed the people are finally free of the all-consuming "you." Rock music abounds in what we might call the "mythical you." "You" dumped me, hurt me, loved me, saved me, screwed me. In crossover Christian videos, "you" functions as a placeholder for God, Jesus, Lord—all of the words that seem to be taboo in the secular music marketplace. One could, of course, argue that the ending of "You Consume Me" is a metaphor for finally achieving salvation, that at the end of the video one is finally "consumed" by "you" (God) instead of being consumed by the things of the world. While the video's images don't do much to support this reading, some DC Talk fans certainly might perform such a reading.

On the other hand, viewers may just see this as a cool video. Band member Kevin Max says, "yeah, part of us is message-oriented; another part of us is entertainment-driven," and Michael Tait says that he'd "like the music to make an impact on as many levels as possible . . . If one person likes the way it sounds, and another likes what the lyrics are saying, both are valid and both are important."[64] So, if one person sees the "You Consume Me" song and video as spiritual, and another sees it as cool or even sexy, it is not a problem. In 2000, DC Talk was clearly marketing themselves for crossover success. Their Web site said that they had "spread beyond the confines of genre" and that they were "willing to let their music speak for itself, without regard for pigeonholes."[65] Although the Web site didn't put it this crudely, what going beyond "genre" and "pigeonholes" really indicated was a desire to escape the stigma of being a "Christian band." They have since suspended the group to pursue solo careers, and it remains to be seen whether they can individually succeed as crossover musicians.

At the opposite end of the spectrum from DC Talk we find Carman, a successful Christian artist who will never escape the Christian ghetto or create videos that leave space for interpretive ambiguity. Carman—technically, Carman Dominic Licciardello, but professionally he goes by his first name alone—is a Christian artist who has struck it rich while staying within the Christian market. His songs and videos veil neither their spirituality nor their politics. In "Revival," Carman shows Satan in Hell delighting over the numbers of daily abortions and the rise of television violence. Carman videos occasionally voice opposition to gays, advocate the reinstitution of school prayer, and ask for the distribution of Bibles instead of condoms in public schools. More often, however, Carman simply preaches about Jesus and salvation. His style is not only didactic but also aggressive, even arrogant. One video shows a man on trial for his sins after his death. In a supreme act of chutzpah, Carman plays four roles: the narrator, Satan, Jesus Christ, and God. Carman's conviction of righteousness, his lack of self-doubt and introspection, and his self-assured first-person address to the camera all make it unlikely that he will speak to people outside of his belief system. It is also alienating to many within the belief system who think Carman is tacky. One person I spoke to made fun of the cheap "Nerf devil" costume used in one video.

In a sense, Carman's music and videos might be seen as the most evangelical of all, as they so aggressively preach about sin, salvation, good, and evil. Yet they only speak to people who already pretty much agree with Carman. They are thus the most evangelical in theory and the least evangelical in practice, in terms of reaching the unsaved. (Not looking to integrate into secular culture, Carman is not the kind of person who would refer to "unsaved" folks as people who are "searching.") There is no way to be certain that un-born-agains never encounter Carman; his videos are shown frequently on the televangelical Trinity Broadcasting Network. They certainly never show up on MTV or VH1, and his music never plays on secular radio. In the spirit of Biblical inerrancy, Carman's music and videos tell it like it is. You might disagree with him, but the videos leave little space for misinterpretation or negotiated readings. In music by other Christian artists, "He" might be understood by listeners to mean a lover, not God. Carman is more likely to simply say "Jesus Christ."

Carman is also exceptional in his occasional inclusion of overt politics. Nonevangelicals tend to assume that Christian music and music videos must be propaganda with a secret, Christian Coalition–type agenda. Most often, however, CCM is as politically innocuous as secular music. Even overt, unambiguously Christian videos usually focus on images of angels and Bible-readers, not people picketing women's health clinics or fighting against gay rights. One might cautiously venture to say that CCM is "conservative," although when politics can actually be gleaned from the music or videos they are fairly vague. In "Carry On," Point of Grace includes images of kids praying around a flagpole, referencing the flagpole prayer movement that evangelicals have promoted as a response to the elimination of school prayer. The title of Big Tent Revival's song "Choose Life" might seem to point to antiabortion politics, but the song does not actually mention abortion, and the video implies that choosing life means choosing eternal life. Audio Adrenaline has a song called "Can't Take God Away," which says that even though the government has removed prayer from classrooms, you can't take God out of people's hearts, an idea that most people who support the elimination of school prayer would not object to. This is an atypically political song for Audio Adrenaline, since most of their peppy songs simply advance the argument that God is a really cool dude. They also sing about feeling good for standing up for your religious beliefs and witnessing to people; such songs probably speak pretty directly to evangelical teens who feel censored or alienated in secular schools. But even when Audio Adrenaline ventures into politics their songs ultimately—like much youth music—deal less with social structures than with individual feelings and adolescent traumas.

To some extent, evangelicals see their music as a reaction against secular youth culture, which they claim "preaches" politics and values to vulnerable audiences. Evangelicals complain that MTV, in particular, shows plenty of videos advocating immorality. In my interviews,

Madonna and Marilyn Manson came up most frequently as examples of preachers of immoral values. Madonna was seen as promoting sexual activity outside of marriage, as well as bisexuality and sadomasochism. Marilyn Manson was seen as promoting the occult. From a nonevangelical perspective, it is easy to dismiss the idea that Madonna and Manson are "preachers" of ideas, yet the more I spoke with people in the Christian music industry, the more I came to see what they were getting at with this line of argument. Many people who don't identify as Bible-believing (saved, walking, living the life) evangelicals think that Christian music promotes a dangerous ideology that has no place in the secular marketplace. Believers, conversely, argue that they don't like the dangerous ideology that they feel has already inundated the media and that they want their turn to compete in the marketplace of ideas. As Squint animator Jonathan Richter explains,

People don't want to be preached at . . . but at the same time there are people preaching in the secular market a lot of things that are even less appropriate [than evangelical Christian ideas], and they're doing fairly well. I think Cher has a song that's called "Sisters of Mercy" that's coming out on her next album, an anti-Catholic song about how she was treated poorly at an orphanage. She's talking poorly about nuns. The New Age ideas, that's probably another really good example. Just social ideas. And you can call Christianity a social idea, too.[66]

The conservative evangelical version of the "social idea" of Christianity is certainly problematic for those who do not oppose feminism, lesbianism, homosexuality, sex outside marriage, abortion, and so on. But most Christian music and music videos do not directly address these issues. In fact, the "social ideas" of most Christian youth music could be boiled down to a few simple things: God loves you, be nice to people, and stand up for your beliefs. It's not deep theology, but it's not a right-wing conspiracy, either. The growth of the Christian music industry may be fueled by the growth of conservative evangelicalism in the United States, and this growth ultimately has political ramifications, but Christian music and music videos do not, for the most part, have political aspirations. CCM is better described as a symptom than a cause of the growth of the religious Right.

MUSIC VIDEO ECONOMICS: PRODUCTION, DISTRIBUTION, MARKETING

The principal force driving Christian music video is one thing: marketing. In fact, that is the raison d'être for any kind of music video. Videos are created, as they say in the business, "to spike sales." The catch, however, is that the distribution of Christian video is limited, and there is currently no consistent national venue for these videos. They are shown sporadically late at night on PAX-TV, an independent national station owned by evangelical Lowell White Paxon,[67] and sometimes they turn up on televangelist shows, especially on the Trinity Broadcasting Network (TBN). But except for the occasional crossover hit, Christian videos are not aired on VH1 or MTV. So why sink between ten and a hundred fifty thousand dollars into something that no one will see? Because of the financial disincentive, Robert Deaton and George Flanigan, a prominent country music production team that started in the Christian market, see little future in Christian video. As Flanigan explains, "It's almost become a necessary evil from the artist's standpoint. The artists think that they have to have a video, and so it's in their contract. It might not be a smart thing financially, but they end up having to do it anyway."[68]

Naturally, people still working in the Christian market have a different perspective. Scott Brickell is optimistic: "I like doing videos. I think that they're important for the band's image, for furthering their career . . . it's a step you have to take in order for the public to feel like you've reached a certain level." It's a catch-22. You have to make the videos to be taken seriously, but if you are overtly Christian there's a good chance MTV won't take you seriously. And it's only by getting airplay that you will increase sales, which will force MTV to take you seriously. Even if you can't get on MTV, however, just having a video is good for your image. It's like dressing for success, but with an enormous price tag. Brickell says that just as Christian radio has grown, video will grow as well, albeit slowly. He concludes that "videos don't pay for themselves in the amount of records you're going to sell or promotion you're going to get out of it, but it's still something that you have to do in order for eventually it to make sense to do video. If we don't do them now, we're never going to get to the point where it is cost-effective."[69]

Producer Cindy Montano feels that Christian video budgets are improving and will continue their upward climb. She explains, "In the last five years the budgets on the projects have come up incredibly. Thirteen years ago, when I started doing Christian video, the music was still of marginal quality. You weren't using the best studio engineers. You weren't using the best studio musicians, the best backup singers, but now you have guys who have come out of the E-Street Band [Bruce Springsteen's backup group] who are producing in the Christian marketplace, like Tommy Simms." Montano further predicts that eventually Hollywood will look to Christian music and video as their standard. Initially, when Montano referred to high standards she was speaking of production values (lighting, editing), but she quickly and seamlessly shifted gears to the other definition of "values," claiming that secular producers would end up looking to the Christian market largely for spiritual reasons. Amoral (or immoral) Hollywood producers, she reasoned, would eventually burn out.

As the current *revival* [her emphasis] continues to spread, and people who are secular-creative start to feel a call or a responsibility to carry their walk into the visual medium or the audio medium, whatever medium they're working in . . . you know, you can't just continue to create the same crap. People will want to be able to go to sleep at night and go, "You know, I was walking in your will today. I utilized the gifts that you gave me in a manner that is edifying to you."[70]

For Montano, Christian videos thus serve a holy purpose, in part, because they will eventually serve as a wake-up call for secular producers. She also referred to specific story-driven videos that have strong spiritual value, such as a Ray Boltz video she worked on that reenacted the death of Christ.

Most of the time, however, the people I interviewed did not speak of Christian music video as having evangelical value; marketing came first. Musician Eddie DeGarmo was disappointed because "videos have become more of a promotional gimmick than a deepening of the art form." He said there's a lot of bad art, but a good video, like Audio Adrenaline's "Some Kind of Zombie," tries "to get the viewer to think about what the artist is saying," that is, a Christian message.[71] Stephen Yake says, "My job is to promote the artist but also to communicate a message. I think we have a higher purpose for music video than just eye candy."[72] Yet he admits that much of the Christian music video currently on the market is eye candy and that it is the story videos (which remain prohibitively expensive for most artists) as opposed to the more fluffy concept videos (which are often cheaper) that are most likely to get people thinking about spiritual issues. Squint animator Jonathan Richter is pleased to see videos that don't preach Madonna's values, but he still has doubts about the evangelical value of video. "Why would people want to preach with music videos? I mean, is that really video's role? It's the same as a lot of people's opinions about church. Church, in some circles, isn't where you convert new believers. Church is where you worship, the place for conversion and education is in the meetings, in the Bible studies, in the meeting of friends who are living the life."[73] Christian music videos are a would-be marketing tool that may occasionally have spiritual value, but there are no delusions in the Christian music business that anyone is going to start "living the life" simply because he or she has seen a five-minute music video.

There is one exception to Christian video's low-key evangelism and high loss of profits, the aforementioned Carman. Carman is only one artist, of course, and he is in a small minority, but the fact remains that he is turning a profit from his hard-core evangelical albums and videos. A number of the people I met with in Nashville were reluctant to discuss Carman. In spite of his success, many seem to see him as the Billy Carter of Christian music, a kind of embarrassing relative to be kept out of sight. This discomfort around Carman is bound up in issues of taste and class. Carman's videos may be slick, with decent production values, but their heavy-handed preachiness evokes old-fashioned, lower-class fundamentalism rather than newfangled, middle-class evangelicalism. His videos are often played on TBN, an evangelical network where artists with a more mainstream (middle-class) and youthful look do not want to show their work. As one person in the business puts it tactfully, "TBN is not our demographic." TBN targets "the blue hairs and the big hairs"—older viewers and lower-middle-class or working-class Southern women. Jan Crouch, TBN's cofounder and female host, sports hair and make-up that would make Dolly Parton blush. While no one I encountered in Nashville had a negative word to say about TBN's spiritual mission, most tactfully distanced themselves from the network, recognizing that it was not the ideal place to show funky MTV-style videos, even though it has a huge viewer base.

This has left TBN wide open for Carman, who is the consummate marketer. Carman uses TBN to promote his music, but one might more aptly call what Carman does not music but theme packaging. Since 1989, Carman has released the albums *Radically Saved, Revival in the Land, Addicted to Jesus, R.I.O.T.* (Righteous Invasion of Truth), *The Standard, Mission 3:16,* and *Heart of a Champion.* Each of these albums is used to promote a music video compilation tape, a concert, and T-shirts. A forty-five-minute film based on the *R.I.O.T.* album was sold on video, and a feature-length movie based on *Heart of a Champion* is also available for purchase on video. In addition, Carman puts together TBN specials, promoting the album, music videos, and films. Sometimes he even produces a making-of-the-video show for TBN. Montano says that after watching Carman TV specials—which are produced by her company, Stephen Yake Productions—a lot of people call TBN, "seeking salvation, and wanting someone to pray with them. What drove those people initially to watch TBN, I don't know. Could it possibly have been the full-page ads they [Carman and TBN] took out in *USA Today* to promote the video? People tuning in purely out of curiosity factor? But supposedly Carman's videos are very effective at touching people."[74] Montano clearly supports Carman's spiritual crusade, yet she also acknowledges how powerful the financial muscle behind the crusade is to its success.

Carman tours the country giving free concerts, since, as he says on his Web site, you shouldn't charge for the Gospel. However, his Web site explains that each concert costs $125,000, so he asks for donations to help bring the Word to people.[75] If you pledge to pay ten dollars a month for a year, you get a free T-shirt and pay for the cost of eight people to attend a Carman concert, but for a thousand dollars per month you can cover eight hundred and fifty people. Plus you get a Bible, shirt, CD, video, leather tour jacket, and platinum record. T-shirts, videos, and other merchandise are, of course, also available for purchase at the free concerts. Through this technique, Carman has sold millions of albums, about half a million videos, and plenty of ancillary merchandise. Clearly, God and Mammon do not conflict in Carman's world. Stephen Yake says that "some people think he's cheesy, and other people just think he's anointed of God," but most folks that I talked to belonged in the former camp.[76] One person in the business went so far as to say, "I try to avoid Carman like the plague, I get too angry. I think he's a heretic. I think it's done more damage, well, maybe not . . . His whole thing, I think it borders on prostitution of the Gospel, quite frankly."

Whether Carman is anointed or a heretic, one thing is certain: he is not shy about the "Christian" label, and his videos never undercut the evangelical messages of his songs. Notably, the videos are made by an evangelical company. One reason that some Christian music videos do not successfully advance a Christian message is that they are not made by evangelicals. According to director Eric Welch, "crew, equipment, and film costs are rising, but the video budgets aren't. Some labels expect you to pull off MTV-quality videos on ten to fifteen thousand dollars," which is not even a tenth of an MTV budget.[77] Welch is a committed Christian and experienced director who manages to work with these small budgets. But many seasoned directors will only take on bigger budget projects. It is common for young aspiring music video directors to come to Nashville to get into the country music business, and when they are turned away by the major players because of their inexperience, they end up getting work making Christian music videos, since they are the only ones willing to take the low salaries and to work with very small budgets. Once the young director has gotten together a demo reel of cheap Christian videos, he or she has something to show prospective employers to get into the country music business. Robert Deaton and George Flanigan, now very successful country video makers, got their start in the early eighties making a video for

Eddie DeGarmo, one of the first Christian singers who explored video. Deaton explains:

We did Eddie's "Good to Be Forgiven" video for one sole purpose: to show it to get work from the people who wouldn't return our phone calls. We wanted it to be hip, to be a good piece for Eddie and a good piece for us. We did it for cost—it actually cost us money to do it. We made it with a country feel, and it got onto CMT [Country Music Television]. And supposedly it was the first video to play on CMT, VH1, MTV, and BET across the board. CBS called us right away and asked to see our reel, and asked for a meeting with us in fifteen minutes. Then they gave us our first country video to do.[78]

Fifteen years later, not all fledging directors find such instant success, but Deaton and Flanigan's strategy still seems to be in play for up-and-comers. If Christian music videos are, in large part, a training ground for people interested in the secular (country music) market, it makes sense that the videos sometimes don't feel very Christian.[79]

It is certain that Christian video budgets will remain low as long as they do not have a mass distribution outlet. To what extent this hinders Christian video, however, remains an open question. Some people on the business end don't see a future for video since it doesn't fulfill its marketing function, while others have a more optimistic and less bottom-line-driven attitude. Interestingly, this attitude toward Christian video is evocative of the attitudes toward low-budget video held by many left-leaning alternative video makers. In her article extolling the virtues of "bargain media," video artist Sherry Milner argues that "many small audiences often add up to much more than one large audience."[80] This is the attitude of a number of people in the Christian music industry with whom I spoke. Teen Mania, a missionary organization, was frequently mentioned as an organization that exposed thousands of kids to Christian music videos. Similarly, Women of Faith, a sort of female version of Promise Keepers that sponsors seminars across the country, exposes thousands of women to adult contemporary Christian videos. While all these audiences probably don't add up to the kind of exposure offered by MTV or VH1, they do add up to a lot of viewers.

Of course, many Christian videomakers aspire toward increased audiences and increased budgets. Indeed, Cindy Montano and Stephen Yake emphatically stressed how much they want their programs to look like the rest of TV. Most channel surfers whiz by public-access shows because they instantly read the poor lighting, sound, and video as signs that this is not "real TV." Montano and Yake, conversely, want channel surfers to stop when they see the high production values of their new series *More than the Music,* which explicitly mimics the conventions of VH1. Montano explains,

We're wanting to go on a broader scale and to create programming that your average viewer who's channel surfing, there's something there about that program that's going to catch them. Whether it's what the production quality looks like— "Oh, that could be VH1's *Behind the Music"*—just looking at the way an interview's framed, the way it's shot, the way it's lit, all of that mise en scène, so to speak. As you're channel surfing, and there's forty-eight million channels with all these biographical and spooky mystery kind of things going on, the *quality* of *More than the Music* will grab you and then you'll get intrigued by the story.[81]

In general, Christian videomakers may be optimistic about the value of multiple small audiences rather than one giant mass audience, but they ultimately want to increase their distribution and their production values.

I have, however, seen two videos that take a different attitude toward production values. Reilly Armstrong is an upbeat pop singer who definitely belongs in the "entertainers who happen to be Christian" camp. The video for Armstrong's "Sleep" is a charming clay animation piece that was made by a member of Audio Adrenaline. Armstrong's clay animated head seems to be stuck onto a G.I. Joe body, he moves jerkily, and it would be an understatement to say that his lips aren't properly synched to the song. The peppy video shows the clay Reilly waking up late, eating breakfast, and trying to get to work on time. It's high-energy and fun and seems to wallow in its own low budget. A second short video, the "Making of Sleep" video carries this wallowing to another level. The clay Reilly explains how much fun it was making the video, thanks Barbie for loaning him her sports car, and explains how tough it was doing his own stunts, especially when he encountered a mischievous Austin Powers action figure and a dog eager for a clay snack. Both videos are good, clean fun, and, while lacking a critical or political edge, nonetheless convey the kind of high-energy enthusiasm one finds in low-budget, independent videos like *Joan Does Dynasty, SPIN,* or *Greetings from Out Here.* While many Christian videos desperately try to look more expensive than they are (with only occasional success), the Reilly Armstrong videos are unique in the world of Christian media for their sense of humor and comfort with the low-tech aesthetic.

CONCLUSION: FROM NU THANG TO OLD HAT

In the early 1990s, Carman was at the forefront of Christian music video production. He was in his thirties, however, seemingly too old to speak to young music fans. Undeterred, he donned baggy pants and shades and became a Christian Vanilla Ice, appropriating hip-hop lingo and coding his voice as black. Perhaps to increase his credibility with the youth audience—and temper his own obvious racism?—he gave DC Talk, a hot new interracial hip-hop group, a major cameo in his "Addicted to Jesus" video. DC Talk had just released their *Nu Thang* album, which included an antiabortion song called "Children Can Live without It." Today the former members of DC Talk are unlikely to take breaks from their solo careers to appear in a tacky Carman video. Nor are they likely to discuss abortion in their songs. "You Consume Me" has made passion for God seem really sexy, and frankly, these guys are looking sexier than ever themselves. If the evolution of DC Talk is a barometer of CCM, does that mean Larry Norman was right? Have Christian musicians prostituted themselves? Do they write songs for consumption, not salvation? Where is the introspection and self-critique one might expect of evangelical artists?

Evangelicals outside the music business have certainly asked critical questions about Christian music. *Christianity Today* often contains articles questioning the mission of the Christian music industry. People within the industry, however, are simply aspiring to do the Lord's work to the best of their ability, and there does not seem to be much time spent debating whether Christian music may be a spiritual dead end. One of the few serious critiques of Christian consumerism advanced by Christian media itself is in a documentary about the annual Creation music festival. In one brief scene, a Stephen Curtis Chapman song called "The Change" plays. The singer explains that he has Jesus T-shirts, jewelry, bumper stickers, and refrigerator magnets but has not experienced "the change," by which he means a spiritual transformation. The images with the song show all the merchandise for sale at the Creation festival, and then show that there are also representatives from missionary, charity, and prolife groups, illustrating what a true "change" might entail.

Ultimately, an in-depth critique of consumerism is unthinkable in most Christian music and music videos, since they themselves would have to be defined as part of the problem. DC Talk's "My Friend (So Long)" is instructive in this regard. This peppy song is addressed to a Christian crossover musician who has gone astray by being caught up in fame. This old friend has an expensive video on VH1 and has been interviewed by *Rolling Stone*. Ending on a charitable note, the song concludes by saying that the singers miss and love their old friend. The high-energy video shows the members of DC Talk being rushed to the hospital in an ambulance, nurses dancing with Las Vegas showgirl fans, and high-kicking businessmen in suits (figs. 24–25). The singers have

FIGS. 24–25 FAN-DANCING AND
HIGH-KICKING NURSES IN DC
TALK'S *VIDEO FOR "MY FRIEND
(SO LONG)"*: PLAYFUL KITSCH OR
SATIRICAL CRITIQUE?

(mock?) serious expressions on their faces, as they lip-synch in a dead-pan style. The video's stylistic excess is perhaps intended as an indict-ment of fame, but it is so much fun that it feels tongue-in-cheek. One segment slows down and shows the guys praying for their friend, but the last image of this sequence shows a man listening to a boom box playing DC Talk's hit song from their last album, *Jesus Freak*. Notably, this was the album in which the band abandoned their hip-hop style, leading some fans to accuse them of being sellouts who changed their music to make a buck. But the moment in which *Jesus Freak* is sam-pled in "My Friend (So Long)" seems more humorous than self-critical. Viewers are thus returned to goofiness, as well as the very self-promotion that the video and song ostensibly criticize. In sum, one is never certain whether the video constitutes playful kitsch or satirical critique.

Perhaps this very illegibility is the key to understanding the con-temporary Christian music industry. Christian music has changed to

compete in the mainstream, and the result is not so much a secularization of the music as a smashing of the literalism that dominated early
CCM, a literalism that persists in the work of artists without crossover
aspirations. The lyrics and images of much of today's Christian music
are nothing if not ambiguous. Searching to appeal to both evangelical
and nonevangelical audiences, Christian music has ended up hitting
some notes that musician Larry Norman never could have imagined in
1973 when he first exclaimed that Jesus was the "rock that rolled his
blues away."

COMMODIFICATION

PART TWO
SEXUALITY

FILMMAKING

CHAPTER THREE

VIRGINS FOR JESUS: THE GENDER POLITICS

OF THERAPEUTIC CHRISTIAN MEDIA

... Girls don't eat much when guys are around. I guess they assume
we're going to think bad of them, or maybe they're too concerned about
their appearance ... many times a girl will look great, but she'll still say
she's fat ... When I go out to dinner with a girl, I want to enjoy the meal
with her instead of just watching her pick at her food.
—Interview with *Breakaway* boys in *Brio* (April 1995)

Unlike crossover Christian music, which is toned down for mass consumption, the prochastity magazines, books, and videos examined in
this chapter are narrowly targeted to an exclusively evangelical audience, which means they can have harder-hitting messages. Christian
musicians like Sixpence None the Richer strive both to reinforce the
beliefs of those within the fold and to reach out to those beyond the
fold, but youth magazines like *Brio* and *Breakaway* are more like Carman, whose music speaks only to fellow born-agains.

Yet even as evangelical youth magazines speak only to believers,
they are not immune to secular ideas. For example, there is nothing
particularly Christian expressed in the epigraph above, in which boys
describe frustration with the female obsession with dieting. This phenomenon would hardly be foreign to readers of mainstream teen magazines; if there is much in Christian magazines that seems strange to
nonevangelicals, there is also much that is familiar. Indeed, except for
the absence of advertisements, these magazines do not, on the surface,
look very different from secular magazines. This is not to say that *Brio*
and *Breakaway* are simply phony imitations of "real" youth magazines.
In fact, they are slick, sophisticated productions in their own right, offering a Christian perspective on issues of interest to teenagers, especially issues of sexuality. Not surprisingly, their take on sexuality—and
gender in general—is quite conservative. Boys in these magazines are
represented as hard and strong, whereas girls are emotional and weak.

Such sexual polarities are consistently deployed in media advocating chastity. Through their representation of sexual abstinence, food consumption, eating disorders, and weightlifting, evangelical youth media define bodily control quite differently for girls and boys. On the surface, evangelical media's gender-specific definitions of bodily control seem to portray boys and girls similarly—as equally chaste—but, as we shall see, Christian bodily control may actually be more oppressive for girls than it is for boys. Chastity can be empowering for teens, a potent symbol of their commitment to God, and it would be unfair to imagine that teens are simply victims of chastity campaigns. At the same time, though, prochastity media call for feminist critique; in this chapter I will make that critique, considering the ways teens may resist the chastity directive while still acknowledging the fact that chastity has deep religious meaning for many teens.

Focus on the Family books, magazines, and videos are major promoters of chastity in the United States and increasingly abroad. Focus's monthly teen magazines, *Breakaway* for boys and *Brio* for girls, are the only nationally distributed evangelical youth magazines. They are sold in some Christian bookstores, but the vast majority of their distribution is subscription-based. There are over 180,000 *Brio* subscribers and 80,000 *Breakaway* subscribers. Parents offer the magazines to their twelve- to sixteen-year-old children as substitutes for secular magazines like *Seventeen*. Readers may have started off with other Focus on the Family publications, such as *Clubhouse Jr.* for four- to eight-year-olds and *Clubhouse* for eight- to twelve-year-olds. As one often finds in secular culture, the magazines for younger children are not targeted to a single sex, but as soon as readers reach puberty magazines start treating boys and girls like separate species. For girls, the transition from the nongender-coded *Highlights* or *Nickelodeon* magazine to the highly feminized *Seventeen* is comparable to the move from *Clubhouse* to *Brio*.

Examining such media cannot reveal all that youth do with them, but it does elucidate how adults—the producers of evangelical youth media—want teens to think about their bodies and how this conceptualization converges with and diverges from secular conceptions of male and female bodies. Evangelical media may promote conservative ideas, but as in the wider secular culture, they discuss sex and gender using therapeutic language. Secular therapeutic discourse "provides a ready-made and familiar narrative trajectory: the eruption of a problem leads to confession and diagnosis and then to a solution or cure."[1] Evangelical therapeutic discourse likewise involves problem resolution, but because of the nature of sin, cures are always precarious. *Brio*, *Breakaway*, and other evangelical youth products such as chastity videos, advice books, and music strive to cure teens of sexual desire and other "problems," but since sin can never entirely be washed away, teens are not really cured of carnality. Rather, one might say that evangelical therapeutic media help teen desires go into remission.

Media that promote chastity are therapeutic in terms of seeking to help teens learn to manage their sexuality, but they are also part of a bigger picture, the wider context of the therapeutic role of contemporary religion. Although evangelicals often criticize narcissistic individualism—the New Age emphasis on "self-realization," for example—as egocentric and ungodly, evangelicals themselves are far from immune to the lure of the therapeutic.[2] David Watt contends that from the mid-twenties until the fifties "fundamentalists did not allow therapeutic ideas to shape their view of the world." Rather, they "mounted numerous direct attacks upon modern psychology."[3] In the 1950s, evangelicals began to lessen their opposition to psychology and to present Christian versions of it. By the 1960s and 1970s, many evangelicals seemed to have fully embraced Christianized psychology, and a significant body of popular evangelical therapeutic literature emerged.[4] James Davison Hunter has argued that this literature, with its "psychological Christocentrism," represents a major accommodation that evangelicals have made to modernity.[5] While sin is certainly not a concept that has been erased from evangelical culture, today one is likely to hear evangelical sermons that speak not only of sin but also of anxiety, sickness, and low self-esteem.[6] God "understands your feelings" and "boosts your self-esteem." He is "your best friend."[7] Hunter argues that such accommodation to modernity strengthens evangelicalism's position in the religious marketplace, where various religious groups compete for believers.[8] Clearly, I would add, such accommodations also enable evangelicals to compete in the market for religious books and media. It can hardly be a coincidence that one of the most successful purveyors of evangelical media, including chastity media, is James Dobson of Focus on the Family. Dobson is also a psychologist with a Ph.D. from the University of Southern California. If contemporary evangelical discourse is infused with therapeutic rhetoric, self-help chastity media should be understood as one piece of this larger picture.

While it is true that evangelicals often use the therapeutic language of health to discuss chastity, we mustn't jump the gun and assume that this shift in language is simply evidence of secularization, for if American religious language is infused with the therapeutic, the reverse is also increasingly true: therapeutic, "secular" self-help discourse is also infused with "spiritual" overtones. In their understandings of chastity, evangelicals may be mixing up the religious and the therapeutic, but these domains were hardly discreet entities before evangelicals began promoting chastity. Evangelicals, thus, are not atypical in their mixing of the medical and the spiritual, but they do seem to have gravitated to the therapeutic with a particular intensity, consistently melding health and religious language when they discuss sex in videos, magazines, advice books, and other media. The teens represented in these media mix together words such as purity, sin, healthy, unhealthy, addiction, recovery, redemption, and temptation. The words chastity and abstinence are both used, the former term clearly having overt spiritual connotations. Abstinence, conversely, is a clinical, medical sounding word that fits unobtrusively into a discussion of how one "struggles" with sexual "issues."

In examining Focus magazines, books, and videos, my main concern will be to understand how these media speak to teens and tell them how to understand their bodies. There is, however, a wider political context to be noted: the national abstinence movement that evangelicals have been promoting since the early 1990s. This wider movement has in recent years been transformed. Chastity persists as a *moral* movement in much of the media addressed to evangelicals, but outside of that community evangelical politicians have transformed chastity into a *health* movement under the banner of "abstinence." Evangelicals have succeeded in bringing abstinence into the public sphere, in part at least, by obscuring the evangelical roots of their anti-sex (and anti-safe-sex) movement.

When Focus on the Family and other conservative Christian groups lobby for money for anti-sex campaigns, they speak not of chastity but rather of abstinence. And they have succeeded using this tactic. As *Focus on the Family* magazine reports, "The 1996 Welfare Reform Act included a $50 million-per-year appropriation for states to provide abstinence education under Title V. The federal Office of Adolescent Pregnancy Programs also awards grants under Title XX for demonstration projects aimed at preventing adolescent sexual activity."[9] The $50 million was given out each year for five years. The pro-abstinence Bush administration pushed for increased funding, and by 2002 annual federal spending on abstinence programs had mounted to $102 million.[10] *Focus on the Family* crows that "even the harshest critics of abstinence grudgingly concede that abstinence is 'mainstream'—so much so that many organizations, such as Planned Parenthood, have tried to co-opt abstinence language to fool the public, calling their programs 'abstinence-based.'"[11] The irony, of course, is that Focus and other groups are themselves guilty of trying to fool the public by pretending that abstinence campaigns do not have evangelical roots. These abstinence campaigns have received much press coverage, but chastity campaigns have received less media attention. In other words, we know how evangelicals try to sell abstinence to outsiders, but how do they sell chastity within their ranks?

CHASTITY THROUGH THE ROOF

Evangelical teen advice books repeatedly state that feelings of sexual attraction are a gift from God. Yet God's gift is dangerous; left uncontrolled, it will lead to premarital sexual activity. To prevent such activity, evangelicals have undertaken a number of nationwide chastity campaigns, and these campaigns are promoted in *Brio* and *Breakaway*. When you open the magazines, chastity pledge cards tumble out instead of subscription cards. In July 1994, the True Love Waits campaign culminated with 25,000 teens planting 200,000 chastity pledge cards in the Mall area between the Capitol and the Washington Monument. These cards read: "Believing that true love waits, I make a commitment to God, myself, my family, my friends, my future mate, and my future children to be sexually abstinent from this date until the day I enter a Biblical marriage relationship." In 1996, thousands of teens filled out "True Love Waits" cards and assembled at the Atlanta Georgia Dome for a weekend-long chastity extravaganza, featuring various speakers and the hottest Christian bands. These cards had the same words on them as the 1994 cards but were designed slightly differently, with a hole in them so that they could be stacked on a pole soaring up to the ceiling of the arena. Further cementing the already bizarrely phallic connotations of the event, the ejaculatory motto of the gathering was "My card's through the roof!" (figs. 26–27).

Assuming that God makes "opposites" attract, evangelical abstinence campaigns address boys and girls as utterly dichotomous: boys are strong and stoic; girls, emotional and nurturing. But their faith and their commitment to chastity unite these opposites. That boys and girls can send their cards through the roof and gyrate to Christian rock to celebrate their shared dedication to chastity may seem strange. Yet chastity celebrations, like Christian youth music festivals, are the ultimate coed road trip. Boys and girls who usually aren't allowed to stay out late, go to wild parties, or even touch each other platonically (there is a three-inch separation rule at one evangelical junior high school in California), pile into buses with their adult youth group leaders and spend three or four days in a hotel or at a campground. Although conservative ideas about gender-appropriate behavior remain firmly in place, the commitment to chastity does bridge the metaphorical and literal sexual separateness of evangelical boys and girls. Chastity—and all the celebratory rallies, concerts, and parties it entails—is, ironically, the only risk-free activity that teen boys and girls can safely engage in together.

Believing that *true love waits*, I make a commitment to God, myself, my family, my friends, my future mate, and my future children to be sexually abstinent from this day until the day I enter a biblical marriage relationship.

Signed: _____

Date: _____

❑ I am making this commitment for the first time.
❑ I made this commitment previously; this is a restatement of that commitment.

Believing that *true love waits*, I make a commitment to God, myself, my family, my friends, my future mate, and my future children to be sexually abstinent from this day until the day I enter a biblical marriage relationship.

Signed: _____

Date: _____

❑ I am making this commitment for the first time.
❑ I made this commitment previously; this is a restatement of that commitment.

Mail the top card to Atlanta; keep the bottom card as a reminder of your commitment.

Please mail card with punch-out to:
True Love Waits
958 Milstead Avenue
Conyers, GA 30207

My Card!
Thru the Roof!
ATLANTA GEORGIA DOME
FEBRUARY 11TH, 1996
TRUE LOVE WAITS

5621-39

FIGS. 26–27 CHASTITY PLEDGE CARD

The conundrum is, how do you create a therapeutic discourse that explains and promotes chastity to teens who have been taught to think of boys and girls as sexual antagonists? How can essentialist notions of gender be maintained—the idea that certain behaviors are simply "natural"—if the "inherent" desires of boys and girls can be restructured? In other words, how can boys still be masculine while resisting their active sexual urges, and how can girls still be feminine while resisting the urge to passively submit? These questions represent the fault lines of evangelical notions of sexual control. To "cure" teens of sexual desire, evangelical adults must sanction the very behavioral traits (masculine aggression, feminine passivity) that supposedly compel unchaste behavior.

At the 1994 True Love Waits conference, girls and boys were taught about chastity in separate seminars. Girls were told a sentimental fairy tale about true, eternal love and the achievement of the feminine dream of romance through the preservation of virginity. Boys, conversely, were directed to loudly chant "We are real men! We are real men!" They were told that abstinence was not emasculating, that "Adam was a real man," and that the Garden of Eden housed "Adam and Eve," not "Adam and Steve."[12] The problem of how one could be a "real man" and a virgin was solved by asserting homophobic machismo. Ironically, in order to control the male body, to save it from its own heterosexual aggression, that body must be constructed as aggressively heterosexual and masculine. Thus, "natural" heterosexual gender roles are maintained in spite of a constant attempt to control and reconstruct "natural urges."

Susie Shellenberger and Greg Johnson, the editors of *Brio* and *Breakaway,* have written numerous teen advice books on how to maintain one's faith and virginity.[13] Their coauthored *258 Great Dates While You Wait* tells teens how to avoid sticky situations in which their hormones might carry them away. Like other adult chastity promoters, Shellenberger and Johnson assume that teenagers cannot control their desires. Heavy petting or even French kissing will almost inevitably lead down the slippery slope to sexual intercourse. Shellenberger rationalizes her argument by referring to the "law of diminishing returns": "each time you go a step further, you find that it takes *more* to fulfill your appetite. So you continually let down your barriers to become more and more fulfilled. The result? Two people have had sexual intercourse without planning on it."[14] By constructing a teen body utterly lacking self-control, a body that can only be controlled or cured by a spiritual commitment to chastity, evangelical books, magazines, and videos may not only be dangerous to teen self-image but also may encourage boys to be sexually violent and girls to see submission to sexual violence as natural. Boys and girls who are repeatedly told that at a certain point they are no longer in control may as a result feel less in control, and it may actually be more difficult to stop sexual activity if one conceives of one's body as a runaway train. Crudely put, when all bodily control is lost, boys give in to their urge to rape and girls give in to their urge to submit to rape.

Evangelical youth media are, in fact, contradictory in their conceptualization of rape. Sometimes it seems that rape per se does not exist for evangelicals. Instead, boys "lose control" or "force themselves" on girls. This is a scenario in one episode of *Family First*, an evangelical sitcom aired on the Trinity Broadcasting Network. A girl ignores her brother's warnings that the boy she is dating has a "bad reputation." The boy eventually forces himself on her, but she simply hits him and escapes. The word "rape" is avoided, and the girl is taught a valuable lesson about being led by the spirit, not the flesh. The unstated implication is that she was "asking for it." A teenager who wrote in to *Breakaway* was less fortunate than the sitcom girl. She explains that she and her boyfriend were sexually "wrestling," and she kept telling him to stop, but at a certain point she felt that she had "let him go so far" that it wouldn't be fair or possible to stop him. She says she should have pushed him off her and run away, but instead she had sex. Again, what sounds like rape is here defined as the victim's fault because she has been so thoroughly instructed in biologically compulsory fornication.[15] Notably, though, when girls write to *Brio* and explicitly say that they have been raped, the editors respond compassionately and do not blame the victims. Here, the evangelical understanding of rape mirrors that of most of the contemporary secular world—that "no means no" and that rape is a violent crime in which women are not complicit.

While *Brio* and other Focus magazines promote an idealized, nostalgic 1950s sexual morality, they cannot escape the fact that attitudes about rape have changed since then. As much as evangelicals criticize feminism, they have been affected by it. In fact, their ideas have been modified, and one might even say made more liberal, in response to changes wrought by feminism. We can see this change in both youth and adult culture. In her study of adult evangelicals in the Women's Aglow organization, Marie Griffith recounts how the group's conceptualization of female submission to men has shifted over time. In the 1970s, Women's Aglow literature emphasized a doctrine of wifely submission. Rather than "merely participating in their own victimization," Griffith explains, "the women themselves claim the doctrine of submission leads both to freedom and to transformation, as God rewards His obedient daughters by healing their sorrows and easing their pain. Thus interpreted, the doctrine of submission becomes a means of asserting power over bad situations, including circumstances over which one may otherwise have no control."[16] Since the mid-1980s, however, the doctrine of wifely submission has changed dramatically. Griffith observes that "as teachings on proper gender roles have fluctuated over time, the strictest interpretation has gradually given way to more lenient, flexible interpretations" of submission or surrender to God.[17]

Today, *mutual* submission of husband and wife is emphasized. This decreasing emphasis on wifely submission must surely be understood, at least in part, as a response to feminist ideas, and here we see a parallel in teen chastity literature and videos that speak of rape using a language that could not exist without feminism. In fact, the very idea that girls have "healthy" sexual feelings is a modern one that owes quite a debt to feminism.

Even if the official prochastity line is that sex is beautiful, natural, and healthy, Christian media have ways of making it seem rather unpleasant, even infusing it with Oedipal overtones. Magazines, videos, and advice books urge sexually aroused teens to stymie sexual feelings by picturing the faces of all their relatives, as well as Jesus. Although the intention may be simply to make kids feel guilty, there is also a creepy Oedipal dimension to picturing your mother's or father's face whenever you are sexually aroused. Boys and girls are encouraged to imagine dates as siblings and to "date" their parents.[18] Articles in *Focus on the Family* magazine even suggest that fathers "propose" to their daughters, offering them purity rings instead of engagement rings (fig. 28).[19] A cartoon in Shellenberger's advice book *Guys and a Whole Lot More* shows a car parked at Lover's Lane and explicitly places the male sexual aggressor in the paternal subject position. In the caption, the girl tells the boy, "Here's a quarter. Call my dad. Tell him what you want to do. If it's all right with him, it's okay with me."[20] Mothers are less often evoked, although one Christian music celebrity does say, "The best date I've ever had was with my mom!"

While this all sounds a bit perverse, evangelical media intend to construct chastity as empowering. One *Edge TV* video, however, illustrates the pressures wrought upon both boys and girls by a commitment to chastity. The first segment in the "Sexual Choices" episode features a dozen kids, many of whom have made sexual "mistakes" in the past. While some feel empowered by their current commitment to chastity, memories of their sexually active histories torture many of them. This video shows emotional, introspective teenage boys, a far cry from the "We are real men!" chanters. An athletic football player type explains that lust is dehumanizing. He is shot in soft focus, a style typically associated with feminine images. Another boy suffers desperately from the urge to masturbate. A third teen is horrified by his homosexual past and remarks that if only he had talked to someone about his homosexual feelings before he succumbed to them he could have properly dealt with his problem, and he would not have engaged in the sexual acts that led to his HIV-positive status.

The antilust football player, the suffering masturbator, and the repentant homosexual offer striking examples of evangelicals' simulta-

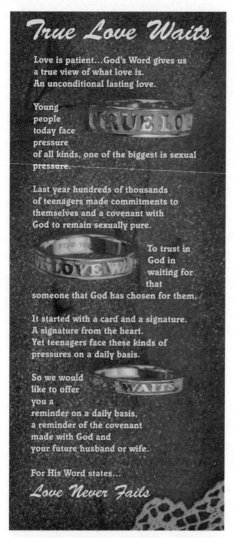

FIG. 28 ADVERTISEMENT FOR 14KT GOLD CHASTITY RING.

neous engagement with and distance from secular media. On the one hand, unlike evangelical media, most mainstream media does not vilify teen sex and even, in fact, encourages it. On the other hand, evangelical media parallel secular media in their emphasis on popularized versions of what Freud called "the talking cure."[21] Through externalizing their feelings, evangelical youth are promised they can cure themselves of their sexual problems. This is also the logic of secular therapeutic media such as *The Oprah Winfrey Show* or mainstream self-help books, even if what constitutes a sexual "problem" is generally defined quite differently in such venues.

THERAPEUTIC SELF-EXPRESSION

Like most media promoting chastity, *Edge TV* videos teach viewers that they desperately need to *talk* about their sexual feelings. In fact, the evangelical invective to speak one's sex is evocative of the forced "infinite task of telling" sexuality that Michel Foucault speaks of in the first volume of *The History of Sexuality:* "[Y]ou will seek to transform your desire, your every desire, into discourse."[22] The organizing principle of much therapeutic evangelical youth media is that translating sexuality into language is liberating, and that if youth could express their sexual feelings to youth pastors or other mature elders, they would be able to control those feelings. Because of the intransigence of sin, the cure from sexuality is unstable, but it is nonetheless within the grasp of those teenagers who can translate their interior self into language.

Importantly, self-narration is a vital part of evangelical culture apart from the issue of chastity. The telling and retelling of conversion stories is a crucial aspect of evangelical identity. The typical witnessing narrative details how one has found salvation; it is a public display of the self that is simultaneously spiritually valuable to the evangelizer and, ideally, to listeners, who are potential converts. Such narratives also help maintain a sense of community, of shared experience. In his essay on the rhetoric of conversion narratives, Wayne Booth notes that "typical Protestant conversions" are "dramatic, sudden, shattering, moving from depravity to a sudden inflowing of grace."[23] Booth argues that the conversion narratives that have the most impact on listeners are those that emphasize the perilous journey between "before" and "after." The distance traveled to salvation must be dramatic, even exaggerated, to make a strong impact on listeners.[24]

Narratives of sin and salvation can be difficult to construct, however, for children raised in evangelical homes, many of whom were saved at the age of seven or eight and who only vaguely remember the moment of salvation. Teenagers who have no "before" to their conversion narratives have not experienced serious worldly transgression, but for many this changes with the arrival of puberty. Sexual desire opens the door to transgression, and even those who only gingerly cross the threshold, perhaps buying a pornographic magazine or watching a dirty movie, will find their conversion stories changing (or coalescing for the first time) as they fight temptation, stumble, and perhaps end up "rededicating" themselves to God. Through rededicating one's self to the Lord one can, in effect, be saved over and over again, and conversion narratives will quite likely be stronger for those who have fallen and then returned to the fold than for those who have never succumbed to transgression and strayed from the flock.

As we saw in the figure of the sensitive football player, it is not only girls who are allowed the emotional, introspective discourse of therapeutic self-narration. Although both genders are expected to reveal their innermost selves through impassioned, public rhetorical displays, in the introspective teenage boy we find a new twist in the gender politics of Christian prochastity media. On the one hand, boys are told that they are driven by strong, even brutal, sexual impulses, and prochastity media provide tactics to harness such energies while maintaining that chaste boys are nonetheless masculine: they are big eaters, into sports, and aggressively heterosexual. On the other hand, evangelical videos also picture a soft and introspective teen boy. This boy is emotionally connected with others and very much in touch with his feelings. I would argue that the more macho boy is a bit old-fashioned. Although some videos mix images of the insensitive tough guy with the new emotionally attuned boy, the older type is most likely to turn up in the least cool youth group videos. These are videos with music and graphics that seem a few years out of date and with an adult rather than teen host. The hipper videos with teen hosts and the newest music, conversely, are more likely to picture the new-fangled boy.

Of course, the sensitive boy featured in chastity videos is not a character type created from scratch by evangelical media makers. To be in touch with one's feelings and to be familiar with the therapeutic language used to express those feelings is increasingly crucial to the contemporary definition of masculinity—at least as expressed in popular culture. To give only one example, the crux of much of the humor of the HBO hit series *The Sopranos* is that the hero is a murderous mobster who is also in therapy discussing his feelings. Even macho action films have increasingly focused on sensitive family men since the nineties.[25] Put simply, masculinity is being "feminized" in much popular secular media, and thus, a Christian youth video that wants to successfully speak to viewers will have to be aware of the recent entry of therapeutic, self-help language into masculine self-expression.

Evangelical teens may well avoid secular television shows such as *Felicity* and *Dawson's Creek,* since these programs picture sexual relationships outside of marriage, gay characters, and other elements that might trouble evangelical viewers. Yet evangelical youth group videos demonstrate familiarity with the kind of boy so often featured in these programs, the hypersensitive, emotionally attuned young man. In one Christian video, a young man in college describes how he bonded with his male best friend: "We both struggled with the same thing—being, or trying to be, 'manly' or 'masculine' as the culture has defined it, to be tough and invincible. But we both connected because we realized that we weren't. We tried really hard to be, but we weren't [manly or masculine] inside." He adds, "I can remember the first time that I ever heard another guy say that he was struggling with sexual temptation, or pornography, and how freeing that felt to hear another man say that . . . The rewards of taking those uncomfortable, awkward steps toward someone to be real and be honest and to admit *feelings* far outweigh the scariness of taking those steps." He concludes that "my relationships have improved immensely because I've been vulnerable with my friends."[26]

In Christian youth videos, such vulnerability is a key issue for boys in support groups. The premise of such groups is that talking about sex with male friends functions as a prophylactic against the committing of sexual acts. The *Edge TV* masturbator, for example, ends his tale by explaining (somewhat unconvincingly) that he feels better now that he has found a support network of tormented fellow masturbators to whom he can confess his sinful feelings rather than acting upon them. Notably, a key premise of the all-male chastity support group is that this is a safe space to talk about sex, since no women are present. Clearly, however, for evangelical boys struggling with homosexuality, the support group will help isolated boys meet others who are gay, and the current evangelical trend toward speaking about homosexuality rather than hiding it may produce some unintended results.

Prophylactic Christian media hope to ease the pressures of the chaste Christian lifestyle by offering pleasurable alternatives to sinful secular culture,[27] and, in principle, prochastity songs ("I Don't Want It," "Ain't No Safe Way"), videos, books, and even nonmedia products such as jewelry (purity rings) and clothing ("Pet Your Dog, Not Your Date" T-shirts, "No Trespassing" underwear), are designed to help kids not think about having sex. But just when sex is ostensibly repressed, it is actually ubiquitous. Indeed, evangelical prochastity media provide a stunning illustration of Foucault's "repressive hypothesis." Evangelicals strive to eliminate sex outside the boundaries of marriage, yet it is precisely outside those boundaries that discourses of sexuality propagate with reckless abandon. Focus on the Family dispenses advice to improve the sex lives of married couples, but the amount of sex talk directed to those *not* allowed to copulate by far outweighs the amount of sex talk directed to those sanctioned to indulge. Prochastity teen media make ignoring sex impossible.

TEEN NEGOTIATION OF CHASTITY

Prochastity media will almost inevitably strike nonevangelicals as bizarre. Most will assume that such media damage their young consumers or, at the very least, that they constitute antisex propaganda. Prochastity media can indeed misfire, teaching teens to think about their bodies in potentially damaging ways. Most obviously, such media can be devastating for gay and lesbian teens. Still, it is simplistic to imagine that Christian teens simply swallow the sexual directives of evangelical media hook, line, and sinker. How might teens negotiate the advice they receive through such media?

Some of the advice dispensed in prochastity books, magazines, and videos is just plain bad and would be rejected out of hand by many teens. In their dating book, for example, Focus on the Family's Susie Shellenberger and Greg Johnson suggest odd food-centered and highly infantilizing group dates.[28] "Kid's day" requires crayoning in coloring books and playing Candy Land. Airport dates involve putting on strange costumes, pretending to meet each other getting off planes, and competing at guessing how many men will go into the restroom immediately after deplaning. Food dates include eating entire meals by taste-testing at a large grocery store, organizing fruit juice tastings (as opposed to wine tastings), making a giant popsicle in a trash can at the local ice plant, and eating all of the leftovers in the fridge. In sum, these adults suggest that one avoid sex by engaging in activities more appropriate for a prepubescent person and by displacing sexual desire onto desire for food. No doubt, many evangelical teens would find these suggestions insulting.

But what about more nuanced advice literature? Do Christian teens seriously question chastity directives that have been explained to them in Biblical terms? Interestingly, letters published in *Brio* indicate a constant negotiation of the idea of chastity among the magazine's subscribers; it seems that readers do indeed look for contradictions in the Biblical chastity mandate. The editors receive 1,000 letters each month, most of them asking questions about boys and sex.[29] *Brio* letters often focus on looking for loopholes in the chastity mandate. A girl from Ohio writes, "This is kind of an embarrassing question, but if the guy doesn't have a name or face, is it okay to fantasize about your wedding night and what sex will be like after you're married?" The answer is no, because you should "strive to fill your mind with things that won't leave you frustrated or wanting what you can't have,"[30] but it's hard to believe that teens who have signed chastity pledge cards don't have sexual fantasies made safe through a prefatory marriage fantasy. Although Shellenberger consistently tells girls that even French kissing is off limits, they continue to ask, "How much fooling around is acceptable by God?"[31] One girl, who signs herself "Feeling Guilty," thinks she has found a potential loophole in her chastity pact with God: "I have pledged to remain sexually pure until marriage. But what if Jesus comes back before I get married? I want to know how it feels to have sex. Is this a horrible thing to want?"[32] Many evangelicals believe that the Bible predicts the end of the world and the Second Coming of Christ. These events will be preceded by the Rapture, when all saved Christians will be instantly removed from the earth. Those who have been raptured cannot have sex, and there is no sex allowed after the return of Jesus and the Final Judgment. This *Brio* reader thus voices a legitimate concern inspired by an evangelical interpretation of the Bible.

Occasionally, *Brio* girls write in to flaunt the fact that they engage in sexual activity without feeling guilty. One particularly outspoken girl writes:

You're probably going to tell me that petting will lead to intercourse . . . [but me and] this guy . . . have done some things that you would probably consider wrong, but I don't think it is, and I don't feel a bit guilty about it. I don't think it will lead to us having sex, because I'm not ready until I'm married. He doesn't pressure me at all and says he respects me for not wanting to have sex. So my question is, what if—because of my own values and beliefs—I don't think it's wrong? And don't tell me to get out of the relationship because I don't want to and I won't.[33]

There's no telling how many such letters *Brio* receives, since it behooves their own agenda to print more letters from guilt-ridden girls than unrepentant ones, but it is clear from the letters that *Brio's* adult editors choose to print that readers do not merely internalize the chastity directive without substantial questioning, negotiation, and varying degrees of resistance. On the other hand, it is also clear that such letters aid *Brio* in defining the chastity directive. From the editors' perspective, the letters prove that teen sexuality really is out of control; the existence of the fallen girl enables the therapeutic salvation narrative to exist.

Breakaway does not represent fallen boys and does not print letters from Christian boys asking if it's OK to make out as long as they don't "go too far." Because their desires are considered uncontrollable once unleashed, the boys given a voice in *Breakaway* avoid any contact, or even being alone with a female: "I prefer group dating because there's a lot less temptation. Because I'm a Christian, I want to stay away from *risky* situations . . . it's better to go out in groups. It's *safer* and it's more fun."[34] Group dates save boys from their own lustfulness and also shield them from the occasional female temptress. When a boy writes that his girlfriend wants to have sex, *Breakaway* advises, "you ought to end this relationship pronto, ASAP, yesterday and real quick. I promise you that your girlfriend is much more likely to bring you down than you are to bring her up. You may think you're strong enough to stay with her without caving in. But be warned: Samson thought the same thing, and before it was all over he was blind, beaten, betrayed and bald (see Judges 16)."[35] This boy, like the girl who feared Jesus would come before she did, is negotiating the fact that his desires don't mesh with Biblical directives.

Teens writing to *Brio* or *Breakaway* often ask questions about Biblical interpretation. Christian parents put forth the Bible as a rule book for their children, but the rule book can backfire when teens study it and recognize the complicated or contradictory dimensions of the textual interpretations that adults put forth as straightforward and unquestionable, or when they notice the differences between isolated Scripture and the same Scripture in its context. Through their own Bible study, teens may end up rethinking, or at least complicating, the very rules that adults say the Bible teaches unequivocally. On the other hand, teens who don't know the Bible well enough will find themselves trumped by well-versed adults. At one Christian school, for example, some boys questioned the rule that their hair had to be short. Their teacher pointed to 1 Corinthians 11:14: "[I]f a man has long hair, it is a disgrace to him." One student thought he had a winning counterargument: "'But didn't Jesus have long hair?' The teacher was indignant and cautioned the students that the pictures they see of Jesus are just representations painted by sinful men. The Bible teaches that long hair is a sin and also teaches that Jesus never sinned; Jesus, therefore, could not have had long hair. Case closed."[36] The boys lost because they countered with a commonsense assertion about Jesus' hair rather than a Biblically based argument for long hair. ("What about Samson and Delilah?" might have been a more productive line of questioning.)

Questioning rules is highly problematic for teens wishing to follow the fifth Commandment: honor thy father and mother. In fact, some teens may not question the chastity directive at all. Why would they want to tamper with their relationship with God and with their community? After all, many teens find great peace and joy through their faith. In addition, belief in a rule book (the Bible) offers believers a sense of stability and order and a place in a community of like-minded folks. Given the tortuous isolation and feelings of helplessness and despair that many teenagers endure, it is not difficult to see why an ordered belief system and a community of fellow believers would be appealing. The evangelical belief system, which to outsiders may seem to be all rules and prohibition, offers structure, stability, and community to youth. Acknowledging the potentially positive aspects of evangelical youth culture, however, does not preclude also looking at the flip side. What are the potential consequences—both personal and political—of imagining male and female bodies as utterly opposite? What kinds of contradictions are bound up in evangelical conceptions of teen bodies?

FEMALE RETENTION AND MALE EXPULSION

The adult compilers of the *Teen Study Bible* tell readers unequivocally that "God is prolife."[37] Psalm 139 is one key text used to support the evangelical antiabortion stance. The New International Version of the psalm reads, in part,

you created my inmost being; you knit me together in my mother's womb . . . My frame was not hidden from you when I was made in the secret place. When I was woven together in the depths of the earth, your eyes saw my unformed body. All the days ordained for me were written in your book before one of them came to be.

While the Bible never explicitly condemns abortion—indeed, inducing miscarriage and killing pregnant women are advanced in the Old Testament as methods to smite one's enemies—Christian antiabortion advocates use Psalm 139 to prove the personhood of unborn life.[38] Evangelicals also use this passage to show how thoroughly God knows you and your body and, furthermore, to show that your body is not only his creation but also belongs to him. Another Biblical passage supporting this idea is 1 Corinthians 6:19–20 in which Paul says, "Do you not know that your body is a temple of the Holy Spirit, who is in you, whom you have received from God? You are not your own; you were bought at a price. Therefore honor God with your body."[39] Crucially, this means that you cannot "choose" whether or not to have sex or to terminate a pregnancy in your body, because it is *not your body.* Your body is simply on loan from God.

Should the *Brio* girl falter in her commitment to chastity, it is assumed she will become pregnant. Like many adult chastity promoters, James Dobson presumes that birth control does not work.[40] He likes to joke, "What do you call a couple that uses condoms? Parents!" The properly containing (and contained) *Brio* body should retain, not abort, any fetuses that may grow inside her. This contained feminine body should not sweat or burp, either. Unlike *Breakaway* boys, whom the magazine portrays as belchers who wear dirty socks and rarely shower, *Brio* girls express great concern about bodily containment: How do I tell a friend she has bad breath? How can I manage my sweaty hair after gym class? The same kinds of anxieties can be found in the letters section of mainstream female magazines, and both kinds of magazines function as public therapy spaces where problems erupt, confessions and diagnoses are made, and a solution or cure is offered. A crucial difference between secular and evangelical girls' magazines, however, is that whereas both tend to promote certain ideas about "proper" (odor-free, nonsweaty) femininity, the secular magazines promote a gendered body that is only implicitly politicized, while the contained body promoted in *Brio* has more explicitly politicized, prolife connotations. The message sent to teen girls is that God created "your" body, loves "your" body, and lent it to you, and His will is that you fill your borrowed flesh with progeny. Although the young female body is urged to be chaste, once married God has designed her body to be penetrated and filled.

The male teen, conversely, embodies the principle of expulsion and impenetrable hardness. *Breakaway* and other Focus publications endeavor to construct the controlled, chaste teen male body mainly by encouraging rigorous bodily activities *besides* sex. Boys maintain self-control through sports and bodybuilding; such vigorous, structured activity is necessary to cure or at least to stymie their lust. Inherently more reckless, boys must exert much more self-control than girls. But unlike girls, they are allowed to express their recklessness through their overflowing bodies. Boys are encouraged to expel spit, vomit, and sweat, but not semen, and *Breakaway* humor often centers on the very bodily humors disavowed in *Brio*. One reader mail column centered on "spew stories," where teen boys wrote about their most embarrassing vomiting experiences.

Breakaway boys' earthly bodies are metaphorically clean (chaste), yet they are literally filthy. One *Breakaway* cartoon shows a boy eating junk food and explaining, "Actually, Mom, potato chips are very good for you! The loud crunching scares away germs!"[41] Since boys are assumed to be insalubrious, scaring away germs is certainly in order. Interestingly, the dirty, spewing *Breakaway* boy never seems to fart; this boy is grotesque in carefully circumscribed ways, transgressing boundaries only from the waist up. The *Breakaway* boy exists somewhere between the "classical body—a refined, orifice-less, laminated surface" that *Brio* constructs, a body whose higher stratum is emphasized while the lower stratum is disavowed, and the vulgar "lower class"–coded body that Laura Kipnis has described as the *Hustler* hard-core porn body: "a gaseous, fluid-emitting, *embarrassing* body, one continually defying the strictures of bourgeois manners and mores and instead governed by its lower intestinal tract—a body threatening to erupt at any moment. *Hustler's* favorite joke is someone accidentally defecating in church."[42] The *Breakaway* body threatens to erupt at any moment, but only through the nose or mouth, and certainly not in church! This body thus violates what Kipnis, following anthropologist Mary Douglas, calls "'pollution' taboos and rituals—these being a society's set of beliefs, rituals, and practices having to do with dirt, order, and hygiene," but it only does so within circumscribed limits.[43] Both unhygienic and unscatalogical, the *Breakaway* body can have its cake and eat it, too, as long as the cake exits through an upper body cavity.

Obsession with the body is considered vain in the *Brio* world, but *Breakaway* encourages boys to build up buff physiques in order to enhance their masculine self-esteem. *Breakaway* never explicitly states that muscles may increase a boy's sex appeal, and while *Brio* advises girls not to unfairly arouse boys with "suggestive" clothing, *Breakaway* never warns boys to hide their sweaty muscles from their horny peers. Yet Christian sports, and bodybuilding in particular, are as erotic or masturbatory as secular sports and bodybuilding. A *Breakaway* feature on weightlifting describes a sexually charged male body that would be unthinkable in a evangelical coed environment:

THE PUMP. It must be experienced firsthand because no sensation compares. Your shoulders throb, your chest aches, your skin tingles. Blood pulses through your veins like a pack of angry earthworms. Sweat streams down the rippled bands of sheer steel you once called your belly. When you stand on your toes, your calves threaten to pop out at the knees. You flex your biceps, and two bowling balls appear. You look at yourself in the mirror and grunt, "Hello, Hulk!"[44]

Although the magazine urges safety and moderation in workouts, here it also applauds (somewhat parodically) the bulging masculine body. Likewise, a youth group study guide on steroid use does not find bodybuilding problematic or vain. While advantages of a drug-free workout include "Your steady loves your new appearance" and "You look fantastic! Members of the opposite sex are keeping an eye on you," steroids are condemned as a "shortcut" that will make you "overly aggressive" and "cocky"—in other words, out of control.[45] By advocating bodybuilding, *Breakaway* and other prochastity media solve the problem of how virgin boys can be "real men." Weightlifting represents not a "feminine" obsession with one's looks but rather a business contract with God whereby if you don't cheat with steroids you will gain self-esteem through your muscles. Only through cheating will you become cocky and aggressive—excessively masculine and therefore no longer self-controlled. Paradoxically, lifting should be a diversion from sexuality, yet onanistic weightlifting produces a more sexually alluring body.

To some extent, autoerotic weightlifting is hoped to function as a substitute for autoerotic genital activity.[46] Although it would be best if boys could avoid erections altogether, according to most evangelical experts erections in and of themselves are not sinful, as long as they are not accompanied by mental images of other bodies. This was the source of the *Edge TV* masturbator's agony. He could not masturbate without fantasizing about girls. If masturbation does occur, it must not be accompanied by lustful thoughts. Caught between a rock and a hard place, as it were, the teen boy is basically denied guilt-free penile tumescence. The weightlifter can at least increase the bulk of the rest of his body.

Girls apparently have less to feel guilty about, since they are generally assumed to be less interested than boys in sex. A cartoon in Shellenberger's *Guys and a Whole Lot More* illustrates a "humorous" reaction to the female's puberty-induced anxieties: a girl asks her pharmacist, "Do you have an antidote to hormone poisoning?"[47] Girls may be sexually curious (hormonally poisoned), but girls' books, magazines, and videos ignore masturbation, since it is considered a boy's problem. Needless to say, weightlifting is not an option for Christian girls wanting to rechannel their sexual energy into the quest for the ideal body.

CHASTE GIRLS AND EATING DISORDERS

As we have seen, evangelical media's messages about sexuality and teen bodies contain a number of contradictions. Sex is normal and healthy; sex is sinful and aberrant. Rape is wrong and not the victim's fault; sometimes girls are to blame for rape. Male bodies are aggressive and eruptive and so should not be sexually aroused; male bodies are aggressive and eruptive, and this is a natural aspect of masculinity to be encouraged. The contradictions of evangelical media offer particular challenges to adolescent girls, I would argue, because there is less space within evangelical culture for chaste girls to rebel against authority. To be sure, both boys and girls are encouraged to see the commitment to chastity as a means of rebelling against peer pressure and the prosex attitudes of mainstream society, but since conservative ideas about masculinity and femininity remain very much in place in evangelical culture, it may be harder for girls to see themselves as rebellious. Their bodies cannot erupt sexually or, unlike boys, athletically, and they are also less likely than boys to have access to the Christian hard rock, tattooing, skateboarding, and other "rebellious" activity that is increasingly part of Christian youth culture.[48] In other words, both boys and girls may be instructed to control their bodies, but boys have more opportunities to blow off steam. Girls, conversely, must remain contained. And while *Breakaway* encourages boys to ravenously consume—as a carnal alternative to sex—*Brio* is less likely to propose that girls stuff their faces with junk food. In other words, *Brio* and *Breakaway* assume boys and girls to have different appetites not only for sex but also for food. As in secular culture, the ways that evangelical girls perceive food and their bodies can have dire consequences, but are there aspects of Christian culture that may exacerbate these consequences?

Food and sensuality are certainly linked for many non-Christian women, but for evangelicals that linkage is more likely to be morally coded as sinful. Marie Griffith, for example, has documented the ways that food is described as an evil temptation in Christian dieting literature directed to adult women. Christian diet books liken love for food to idolatry and declare eating chocolate or fried foods to be sinful. There is an obvious carnal dimension to the Christian dieter's relationship to food. One diet book author writes, "This flesh of mine is like a hungry tiger, always ready to break out of the cage of discipline and gobble everything in sight. And I am the one who opens the door."[49] Gwen Shamblin, who wrote several bestselling Christian diet books in the 1990s, particularly emphasizes the sexual dimensions of food consumption. Griffith argues that for Shamblin food is "a devilish lover, tempting human beings to betray their covenant with God and enter a lascivious relationship with food."[50] Most Christian dieting literature is directed to white, middle-class married women with children. In fact, I would argue that part of the reason that relationships to food and dieting can be so overtly eroticized in Christian diet books is that the reader is assumed to be an adult who engages in marital sex. To speak of the illicit temptations of chocolate donuts and the need to submit to a higher authority would be a dangerous discourse if directed to chaste girls, for it would acknowledge too overtly that teen girls have carnal desires. To acknowledge this in an adult married woman is one thing, but to speak of teenage girls as tempted by sin would be to go too far.

While Christian dieting literature speaks of food in illicit terms, the opposite tact is taken in chastity advice books, which suggest food consumption as a means of sublimating sexual feelings, especially for boys. Of course, transferring desire from sex to food may be easier for the gluttonous *Breakaway* boy than for the abstemious *Brio* girl. Appropriating liberal feminist discourse, Christian books and cassettes on eating disorders argue that secular notions of the "ideal female body" have a negative effect on girls' self-esteem. At the same time, these self-help media also tend to replicate secular culture's tendency to see excessive food consumption as normal for boys and abnormal for girls. One group date described in *258 Great Dates While You Wait* involves driving to various fast food restaurants and eating a little bit at a time until you're full: "Still hungry? Though the girls may not be, the guys are!"[51] A *Breakaway* cartoon illustrates the boy's insatiable appetite. As a happy cat enters the kitchen through a hinged cat door, an equally happy boy, licking his chops, exits the refrigerator via a hinged boy-door.[52]

Another cartoon in *Breakaway* shows a girl speaking to a boy whose mouth is obscenely crammed full of milkshakes, pizza slices, hot dogs, and fried chicken legs (fig. 29). It is unclear from the image whether he is consuming or expelling his lode. The cartoon was part of a contest where boys saw the image without the artist's caption and competed to come up with the best tag line. The artist's caption, printed with the contest winners', interpreted the image as referencing consumption rather than expulsion: "How much weight does Coach want you to put on for football?" Several contest winners interpreted the cartoon as picturing expulsion: "Biff attempts the world's first atomic burp"; "After hearing what goes into processed food, Hank coughed up every single burger, hot dog, and slice of pizza he had ever eaten." One winning caption reads the image as representing both consumption and expulsion: "Suddenly, Warren was forced to admit he had an eating disorder." The humor of this caption would be impossible were it not for the assumption that boys consume excessively, but that such consumption is not pathological. If boys really binged and purged, it would be un-Christian to laugh at Warren. This cartoon is symptomatic of how *Breakaway* approaches boys and food. While food articles in *Brio* focus on baking cookies for others or making low-fat milkshakes, in *Breakaway* one finds articles with titles like "More Thanksgiving Maggot, Anyone?"[53] The gendered attitudes toward food expressed by these two magazines could not be more opposite.

Of course, if one were to compare secular magazines like *Vogue* and *Maxim*, one would also find men and women treated as opposites with different sexual and culinary appetites. So while *Brio* and *Breakaway* are unique in promoting chastity, their approaches to food are hardly earth-shattering. What is interesting, then, is that by virtue of their religious focus these magazines seem to be far removed from the secular world, but that they nonetheless strongly mirror aspects of that world. Notwithstanding this fact, evangelical media maintain that eating disorders are problems that are induced by the *secular* world and that can be cured by spiritual means. Because of society's pressure on women to

ARTIST'S CAPTION:
"How much weight does coach want you to put on for football?"

step out as a radical witness for Jesus. We'll print your suggestions in an upcoming issue.

GLASBERGEN

Toon Caption Winners

FIG. 29 BREAKAWAY CARTOON ILLUSTRATING BOYS' EXCESSIVE APPETITES.

have a certain kind of body, girls lack self-esteem; an improved relationship with Jesus is the key to solving this problem. By studying the Bible, eating disordered girls will come to see their bodies as "temples of the Holy Spirit." Thus, according to evangelical books, magazines, and videos, the cure for eating disorders is religious, but the causes are not. Evangelical youth media rarely portray girls' eating disorders as stemming from family pressures, an authoritarian home life, or the tremendous pressures that being a "good Christian" can entail.

Focus on the Family offers therapeutic media addressing virtually every difficulty of daily life, so it's not surprising that they've produced a cassette on eating disorders. On this tape, former bulimic Jackie Barrille offers some insight into evangelical perceptions of eating disorders and the female body. Barrille argues that eating disorders are primarily a matter of taking control of one's life. She says, "In eating huge amounts of food I felt a release, a freedom I had never felt in my life," and she explains that by surrendering control to the Holy Spirit, you won't need to binge and purge to seek control over your body.[54] (Interestingly, the same rhetoric can be used to describe both dieting and controlling compulsive dieting. A testimonial printed on an evangelical weight loss manual reads, "Thanks to First Place, I'm controlling my weight with a power greater than my own.") Barrille does not address how devout evangelicals who already have a personal relationship with God nonetheless develop eating disorders. Might resistance (conscious or unconscious) to giving all control to the Lord be one of many factors contributing to developing eating disorders in the first place? Or might the imperative to surrender oneself spiritually actually contribute to a woman's desire to have total control over her earthly body?

Eating disorders are a way to assert control when faced with difficult and disempowering personal and familial situations. The surrendering of control to parents that is mandated by disciplinary child rearing, the typical evangelical parenting style, may thus play a pivotal role in the development of teen anorexia and bulimia. As we saw in discussing Dobson's theories in chapter 1, disciplinary child rearing demands the child submit both will and body to parents. For example, anorexic Cherry Boone O'Neill, daughter of Christian singer Pat Boone, recounts how her authoritarian parents made her feel bodily shame when they forced her to wear children's clothing at age twelve, even though she had the sexually mature body of a sixteen year old. At eighteen, when she resisted their directive not to vomit, they said she was acting like a child and spanked her. The drive to make her submit to parental control, a crucial principle of authoritarian child rearing, backfired when her resistance was bound up in the development of eating disorders. O'Neill asserted herself, but only at the expense of herself.

O'Neill begins her autobiography, *Starving for Attention,* by explaining how religious rituals helped her maintain her anorexic regime:

Fasting on Thanksgiving Day had really saved me . . . when I was asked why I had not loaded up my plate like everyone else I just answered with spiritual overtones, "I'm fasting today," and that was that! . . . my mother called from the kitchen . . . "Daddy wants to have Communion together before we say the blessing, okay?" . . . my mind was computing feverishly: crackers are about twelve calories and I'll probably eat about one twelfth, so that's one calorie, and . . . how many calories does a six-ounce glass of grape juice have? . . . Too many. I'll just pretend to drink the grape juice . . . maybe I can pretend to eat the cracker, too![55]

Religion is uncannily woven throughout this family melodrama, as "fasting" sanctifies self-starvation, and Christ's blood and body become an impediment to weight loss. Boone's eating disorders continued long after she married and left home. Patriarchal evangelical doctrine, she explains, demanded that she submit to her husband in the same way she had submitted to her father, and she continued to resist such submission. Only by finding a more liberal way to live out her faith could Boone finally cure herself.

It would be foolish to valorize evangelical anorexics' resistance as a feminist tactic or to hold up Boone as emblematic of all evangelicals with eating disorders, but her story does help us to begin to think through what eating disorders might mean for women and girls of strong faith. Across disciplines (medicine, psychology, feminist sociology), researchers tend to assume that eating disorders are nonreligious. One exception is Michelle M. Lelwica, who argues that the distinction between "secular" and "religious" behavior fades when one examines how "for many girls and women, creating a slender body has become a matter of all-pervading significance, an end whose achievement feels tantamount to ultimate salvation."[56] In other words, dieting itself has much in common with religion. Lelwica even suggests that "women's subordination within traditional religion makes them prime candidates for this 'secular' substitute [dieting]."[57] I would argue, however, that dieting might function not so much as a *substitute* for religion but as something that could meld with a girl's previously existing religious belief system.

Some researchers have argued, erroneously, that anorexia can be traced back to the fasting practices of medieval nuns and other religious women. The assumption is that eating disorders have always existed but that now they have been drained of their religious impetus and are a result of consumer culture's images of slender female bodies. Historian Joan Jacobs Brumberg has quite rightly argued that tracing eating disorders back to the tradition of medieval fasting women is highly problematic:

> To describe premodern women . . . as anorexic is to flatten differences in female experience across time and discredit the special quality of eucharistic fervor and penitential asceticism as it was lived and perceived. To insist that medieval holy women had anorexia nervosa is, ultimately, a reductionist argument because it converts a complex human behavior into a simple biomedical mechanism. (It certainly does not respect important differences in the route to anorexia.) To conflate the two is to ignore the cultural context and the distinction between sainthood and patienthood.[58]

Calling medieval saints anorexic certainly erases the complexity of their faithful practices.[59] But Brumberg's argument against reading modern anorexia in light of the history of fasting seems to assume that the contemporary faster lacks spirituality. As she further argues: "From the vantage point of the historian, anorexia nervosa appears to be a *secular* addiction to a new kind of perfectionism, one that links personal salvation to the achievement of an external body configuration rather than an internal spiritual state."[60]

There may be no transhistorical link between Catholic medieval fasters and contemporary evangelical Protestants like Cherry Boone O'Neill, but this does not mean that twentieth-century eating disorders must be, by their very nature, "secular addictions." O'Neill is surely not the only evangelical for whom eating disorders have a spiritual dimension. Some evangelical anorexics may even see ridding themselves of the flesh as an act of spiritual purification. For example, Barille recounts how when one evangelical anorexic came close to dying her soul left her body and felt weightless as it headed toward the proverbial white light, but Jesus told her that it was not yet her time, and she returned to her body. In contrast to her freed spirit, her anorexic body seemed unbearably heavy. For her, the desire to lose her body was intricately bound up in the desire to be more spiritual: less body meant more spirit.

Of course, loss of flesh not only means less body, but also a transcendence of sexuality through the reduction or elimination of breasts, of menstruation, and of the wider hips that puberty brings to teens. For both secular and religious women, eating disorders are intricately bound up in feelings about sexuality. By not eating, a girl erases many of the bodily changes wrought by puberty, and for the evangelical girl under tremendous pressure to remain bodily and spiritually pure, the desire to erase sexuality may be particularly strong. The desire to drive out sin, to find "an antidote for hormone poisoning," may well be a motivating factor for some teen anorexics. After all, the strictures of eating disorders bear a strange resemblance to those of chastity: maintain bodily control, subdue carnal drives, attempt to displace desire for food/sex onto other activities. Teen consumers of therapeutic prochastity books, magazines, and videos may find in eating disorders their own cure for their sexuality.

WALKING THE STRAIGHT AND NARROW

Evangelical youth media are designed to straighten teens on already narrow paths, directing them toward God and away from sexual activity, liberalism, New Age religion, prochoice sentiments, and other dangerous territory. But these media are about much more than "indoctrination." Evangelical culture offers community and a sense of belonging, and evangelical media bolster the potency of that community.

It is easy for nonevangelicals to imagine that Christian teens are oppressed by their faith, but we must be careful not to conceptualize teen religious choices in the same way that much of evangelical media conceptualize teen sexuality. That is, we should not see teenagers as passive victims of religion, just as so many Christian magazines and videos portray them as victims of their own sexually maturing bodies. Many teens find that their faith helps them get through their difficult adolescent years, while others—gay and lesbian kids in particular—find evangelical beliefs to be quite oppressive. What is crucial to remember is that evangelical teens are capable of making informed decisions. Some of these teens decide to follow in their parents' religious footsteps, while others may leave the church. Nancy Tatom Ammerman observes that "although few people who grow up as sectarians drop out of religion entirely, at least forty percent switch to other denominations by adulthood."[61] In her year-long participant observation study of an evangelical church, Ammerman found that many youth "drop out of church when they are old enough to say 'no' to their parents . . . Rather than leaving religion entirely, many 'convert' to other denominations and become among the most committed leaders of the same liberal churches they grew up disparaging."[62]

Gay and lesbian teens are those who are perhaps most likely to leave conservative evangelical Christianity. While evangelical media promise heterosexual teenagers that one day they will marry and have great sex, gays and lesbians do not have the option of delayed gratification. Rather, they are told that homosexuality is denounced by the Bible. Interestingly, however, in recent years Christian youth have shifted their approach to condemning homosexuality. If therapeutic discourse infuses chastity media in general, it is particularly central to media specifically addressing homosexuality, where being gay is increasingly understood not as a venal sin but as a kind of addiction. Thus, being gay is no worse than being an alcoholic. While hardly liberating, this is nonetheless a conceptual shift that allows gays and lesbians a place to exist as gays and lesbians (at an ontological level, if not at the level of lived sexual practice) in evangelical culture.

This shift in thinking is slowly spreading throughout evangelical culture, but why is it already so clearly in place in youth culture? I would argue that evangelical youth are more attuned to the wider culture's discourses of therapy, addiction, and healing than the generation before them. Further, as sociologist Richard W. Flory argues, evangelical GenXers are strongly committed to "inclusiveness."[63] Thus, magazines and youth group videos contend that as long as you are "struggling" with homosexuality, not accepting your sexual identity, there is a place for you in Christian youth culture. Here it is strikingly clear how the broader secular culture, in which ideas about homosexuality have shifted significantly over the past thirty years, has inflected evangelical culture. While evangelical gay and lesbian teens continue to see homosexuality as morally wrong, their approach is liberal compared with the uncompromising, punitive stance of the previous generation. In chapter 4, I will turn to the gay and lesbian "rejects" of this older generation.

HOLINESS CODES AND HOLY HOMOSEXUALS:

INTERPRETING GAY AND LESBIAN

CHRISTIAN SUBCULTURE

As gay and lesbian Christians, we are kind of in this catch-22 situation in terms of the way the religious Right responds to us but also the ways in which non-Christian folks from our own community respond to us.[1]
—Rev. Dr. Mona West, director of spiritual development, The Cathedral of Hope

In 1998, the popular Christian band Audio Adrenaline released a discussion video for use in youth groups. The tape addresses issues of interest to evangelical youth such as racism, profanity, chastity, body piercing, and homosexuality. The segment on homosexuality aptly illustrates the generational differences discussed at the end of the last chapter. While teens rap in an open-ended way about the "sin" of homosexuality, an older youth pastor repeatedly lays down the law. One teen talks about his friend who, he explains, is a celibate gay who is nonetheless totally saved. The youth pastor asks scornfully if the friend thinks he can be a "gay Christian." Even though conservative evangelical kids agree with adults that the Bible condemns homosexuality, unlike older believers they are likely to look for ways to embrace their "different" peers. After all, evangelical teens are all struggling with things like abstinence, masturbation, pornography, drugs, and alcohol; in this context, homosexuality is perceived by many straight teens (at least in Christian videos) as just one more problem to add to that list. "Gay Christian" does not seem any more unfathomable to them than "alcoholic Christian." They seem to be more sympathetic to gays and lesbians than their parents and grandparents, even if they still maintain that homosexuality is sinful.

Twenty years ago, a "gay Christian" was virtually unheard of in evangelical circles. If you were gay, you were expelled from church. This still happens today in many congregations. Increasingly, however, conservative evangelicals are trying to "cure" gays through counseling and ex-gay ministries such as Exodus.[2] Evangelicals who give up on curing themselves may leave religion altogether, or they may end up at a progay church where they can maintain many of their evangelical beliefs while also learning new, positive ways to interpret the Bible's stance on homosexuality. This chapter will focus on what one might call an ex-ex-gay ministry, the Cathedral of Hope, a Texas church that has become home to many who have tried to cure themselves of gayness or who have simply been thrown out of their churches for being gay. While the previous chapter examined issues of Christian sexuality through close analysis of media, this chapter investigates Christian sexuality by focusing on firsthand accounts of those who have rejected the kinds of sexual prescriptions described in chapter 3. This case study will also complicate what "evangelical" means by turning from conservative evangelicals to look at Bible-believing Christians who are more difficult to peg politically. To the right of the queer Left, to the left of the Christian Right, and generally uncomfortable with the "liberal" label, members of the Cathedral of Hope do not fit into any simple taxonomies.

The queer Left and the Christian Right often appear diametrically opposed to one another. Queer activists and theorists tend to preach against assimilation, against the normative. Normality is a lure to get queers back into the closet. For such believers, the rights-based discourse of liberal (politically "moderate") gays, while sometimes strategically necessary, nonetheless constitutes a procrustean bed because of the way it codifies "homosexual" and "heterosexual" as stable legal categories.[3] A place at the table? Throw out the table! Conservative Christian Pat Robertson, conversely, believes in an absolute standard of "normality." He preaches for the family, for conservative values, for heterosexual monogamy, for the "right" of heterosexuals to deny gays and lesbians the "special rights" (civil rights) they demand. Yet in spite of all their differences, queer leftists and right-wing fundamentalists in the United States do seem to share at least one belief: gayness and Christianity do not go together. For fundamentalists, gay Christians are sinners, "an abomination before the Lord." For many secular queers, gay and lesbian Christians (evangelical or otherwise) are perceived as hopelessly conservative and accommodationist.

The existence of the Cathedral of Hope, the world's largest gay and lesbian church, demonstrates empirically that "gay Christian" is not oxymoronic. Moreover, the Cathedral offers a compelling case study in how a community finds cohesion in its common readings of the Bible, in its common reliance on the self-narration of the coming-out story, and in its common opposition to the Christian Right. As the Cathedral is situated in Dallas, Texas, "the buckle of the Bible Belt," and its congregation is composed largely of former conservative evangelical Protestants (or, in the preferred language of Cathedral congregants, "fundamentalists"),[4] this church offers a unique opportunity to look at discursive strategies not only for fighting the Right but also, more precisely, for fighting the Right with its own favorite weapon: the Bible. In effect, fundamentalists and queer Christians are engaged in an interpretive battle over what the Bible "really" has to say about sexuality. The Cathedral is not a radical activist group, and it does not offer practical models for fighting the Christian Right's policy initiatives, but the Cathedral does offer an intricate picture of how the Bible can be interpreted to support political and spiritual beliefs at odds with the Right.

The Cathedral also offers an interesting case study in the use of grassroots media to spread religious messages. Via their weekly cable access broadcasts and their *Holy Homosexuals* infomercial, the Cathedral offers images that challenge the assumptions of both the secular left and the Christian Right. Conservative evangelicals have made exceptional use of print, radio, television, and video to spread their antigay and antilesbian messages. While a comparatively minor media player, the Cathedral has also found effective ways to use media to get their Biblically based prolesbian and progay message out. The form of that message, a traditional-looking TV sermon, can be disorienting for secular viewers. When non-Christian viewers see a TV preacher with a Southern accent, they are likely to assume the worst. When the preacher speaks of God's "inclusive love" for gays and lesbians, the scenario feels fishy. Does this preacher support a conservative "family-values" agenda? Does he advocate gay marriage as a means of "normalizing" gays? Even as the program defies expectations, many viewers will be wary to label it "progressive," but the incongruous image of the prolesbian and progay preacher cannot be read as simply left- or right-wing, either. To many on the queer Left, gay and lesbian Christians are conservative or even right-wing. To the Right, they are heretical left-wing activists. The Cathedral congregants I spoke with by and large described themselves as politically "moderate," a label that does not quite ring true, since the church challenges such political taxonomies.

Even as they are reluctant to identify as "left," Cathedral congregants do freely identify as being against the Christian "right," in large part because so many of the church's members have emerged from conservative evangelical backgrounds. The Cathedral's senior pastor, Rev. Michael S. Piazza, even opens his book *Holy Homosexuals* by citing Tim LaHaye's *The Unhappy Gays,* a classic of Christian gay-bashing. Cathedral congregants reject fundamentalist antigay arguments, but like fundamentalists they revere the Bible. Cathedral services balance

familiar evangelical elements with liturgical elements evocative of Roman Catholic or mainline Protestant services. In other words, the
Cathedral defines itself, in large part, as a response against conservative evangelicalism, but it also includes elements of that culture. Similarly, as we have seen, evangelicals reject much of secular popular
culture, even as they have created a counterculture of music, videos,
and books that in many ways mirrors the rejected culture. Neither subculture fully breaks off from the culture against which it defines itself.

THE PEOPLE AND THE PLACE

The Cathedral of Hope is located on the far edge of Oaklawn, a small
gay and lesbian neighborhood in Dallas. Its main street sports queer-
owned businesses, identified by pink triangle decals and rainbow flags.
The neighborhood is home to the Gay and Lesbian Community Center,
as well as J. R.'s and Sue Ellen's, gay and lesbian bars, respectively. In a
Bible Belt city where it is particularly difficult to be out of the closet,
this neighborhood symbolizes a fraught visibility. Some same-sex couples walk down the street holding hands, but others park on a side
street at night and move quickly into one of the bars, safe behind their
darkened windows.

A few miles down the road lies the Cathedral of Hope, a modest
white brick building. The exterior is not marked as gay or lesbian, except that cars in the parking lot sport rainbow bumper stickers, some in
the shape of the state of Texas. The construction of the Cathedral had
been fraught. Banks were reluctant to lend money to gays and lesbians
to purchase a building, and property owners were unwilling to sell,
one declaring he would burn his church to the ground before he saw
gays and lesbians worshipping there. The congregation finally decided
to buy land and build a church from scratch, raising the money from
bonds sold to its own members. When Rev. Piazza came to the Cathedral in 1987, the building, which held just under a thousand people,
seemed more than adequate, since there were only four hundred people in the congregation. By 1998, the congregation had grown by two
thousand, and by 2003 the Cathedral had 3,200 members[5].

As you enter, the sanctuary is to the left. On the right, glass doors
lead to a small memorial site with plaques dedicated to people who
have died of AIDS. The Cathedral has lost over 1,400 people to AIDS.
The pulpit and altar are large pink marble triangles. On either side of
the pulpit, there are large screens where the lyrics to hymns are projected, as well as special event videos (the *Ellen* coming-out episode, a
gay pride film festival). On either side of the screens stained glass windows picture pink triangles and linked symbols of male and male, fe-

male and female, and female and male. The window on the left says "Hope," and the window on the right says "Esperanza," Spanish for hope. As one congregant observed, this is symbolic of both the Cathedral's sincere attempt to speak to Dallas's Latino community and, as a largely white, middle- and upper-middle-class congregation, its ultimate separation from that community. Excluding the grammatically necessary article before "Esperanza," the very architecture of the building contains a syntactic error symbolic of the separation of this church from Dallas's largest, most impoverished minority community. The church has succeeded in reaching middle-class, "acculturated" members of that community, Piazza explains, further noting that about 20 percent of the Cathedral's mailing list is composed of people with Latino surnames. The percentage of African Americans in the congregation is very low.

The Cathedral is currently undertaking a massive fundraising campaign for a new building. In the first three and a half months, they raised $6 million in pledges toward their initial $20 million goal. Right now, "cathedral" is a symbolic idea; the current building is clearly a "church." The new building will be an eleven-story cathedral designed by the famous gay architect Philip Johnson. The building will look something like an iceberg, a mammoth concrete structure designed to announce to the world the permanence and strength of gays and lesbians (fig. 30). Lisa Carver, the church's director of communications, explains that

each of the walls leans, and there's no two lines that are alike, and that reflects diversity. You have all these very different lines and unusual walls that individually may appear weak, but all together they create real strength, that presence, that immense structure that's going to rise up. Once you build that eleven-story-tall structure, everybody will be able to see you. As an organization we think that that's a statement to the world that gay and lesbian Christians aren't going to hide anymore. We really hope that it becomes a symbol of pride, strength, confidence.[6]

I arrived in Dallas on a typically sweltering day in June. That night I attended a quiet service with candles, music, prayer, and no preaching, which reminded me a bit of Quaker services I had attended as a child. A group of four people approached me as I left, pegging me as a visitor. Despite the oppressive heat, we stood outside and talked about the Cathedral for almost an hour. The two men were gay, the two women, straight. One of the women, who had come to the cathedral when her husband came out, told me, "They accept me and love me even though I'm straight." There are some lesbians in the congregation, but these

FIG. 30 THE EX-FUNDAMENTAL-
ISTS OF THE CATHEDRAL OF HOPE
SAY THAT THEIR NEW BUILDING,
A MAMMOTH CONCRETE STRUC-
TURE, WILL ANNOUNCE TO THE
WORLD THE PERMANENCE AND
STRENGTH OF GAYS AND LES-
BIANS.

two women matched the profile that soon emerged; many women in the congregation are straight and started to attend the Cathedral when a family member came out. This presents problems for lesbians looking to meet other lesbians. At the services I attended, about 80 percent of the worshipers were men, although the staff is evenly split along gender lines. All services use "inclusive language," which means that God is never referred to as he or she.

Everyone I met praised the "unconditional love" that they felt at the Cathedral, their "church home." At the annual Sunday gay pride service, I rose when the pastor asked all the straights in the audience to stand, and I was greeted by thunderous applause from the room of over a thousand people. The warmth was sincere, and it was impossible not to be moved. Although it is fair to say that the people here are "evangelical" in their desire to spread the word about the church and that they give "testimony" about their experience (all of which reflects their emergence from conservative evangelical churches), I never felt put on the spot about my own religious beliefs here. The sense of urgency to convert others, so common among conservative evangelicals, was pleasantly lacking here.

REACHING POSTFUNDAMENTALISTS

Metropolitan Community Church (MCC), the Cathedral's denominational home, was founded by Rev. Troy Perry in California in 1968. MCC, the first denomination with a primarily gay and lesbian outreach, now has over three hundred congregations all over the world, and all of them are smaller than the Cathedral of Hope. Dallas is very religious compared with other large cities like New York City or Boston, and this might in part explain why a gay and lesbian church could flourish there. Social life is centered around church life, and it would be difficult for a religious person to survive without a "church home." Chances are, queer Dallas Christians who leave or are thrown out of their churches will eventually find a home as "postfundamentalists," as I call them, at the Cathedral. But these sociological factors alone cannot account for the Cathedral's phenomenal growth. After all, the MCC congregation in Birmingham, Alabama, also a Bible Belt nexus, hovers at about one hundred fifty. It seems that the Cathedral has grown, and will continue to grow, because of the way it balances key elements of evangelical culture and mainline Protestant culture, all the while managing to maintain a basically ecumenical image.

Cathedral services eschew fundamentalist fire-and-brimstone rhetoric, and many of the sermons resonate with the therapeutic, self-help discourse common in both mainline Protestant churches and many evangelical churches. Most MCC congregations, conversely, have roots closer to the fire-and-brimstone style. The only place MCC appears at all at the Cathedral is on the cover of the hymnals, which are largely ignored since song lyrics are projected on large screens. As Piazza explains, "MCC is almost an invisible reality around here. Part of the reason is that this church is *very different* than most MCC churches. The denomination is very evangelical, conservative, sometimes even fundamentalist in certain places." Raised Pentecostalist, Rev. Perry takes a more conservative, less ecumenical approach to worship than Piazza. The denomination's affirmation of inclusive language, its inclusion of women clergy, and of course, its outreach to gays and lesbians are clearly elements that put it light-years ahead of many mainline Protestant churches. Yet, while disagreeing with the religious Right's interpretation of the Bible, Perry remains a Pentecostalist at heart, a person who has visions, feels the presence of angels, fasts in the desert, and occasionally speaks in tongues. Perry describes a desert pilgrimage taken when he was concerned MCC might stray too far from Biblical doctrine: "There were no great visions, but within my being I reaffirmed my knowledge that I had to keep our Fellowship firmly rooted in doctrine. Some of our pastors had sought to become more Unitarian and less evangelical, but our Lord let me realize in the majesty of God's living desert that so long as our church continued to follow Jesus, all would be well."[7] In his evangelical fervor, Perry is typical of MCC pastors. Rev. Piazza, then, is atypical in his projection of a more broadly ecumenical image. As mainline Protestant churches are shrinking and dying across the United States, the Cathedral of Hope's growth is anomalous, yet it makes sense, given the flip side of the equation, the growth of evangelical churches. The Cathedral draws from a pool of people discarded by conservative evangelical churches, and it keeps this pool by balancing mainline Protestantism and evangelical elements.

Piazza has a deep respect for Perry's achievements, yet it is clear that the Cathedral's success stems in part from its tactical distancing from its own denomination. As Piazza explains,

Because Perry's background is Pentecostal, he has created a Pentecostal, evangelical fervor in this denomination. He never graduated from high school, which makes it even more remarkable that he's created this whole movement. But what it's also done is create a movement that doesn't particularly value education. It's only in the last four years that we've even required clergy to be college graduates . . . In some places, Austin, for example, anybody in Austin would be a fool not to go to the MCC. It's a fabulous church. San Francisco, Washington, those are great places. But there are other *big* places that are different . . . I wouldn't go to MCC in Chicago. There are six of them there, and all six of them have thirty, forty, fifty people at the most, in a city of nine million people. But there are some *great* liberal churches there where lesbian and gay folks would be welcomed.[8]

As this passage indicates, one aspect of the Cathedral that distances it from MCC is that it "values education," a euphemistic indicator of the Cathedral's middle-class population. Many of the smaller MCCs are more working class in their orientation. One Cathedral congregant says she knows a "well-to-do" couple who would never go to their local MCC because it is in a "really poor part of town" and attended by "very OUT people, hairdressers, who can carry off their existence in a very open way." While this is perhaps not a conscious tactic on the Cathedral's part, it is clear that the toning down of evangelical elements in the service may appeal, in part, because it marks a stylistic distance from a stereotypical "white trash" kind of fire-and-brimstone service. There is no speaking in tongues or snake-handling at the Cathedral of Hope. Piazza may have evangelical roots, but he is not Pentecostal.

Under Piazza's leadership, the Cathedral has undergone a political sea change. The pastor explains:

When I first came here this was a *very* conservative congregation. The first time I talked about Jimmy Carter, there were people in the congregation who booed and hissed. They were *rabid* Republicans who had recently voted for Ronald Reagan . . . Last year we gave away about $350,000 to the poor. The clinic that we opened for the homeless, the kids we tutor, the school uniforms we paid for, those are all things that would have *never* happened in this community a few years ago. But there's been a huge shift in values, and I think it's mostly been that I tried to teach them that that's what it means to be a Christian. By this all will know that we are Jesus's disciples, that we should love one another, and that this is what love looks like.[9]

Piazza's dream is that Jimmy Carter will speak at the dedication of the new building. As additional evidence of the Cathedral's shifting politics (and its stupendous growth), Piazza explains that years ago the board refused to recycle; in March of 1998 the church recycled 32 *tons* of paper. Supporting recycling, giving money to the poor, and liking Jimmy Carter may not sound particularly radical, but in an intensely conservative community within the Bible Belt, these constitute "liberal" values. The church's charity for school children is of particular symbolic importance in the context of a homophobic Southern culture that continues to see "homosexual" and "child molester" as synonymous.[10] In the conservative deep South, that an impoverished school would accept clothing from gays and lesbians is a sign of respect, a sign that the church has, as director of spiritual development Rev. Dr. Mona West explains, "proven itself to be a good citizen of this community."[11]

Piazza estimates that 70–80 percent of his congregation comes from conservative, evangelical Protestant ("fundamentalist") backgrounds, and my conversations with the congregation supported this statistic. When I told one man I was researching the Christian Right, he said, "Oh, I was part of that until a few months ago," when he came out and was immediately denied access to his church and his children. This man was splitting his churchgoing between the Cathedral and a much smaller (and more working-class) MCC church in Fort Worth. He likes the Cathedral, saying that "I thought it would just be a bunch of self-hating queers trying to justify their lifestyles, but actually there is theological depth here and belief in the Bible." This is a good example of the challenge the church faces in helping people deal with deep-seated homophobia fostered by years of evangelical attacks. But it also shows how the church succeeds; like conservative evangelicals, the congregants of the Cathedral take the Bible very seriously.

Nonfundamentalist scholars understand the Bible as a text written and edited by different authors with different religious and political motivations.[12] This approach to the Bible holds little interest for literalists, who prefer to see the Bible as the directly inspired word of God. At the Cathedral, the Bible is understood as a both a spiritual guide and an historical and cultural artifact. Rev. West, for example, has a Ph.D. in Old Testament studies and incorporates her scholarly perspective on the Bible into services. Piazza explains that respect for the Bible is crucial for reaching congregants from traditional evangelical backgrounds. When

Bishop Jack Spong, a radical critic of contemporary Christianity, gave a visiting sermon at the Cathedral he tore pages from the Bible and said, according to Piazza, "Just don't pay any attention to that!" Piazza says,

That's not how I deal with Leviticus [which contains the "Holiness Code," which includes the statement that for two men to lie together is an abomination before the Lord]. This is how I deal with Leviticus: I have to honor it and say that, while one point—not working on the Sabbath, for example—isn't really a law we keep today, the truth that's behind it is valuable. And as far as Sodom and Gomorra goes, we've worked very hard in this church not to throw that story away, because it speaks to some very important issues for us, issues about hospitality, God's disdain for abuse and violence, and all that kind of stuff. It's really not about sexuality. Even the first chapter of Romans, you know, I wouldn't throw that away at all, because read in its whole context it's about something that is of value to *us*. It's against idolatry and says that *all* of us need God's grace. If you read the whole first three chapters, *all of it*, you understand that . . . And so we're not willing to just say, "Well, Paul just didn't know what he was talking about." And Spong was willing to do that.[13]

Piazza consciously works *not* to avoid what he calls the "clobber passages" of the Bible, those passages that fundamentalists use most often to attack gays and lesbians. Instead, he argues that fundamentalists have incorrectly interpreted those passages, and he offers alternative interpretations. While some postfundamentalists reject the Bible, and religion in general, Cathedral congregants seek new readings of the Bible. Biblical reverence is a crucial part of their identity that they cannot throw away, even when they come out and the church that taught them to honor the Bible throws *them* away.

The Christian postfundamentalist must find new decoding strategies to decipher the Bible. A code is both a system of signals for communication and a systematic statement of a body of law. Those who identify as "Bible-believers" decipher the Bible with reverence, evoking these two different meanings of code.[14] For such readers, fundamentalist or postfundamentalist, the Bible functions as a statement of a body of law, an inspirational guidebook for life. However, the postfundamentalist must find new ways to decode this body of law. The very meaning of the law must be reinterpreted, and this must happen not just at an intellectual level but also at a spiritual level. The new understanding is not simply known but also felt, *believed*.

In addition to respecting the Bible and reinterpreting the clobber passages, Piazza appeals to his postfundamentalist congregation through the use of personal testimony. Both his *Holy Homosexuals* book and the Cathedral's infomercial include autobiographical stories because while liberal Christianity doesn't particularly value that sort of evangelical witness, the witness of the spirit is really important to evangelicals. And I used sermon material in the book and in the infomercial because that stuff is authoritative for people from evangelical backgrounds, and they can *hear* it.[15]

The testimonials are personal stories of the transformation that comes through embracing one's sexuality, with the help of the Cathedral. As we have already seen, witnessing—giving testimony of being "born again" and accepting the Lord as a "personal savior"—is crucial to evangelicals. Although evangelicals emphasize the importance of having a "personal" (and, implicitly, unique) relationship with God, their witnessing narratives are remarkably formulaic in how they describe the sin and despair that precedes salvation, salvation itself (being born again), and postsalvation peace and joy. The result is an evangelical "autobiography-in-common that comes to constitute a collective identity."[16] Witnessing is a deeply meaningful speech act, not simply a pragmatic conversion tool. The act of witnessing creates and defines the self, both on its own terms and in relationship to the community.

At the Cathedral, the most common mode of self-narration is not the born-again story but the coming-out story. Not surprisingly, among those for whom witnessing is a salient aspect of identity, the coming-out story (often climaxing at the Cathedral) replaces the story of being born again. The before-and-after formula of the salvation narrative is parallel to the coming-out story: one feels lost and alone, discovers/admits the truth, and having claimed this new identity, can now become part of a community of like-minded people, all of whom have similar stories to tell and retell to affirm the common bond of the community. This self-narration is one factor that enables the transition from a conservative evangelical identification to a gay Christian identification. Self-narration as a crucial aspect of identity need not disappear, because one can change the contents of the story that is told while retaining the before-and-after structure. In evangelical circles, the born-again story is told not only to the community but also to those outside the community, as an evangelical tool. Here's where the coming-out story differs: Cathedral worshippers do not conceive of listeners as potential converts whose very souls hang in the balance. However, their stories do stress the importance of the Cathedral as a source of "unconditional love," and there is a sense in which these stories function to convert the listener into a believer in the Cathedral's organizing doctrine—that God's love is all-inclusive.

Cathedral services themselves have qualities that will resonate for those from an evangelical background. Piazza explains:

We try to keep the energy of the evangelical service, the emphasis on preaching. I preach twenty-two minutes every service. I don't do a *homily,* I do a *sermon.* It's a Biblical sermon, and I often walk with a Bible in my hand. There's enough of those elements to make evangelical folks feel at home.[17]

On the other hand, the appeal to postfundamentalists can go too far, as in the discontinued Sunday night service, which was more traditionally evangelical. Piazza explains that this service

just never really worked, because there was a sense in which those old songs, and that old sort of stuff, kind of caused tapes to play in people, evoked what they were trying to get away from. It really pushed those old buttons that brought up all that shame and guilt and all those traumatic experiences that they had in church as young people trying to escape their sexuality. The regular Sunday morning service is a safer way to approach people from evangelical backgrounds. It sounds familiar enough, and yet different enough to feel safe.[18]

In addition, the Sunday morning service looks different than a traditional evangelical service in that it is more liturgical. Piazza wears robes, enters in a processional, and ceremoniously offers communion. This is quite different from evangelical services where, as Randall Balmer has observed, a certain amount of "aesthetic deprivation" is expected,[19] and where typically there is no procession, no interest in rituals linked to church history and creeds, and an aversion to a sacramental approach to worship. Referring to the centrality of the pastor in the evangelical tradition, Balmer further notes that "evangelicism in America, lacking the confessional emphasis and liturgical rubrics that bind other religious groups, has been susceptible to the cult of personality."[20] The Cathedral's liturgical emphasis, conversely, helps deflect attention away from Piazza and marks the services as different from those old services, where, as Piazza explains, gays and lesbians always felt the "danger that a service could turn against them. Because, you know, you went to church never knowing when you might just get it!"[21]

QUEER THEOLOGY

Like conservative evangelicals, Cathedral of Hope Christians look for ways to apply Biblical lessons to daily life. They expect the Bible to be included in services, and they reject the more liberal Spong approach, whereby one might simply ignore seemingly antigay parts of the Bible. As so many congregants were raised in conservative churches, this should not be surprising. Yet it may surprise some people outside of gay and lesbian Christian culture, who would assume (often correctly) that evangelical gays and lesbians are so fiercely rejected by their churches that they often turn from religion altogether. As one non-Dallas MCC member explains,

There is a stereotype of a gay Christian as a person who was brought up in a religious home, who as an adult discovered themselves to be gay, suffered great guilt because they thought themselves to be sinful and who spends their life on the fringes of Church life being rebutted by the Church until they give up and become a militant humanist.[22]

It is difficult for an outsider attuned to this stereotype to understand how a gay or lesbian person could possibly remain in an evangelical Christian church. Many gay Christians, however, may find that they can remain Christian not *in spite* of their fundamentalist background but rather *because* of the parallels between fundamentalist culture and Cathedral culture. Notwithstanding obvious differences—the Cathedral's ecumenicism and what we might loosely label "moderate" politics—fundamentalist and postfundamentalist gay culture share some crucial common ground. We have already seen the parallel between fundamentalist and gay postfundamentalist modes of self-narration via the witnessing and the coming-out story. There is another parallel between how the two communities undertake Biblical interpretation. Although fundamentalists and gay postfundamentalist Christians find very different meanings in the Bible, they both take the act of Biblical interpretation as crucial to faith.

While the Christian Right uses the Bible to attack gays and lesbians, gays and lesbians use the Bible as ammunition for their rebuttals and, in a more proactive mode, as a text offering inspirational models for self-definition. An overview of some of the key Biblical texts for gay and lesbian Christians illustrates how such Christians use the Bible to argue against the Christian Right. As many Cathedral congregants grew up hearing the "clobber passages" of the Bible, it is important once they come out and move away from their original churches that they learn different ways to interpret these passages. For example, Cathedral congregants understand Sodom as a story of punishment for inhospitality and violence. In this Biblical tale, God sends messengers (or angels) to Lot to warn him that Sodom will be destroyed for its wickedness. The people of Sodom demand that Lot hand over the messengers so that they might "know" them. Piazza argues that

in that day, homosexual rape was often a way conquerors degraded and devalued a vanquished foe. There is no basis for comparing the proposed abuse of the strangers with loving acts between consenting adults. To condemn homosexuality on the basis of this story would be as irrational as condemning heterosexuality on the basis of the rape of Tamar (II Samuel 13:1–33).[23]

Furthermore, Piazza notes that Lot offers up his daughter to be raped by the crowd in the messengers' stead, so this is hardly an ideal story to turn to for guidelines on contemporary sexual practices. Pointing out this problematic aspect of the story enables gays and lesbians to use the Bible to fight fundamentalists. John Wimberly of the Dallas Gay and Lesbian Alliance, the city's main queer activist group, often quotes from this story when he encounters Christian antigay sentiment in the sensitivity workshops he leads with the Dallas police force:

I love Sodom and Gomorra. How can you interpret this as a Biblical attack on contemporary gays? The whole town is gay? And the father says, "Here, take my daughters!" One, why would he be giving up his daughters? That's kind of shitty. But two, it's a gay crowd! What are they going to do with them?! None of this makes sense![24]

To Piazza, the story makes sense as a tale of God's disapproval of inhospitality, and like Wimberly, he does not reject the story as a useless part of the Bible. Instead, Piazza explains that the story does not teach anything that condemns modern homosexuality.

Romans, Corinthians, and Leviticus contain the other key passages often cited by religious conservatives. Again, rather than rejecting these passages, lesbian and gay Christians argue that fundamentalists do not interpret the passages properly. Leviticus contains the infamous "Holiness Code," which contains a list of prohibitions that fundamentalists draw from selectively. In his marriage manual, the religious Right's Tim LaHaye explains that certain Levitical injunctions are now obsolete because of scientific advances and changes in sanitation. For example, he reasons that having sex with your wife during menstruation is no longer a hygiene hazard. Piazza notes the hypocrisy in LaHaye's selective interpretation:

The irony is that LaHaye draws heavily on the Levitical passages to explain his condemnation of homosexuality. He quotes a verse commanding the death penalty for a man lying with another man and follows that verse with these words: "This may seem cruel and inhuman treatment by today's standards, but our leniency has caused today's widespread problems."[25]

Piazza notes that

more thoughtful people dismiss these passages in Leviticus as irrelevant, since we do not follow the remainder of that book's instructions. We eat pork and shellfish, wear clothes made from two kinds of fabric, allow women to wear red, and plant two kinds of seeds in the same field. The Holiness Code prohibited all these things.[26]

Piazza also argues that the same-sex sex acts referenced in Leviticus probably referred to temple prostitution practiced by pagans. "Judaism was one of the few faiths that did not utilize temple prostitutes. For the Hebrews, male homosexual acts became associated with the idolatry of worshipping the gods of the surrounding people."[27] Gay and lesbian Biblical scholars tend to agree with this interpretation, and extend it to Romans, arguing that in condemning "unnatural acts" Paul is probably attacking those who worshipped pagan gods through temple prostitution. As Piazza explains, "Paul didn't let anybody off the hook! . . . fornicators, idolaters, adulterers, male prostitutes, sodomites, thieves, greedy people, drunkards, revelers, robbers—none of these will inherit the kingdom of God (I Corinthians 6:9–10)."[28] In sum, Piazza feels we can learn about the ungodliness of idolatry from Paul's lessons. On the other hand, Paul also taught a number of things that Piazza has no trouble rejecting. Paul encouraged slaves to obey their masters, taught that women should be submissive and obedient to men, and taught that women should not teach men. So, while not rejecting the "clobber passages," Piazza does criticize other passages that he thinks modern Christians should view skeptically.

While arguing that the authors of the Bible had no understanding of the modern conception of homosexuality, queer Christians do find parts of the Bible that offer particular inspiration to contemporary gays and lesbians. One of the earliest books of gay and lesbian theology, *Jonathan Loved David,* argues for the importance of the intimate same-sex relationship between Jonathan and David.[29] This relationship was not gay in the contemporary sense, but according to queer theologians it is a striking example of same-sex passionate feeling, and one that gay Christians should find inspiring. When Jonathan heard the story of the defeat of Goliath, he fell in love with David:

the soul of Jonathan was bound to the soul of David, and Jonathan loved him as his own soul . . . Jonathan made a covenant with David, because he loved him as his own soul. Jonathan stripped himself of the robe that he was wearing, and gave it to David, along with his armor, and even his sword and his bow and his belt (1 Sam. 18:1–4 NRSV).

When they were forced to separate, David "fell on his face to the ground, and bowed himself three times: and they kissed one another, and wept one with another" (1 Sam. 20:41 NRSV).[30] When Jonathan died, David said, "How I wept for you, my brother Jonathan; How much I loved you! And your love for me was deeper than the love of women" (2 Sam. 1:26 NRSV).

A similarly intense same-sex relationship exists in the Old Testament story of Ruth and Naomi, the topic of Rev. Dr. Mona West's dissertation. Ruth (the great-grandmother of King David) and Naomi were childless widows from Moab; Naomi was Ruth's mother-in-law. Naomi urges Ruth to leave her to find a new husband in Moab, but Ruth exclaims,

Do not press me to leave you or to turn back from following you! Where you go, I will go. Where you lodge, I will lodge; your people shall be my people, and your God my God. Where you die, I will die—there I will be buried. May the Lord do thus and so to me, and more as well, if even death parts me from you! (Ruth 1:16 NRSV)

West notes the irony of the fact that Ruth's declaration of commitment to Naomi is a traditional text of heterosexual wedding ceremonies. She argues that Ruth's "words and actions present the closest physical relationship between two women expressed anywhere in the Bible."[31] West further notes that

the Hebrew word that describes Ruth's "clinging" to Naomi is the same word used in Genesis 2:24 to describe the relationship of the man to the woman in marriage. He leaves his father and mother and *clings* to her, and the two become one flesh.[32]

While some queer Biblical scholars have laid claim to Ruth and Naomi as a lesbian couple, others remain more circumspect, taking caution not to apply an anachronistic conception of lesbianism to an ancient Bible story. All seem to agree, however, that the relationship between Ruth and Naomi offers a powerful Scriptural example of same-sex intimacy. This is an empowering thought for Christians who have been taught, via the clobber passages, that the Bible excludes them because of their "sinful" sexuality.

The very idea of "same-sex intimacy," though, is a contemporary one, and these progay and lesbian readings of the Bible can hardly be located as "intentional" in the minds of the ancient authors of the Bible. Noting a parallel between their own interpretive strategies and those of feminist historians and Biblical scholars, queer Christians argue that their stories were omitted from the Scriptures because ancient same-sex relations were invisible or irrelevant to the Bible's authors and to its later editors. A certain amount of "reading between the lines" is thus justified in order to claim a history that many antigays claim does not even exist. Conservative evangelicals attack these readings as crazy interpretations, yet they are no more convoluted than any number of evangelical readings. According to prophecy theology, for example, the Bible predicts the Rapture, the coming of the Antichrist, the tribulation, and the end of the world. As we will see in discussing prophecy media in chapter 6, queer Biblical readings are no more interpretive than such prophetic "literal" readings are.

The most controversial figure in queer theology is probably the eunuch, which some scholars hold up as the ancestor of gay, lesbian, bisexual, and transgendered people.[33] As nonprocreative men, eunuchs were socially stigmatized in the Bible. Deuteronomy states that "no one whose testicles are crushed or whose penis is cut off shall be admitted to the assembly of the Lord" (Deut. 23:1 NRSV), and Leviticus includes crushed testicles in its list of physical deformities that bar a man from priesthood (Lev. 21:16–23 NRSV). The New Testament contains the passage on eunuchs most often cited:

For there are eunuchs who have been so from birth, and there are eunuchs who have been made eunuchs by others, and there are eunuchs who have made themselves eunuchs for the sake of the kingdom of heaven. Let anyone accept this who can. (Matt. 19:12 NRSV)

This passage has been used by the Roman Catholic Church to justify the celibacy of priesthood, and some ancient Christians took the text literally and castrated themselves.[34] While many believe that Jesus was calling for celibacy in these passages, the queer theology interpretation is that he is speaking of nonprocreativity. Thus, a person born a eunuch is, in modern terms, gay, in that this sexual orientation is an incontrovertible fact, like eye color. (Queer theology generally speaks of sexual orientation as an innate biological fact.) A eunuch made by others would be a castrated man, and someone who makes himself a eunuch would be a nonprocreative celibate. Some queer theologians believe that in Biblical times "eunuch" referred not just to a castrated or celibate person but also to men who refused to marry.[35]

That Jesus implies that he himself is someone who made himself a eunuch for the sake of the kingdom of heaven is read by queer theologians as a defense of nonprocreativity. Victoria S. Kolakowski argues that Jesus

created a third category of the procreatively deviant, those made eunuchs for the sake of the kingdom, which he clearly implies includes himself . . . By making this statement, Jesus identifies himself boldly with the eunuch, whom his society considered sexually deviant, *Queer* . . . I believe that the word *eunuch*, applied to Jesus, was as derogatory and hateful as the word *Queer* is in modern times . . . But Jesus took that derogatory slang word thrown at him and proudly claimed it as part of his own identity. This is exactly what modern activists have done with the word *Queer* . . . We need to proudly acknowledge this and inform our fundamentalist Christian detractors that Jesus was "Queer" in his society's eyes and that he claimed us to be his family.[36]

Kolakowski is not claiming that Jesus was gay but, rather, queer, in the sense that he embraced "deviancy" by associating himself with eunuchs, a social outcast group that some scholars point to as the closest thing to a gay person that the Bible offers.

Like many queer theologians, Kolakowski cites Acts 8:26–40, where the first Gentile, an Ethiopian eunuch, is converted to Christianity by the disciple Philip. This well-known story is popular with evangelicals because it is a powerful conversion story. The story is also popular among African American Christians, since it shows a black man as a major early convert. Kolakowski argues that the story should also have special resonance for queer Christians because the convert is a eunuch. In fact, Kolakowski argues that gays, lesbians, and transsexuals may have been lumped together by ancient people under the term "eunuch." Herself a lesbian transsexual Christian, Kolakowski wants to argue that the Scriptures actually offer a radical message to contemporary queers. Pointing to the existence of hierarchies, prejudices, and divisions within Christian queer communities, she concludes that it is "particularly ironic that the most compelling Scriptural argument for gay and lesbian affirmation in the Christian Scriptures may come from teachings about the transgendered eunuchs, because transgendered people are second-class citizens in the Queer Christian community."[37]

MEDIA AND THE CATHEDRAL OF HOPE

In my exchanges with staff and congregants of the Cathedral of Hope, televangelism was often used as shorthand for fundamentalism or the Christian Right. The congregants held up the Cathedral as a counterexample, and one which more and more people would become aware of as the church's national visibility grows. Marty Ruggles was director of the Cathedral's prayer ministry from 1995 to 2000. The prayer ministry handles prayer requests via phone and e-mail, and sends out daily e-mail devotionals to over two thousand people. Ruggles is a heterosexual Catholic who says she would have become a nun if she hadn't disagreed with the church's policy on gays and lesbians. She explains that

many kids growing up today don't have a church foundation, and when they think of Christianity they think of the right-wing fundamentalists. When they look for God, they see those people on TV, and they see God as someone who's hateful and judgmental and white and male. And that's not God! That's why I think this church is so important, because I really think it's going to be the first church of the new reformation. Reclaiming God. This is the God that the world needs to see. It really frightens me that a hurting gay or lesbian turns on these televangelist shows and says, "God doesn't have time for me because I'm a sinner." It breaks my heart.[38]

To counter the televangelism message, the Cathedral has developed a number of media tactics. Lacking the financial resources of Pat Robertson and other high-profile right-wing broadcasters, the Cathedral has found cheaper ways to spread the word, through their position as a resource for the mainstream press, through their use of public access television, and through their infomercial.

The Cathedral has developed an ongoing relationship with the mainstream press, acting as a source of sound bites on religion and gay issues. Unlike secular opponents of the Christian Right, the Cathedral argues against religious bigotry on its own Biblical terms. In the summer of 1998, when then-Senate Majority Leader Trent Lott of Mississippi and then-House Majority Leader Dick Armey of Texas pronounced homosexuality to be a sin, the press turned to the Cathedral for spiritual counterarguments.[39] The Cathedral quickly prepared a press release, and Piazza sent out editorials to newspapers. The Cathedral also invited Lott and Armey to visit the Cathedral, but, needless to say, the invitations were declined. The Cathedral countered Lott and Armey not on political but on religious grounds. Many Americans who identify as Christian and who may agree, in the abstract, that discrimination against gays and lesbians is wrong, still believe that the Bible says that homosexuality is a sin. The Cathedral wants to speak to such people, to show them that there is a different way to read the Bible and, therefore, a different way to understand gays and lesbians.

As the Cathedral's national and international reputation grows, the press more and more frequently calls upon it to comment on the religious aspects of the Right's attacks on gays and lesbians. Lisa Carver, director of communications, says that, "the Cathedral has increasingly become a Rolodex card to the media on the issue. That's my goal. If I ever left here I would want to know that I left it as the golden Rolodex card in various media sources' back pockets."[40]

While the mainstream media has increased its interest in the Cathedral, Piazza notes that

the gay press—not here in Dallas, but the national gay press—really are antireligious. For example, *every major newspaper in America* and *almost* every major newspaper in the world has done stories on the Cathedral of Hope. *The London Times* has done four or five, and the *London Herald* has done a couple of major pieces. *The Advocate*, which is the largest lesbian and gay newspaper, has *never* done a story about the Cathedral of Hope. Nothing.[41]

This confirms Mona West's observation that gay and lesbian Christians are caught in a catch-22 in terms of how both the religious Right and non-Christian gays and lesbians respond to them. The religious Right rejects Cathedral congregants as sacrilegious, left-wing crazies, while secular gays and lesbians (at least the journalists) reject the Cathedral as assimilationists, or at best, irrelevant.

In addition to serving as a "Rolodex card" for the mainstream media, the Cathedral actively engages in media outreach through "COH-TV," their weekly half-hour public access TV program, which is shown in Dallas and thirty-one other cities. There are no audience figures (ratings) for public access, but the Cathedral's potential viewer base (number of cable households) was four million in 1998. This use of public access is unique, since by its very definition, public access is local.[42] The Cathedral gets on the air around the country by finding local sponsors who sign on as the official show "producer," dropping off and picking up the tapes at the public access studio once a month. There is a thirty-second space at the beginning of each tape where sponsors have the opportunity to produce their own short introduction plugging their local MCC or other gay or lesbian group. The Cathedral has had few problems getting the show on access channels outside Dallas, although a few access centers have refused COH-TV, in cities where public access is dominated by local conservative churches.

COH-TV is a half-hour version of the Cathedral's Sunday service. It is conceived in large part as a nationwide attempt to reach gay and lesbian teenagers "who were getting pounded by this Christian fundamentalist idea that it's a horrible, horrible sin, and God hates you."[43] The show seeks to function as a spiritual antidote to fundamentalism in general, and televangelism in particular, an antidote specifically addressed to gay teens, who have a significantly higher suicide rate than straight teens.[44] Piazza observes that some studies have found the attempted suicide rate for religious gay and lesbian teens to be even higher than it is for nonreligious gay and lesbian teens. COH-TV is for viewers of all ages, but services often speak directly to the issue of gay and lesbian youth. At the Cathedral's June 1998 gay pride service, the Sanctuary Choir sang "For Gay Generations to Come," a song that asks adults to remember their isolation as youths and to reach out to today's gay and lesbian youth:

Take a look around you, there are children in despair, powerless to find us in the dark. Let them see you shining like a rainbow past the rain, proof that God can love them as they are . . . Join us if you can by coming out to tell your truth, for the price of hiding is our youth.

Piazza's books and sermons, the Cathedral's pamphlets, and COH-TV productions make frequent references to gay and lesbian youth. Cathedral media respond to a Puritanical and homophobic culture that treats childhood as a sacred space to be preserved from the adult world of sexuality, a culture in which many adults seem to believe that children are, paradoxically, both asexual and heterosexual. Many gays and lesbians, still pegged by right-wingers as "child molesters," are wary of taking up gay and lesbian childhood as a subject of public discussion.[45] There's no way to tell how many teens channel-surf past COH-TV programs, but it is certain that there is no other space on television that so openly acknowledges the existence of gay and lesbian children.

COH-TV services open with Positive Voices, the choir for HIV-positive men. Then the show moves on to Piazza's sermon, and later back to the Sanctuary Chorus. The taking of communion is omitted, and some of the songs are pared down, but the service is basically intact. Many of the hymns include lyrics about gays and lesbians. For example:

Once we were not a people,
God's people now are we.
A proud, determined people
Still striving to be free.
A gentle, loving people
with justice as our aim;
a gay and lesbian people
United in Christ's Name.[46]

The Cathedral also sings more traditional hymns but none that do not use inclusive language. Old hymns such as "Faith of Our Fathers" and "Rise Up O Men of God" have been deliberately excluded. COH-TV *looks* like many other Sunday morning TV church services, but it *sounds* different. The disjunction between, on the one hand, the chorus, robed preacher, slow organ music, and dissolves between every shot, which look so much like the typical TV church service, and on the other hand, songs about gay kids or expositions on eunuchs as gay Biblical models, make for an uncanny TV viewing experience. It is all so utterly familiar yet completely unfamiliar.

In addition to making unorthodox use of public access to distribute COH-TV, the Cathedral has created a half-hour infomercial, originally titled *Holy Homosexuals*, for commercial television. *Holy Homosexuals* does not share all of the qualities of the infomercial genre. It is not highly repetitive, and unlike the average infomercial for hair replacement products or exercise machines, it does not imitate the talk-show or news show genre. The program does, however, repeatedly flash the Cathedral's phone number at the bottom of the screen. It directs viewers to the Cathedral's Web site, promotes one of Piazza's books, and offers a free book about mourning the death of a loved one to AIDS. The final sequence of shots showing a variety of singles, couples, and families in a brightly lit, white studio space is accompanied by inspirational music, and again, the Cathedral's phone number is shown on the bottom of the screen. This sequence in particular has a professional, corporate video look.

The video was slated to be shown five times in August 1998 at 1:00 in the morning on WGN, an independent station based in Chicago and fed by satellite to cable systems around the country. Like using cable access to show the Sunday morning service nationally for free, this was a cost-efficient strategy to circumvent the high prices of network television, although at nine thousand dollars per showing it certainly represented the Cathedral's biggest media expenditure to date.

In the course of getting the infomercial on the air, the Cathedral encountered many roadblocks. Before it was finally accepted by WGN, the program was rejected by the Odyssey Network, the Discovery Channel, Lifetime, BET, and the USA Network.[47] In 1998, the Cathedral filed a suit against WGN because it broke its agreement to broadcast the infomercial, deeming it "too controversial." WGN had already suggested changes, which the church had agreed to. They changed the title to *A Cathedral of Hope*, and they "agreed to blur the image of Pat Robertson . . . to make his face unrecognizable."[48] Defending their decision, WGN lawyers observed that in the past they had also rejected programming with gay-bashing themes. However, as Piazza observes, newspapers regularly accept ads from conservative Christian groups: "We just wanted to make our voice heard against the overwhelming onslaught of people using the media to say how bad gay people are."[49] After months of legal battling, WGN finally agreed to broadcast the program in April 1999.

If the relatively mild *Holy Homosexuals* is "too controversial" for late-night TV, it is a sign of how homophobic the culture remains. The video is prefaced by a short montage sequence of Christian right-wing hatred. This segment includes picket signs saying "Yes, God *Does* Hate Fags" and "Repent or Perish," a mouth in close-up saying "God's going to condemn you to Hell," and several short video clips and sound bites of Pat Robertson attacking gays and lesbians. Next, the video cuts to testimonials of church members and gives a short history of the Cathedral, noting that it is situated in an area dominated by fundamentalists. The story of architect Philip Johnson and the new Cathedral is told, followed by an overview of some of the Cathedral's charity projects and a quick overview of queer theology, which concludes that Jesus taught nothing about homosexuality and that his message was one of love and inclusivity. A large part of the infomercial is given over to a music video for a sentimental song, "Everything Possible." The music video shows children playing. A girl gives a boy a flower, which he gives to a girl, who then gives it to another girl. At one point, a low angle shot shows a butch little girl looking defiantly at the camera to the lyrics, "Some girls grow up strong and bold" (fig. 31). Then, a high angle shot shows a small boy offering a flower to the camera to the lyrics, "Some boys are quiet and kind" (fig. 32). Finally, a series of studio shots runs as the Cathedral's theme song plays. Each shot shows different configurations of people, mostly gay and lesbian couples but also some singles and heterosexual couples. Some of the gay and lesbian couples have children. At one point two men lean forward to kiss their daughter on the cheek. At the last moment, she giggles and ducks, and the men kiss each other on the lips. The kiss is playful and chaste.

Holy Homosexuals strives to present "positive images" of gay and lesbian adults and children. While the Right attacks gays and lesbians as a threat to the "American family," this video shows alternative "families of choice," *without* trying to say "We're just like you." As Mona West explains,

we don't want the video to send the message, "See, we're just like everybody else," because I think that is falling right into that trap where we're feeding into the rhetoric of the religious Right, if we say, "Oh, yeah, we have family values, too. They're just like yours."[50]

The studio images include single people, couples with and without children, and groups of people to symbolize the idea of extended "families of choice." The video's picture of alternative families is mild, and West's argument is not altogether convincing, but the intention was certainly not to buttress a gay version of the Christian Right's family values. As Piazza writes in his self-help book for lesbian and gay couples, "Enemies of the 'American family'? I hope so!" meaning that the traditional fam-

FIGS. 31–32 THE CATHEDRAL OF HOPE ACKNOWLEDGES THE EXISTENCE OF GAY AND LESBIAN CHILDREN: "SOME GIRLS GROW UP STRONG AND BOLD . . ."

". . . SOME BOYS ARE QUIET AND KIND."

ily was never the ideal that conservative evangelicals imagine and that it is time for gays and lesbians to come up with new models for nonbiological families of choice.[51] Piazza and his partner, for example, have two children, whom they coparent with a lesbian couple. Piazza is the father of both, and one of the women is their mother.[52] In *Holy Homosexuals*, we see Piazza, his partner, and their kids, but there is no visual indication of the four-way parenting schema. In other words, the video could probably challenge the "American family" more aggressively. On the other hand, it does push homophobic panic buttons by showing queer kids. While many on the Left may see images of gay Christian families as conservative and assimilationist, the Right sees these images as directly confrontational, and even evil. In a culture that is both terrified of childhood sexuality and generally homophobic, images of gay and lesbian children are far from neutral.

However, I would like to stress the paucity of terms like "liberal," "conservative," "Left," and "Right" to describe the image dynamics at work here. An image of a lesbian child in a Christian video cannot be simply pegged "liberal" or "conservative." The sentimental image of the child is a cipher used by all political camps to make their arguments. While all sides feel they are helping children by showing such images, they are producing the images in the name of an imaginary, symbolic child, and ultimately, in the name of advancing very adult ideas about tolerance and intolerance, rights and the denial of rights, normality and abnormality.[53] To oppose civil rights for gays and lesbians in Colorado, Colorado for Family Values created an ad showing a child at a gay pride parade. "The ad ends with freeze-frame blowups of the child that move progressively closer until her screaming face fills the screen."[54] The Cathedral uses the image of the child toward a nobler end, but it still *uses* the image of the child. A key difference, of course, is that the Colorado group shows a youth endangered by adult sexuality, while the Cathedral shows a youth whose sexuality is represented as "innocent" and far removed from the adult world, but one could easily imagine the iconography reversed, with the Cathedral showing a crying youngster in the arms of an antigay picketer, and Colorado for Family Values picturing happy heterosexual children playfully expressing "innocent" opposite-sex attraction.

While COH-TV does respond to the Christian Right and, more specifically, to televangelism, the Cathedral does not see its media outreach as a purely reactive or defensive maneuver against the Right. In fact, while acknowledging the tremendous damage that the religious Right does in spreading hatred (and self-hatred, for many queer Christians), the Cathedral also sees the Right as actually *helpful* to the Cathedral. As COH-TV director Paul Taylor explains,

We're counting on the religious Right, and the Christian Broadcasting Network, and anybody else who's against us out there to do our media for us. Because they only further our cause by showing their true colors and talking about what horrible people we are. And the rhetoric of intolerance, the rhetoric of hate that they put forth, only shows the rest of the people in the world that those Christian fundamentalists, the religious Right, are the ones who are in the wrong. We are not who they say we are.[55]

Knowing they can count on the religious Right to use the Bible to attack gays and lesbians, the Cathedral is always prepared to issue counterstatements and press releases, as they did in the wake of the Lott and Armey incident. Carver notes that "we *always* need to be in a position of responding to hatefulness that the religious Right spews out. They are opportunistic about gay and lesbian stuff. Well, we can turn that into an opportunity for us as well."[56]

Paul Taylor gives one example of how the Cathedral turned an attack into an opportunity. Pat Robertson's Christian Broadcasting Network (CBN) reported on the Cathedral's new building, concluding that
so far the church hadn't even raised the hundred thousand dollars they
needed for the architectural model and the architect's commission fee.
Piazza played the CBN clip at both Sunday services, and as Taylor recounts, he said,

"Now, we want to say something to Pat Robertson and CBN. They're wrong.
We have the money to pay for the model, we just haven't collected it yet. And
that's what we're going to do right now." And with that he took his pledge en-
velope, and we had these wheelbarrows up front, and he put it in. It was a little emotional! At that point, the congregation came forward and put their
envelopes in, and we raised a hundred and thirty-four thousand dollars. And
that's how you use media![57]

Perhaps this sounds a bit opportunistic, like a televangelist's fundraising strategy, but the picture conjured is phenomenal. Imagine a church
full of gays and lesbians, many of them raised in conservative evangelical households where CBN was a staple. Now, they are in the world's
largest gay and lesbian church, listening to a pastor preaching from a
pink triangle pulpit, flanked by stained glass showing linked male-
male and female-female symbols. Suddenly, Robertson is projected on
two huge screens sandwiched between the pulpit and the stained glass.
The usual antigay sentiment spews out, but in this reception context,
the words have the opposite of their intended effect. The viewers' donations are not only for a new building; the donations also resonate
with symbolic importance as an action against the religious Right.
Congregants are not victimized by the clip, as they might be in a different viewing context but, rather, empowered by the collective experience. It is a way to use the Right that serves the Cathedral's purposes.
As Piazza explains, he gets invitations all the time, but he no longer debates the Christian Right unless he feels it will benefit the Cathedral.
He turns to the Bible to explain this:

There's an interesting verse in Nehemiah, where Nehemiah, who was a eunuch, probably a homosexual man, went back to Jerusalem to rebuild after it
had been destroyed. He's up on the walls rebuilding them, and some of his fellow Jews are afraid that if he rebuilds the wall they're going to be attacked
again, and they've sort of gotten some benefit out of the dysfunction of the
whole situation. They're profiting off of it, and so they send for him to come
and talk to them about this strategy of rebuilding, and he says, "I am doing a
great work, and I cannot come down." And that's been sort of my perspective

about this church. You know, Trent Lott and all of them can say what they want to, but we're doing a great work, and we are not going to come down, *except* in as much as it helps us build up what we're doing.[58]

With the help of COH-TV and the *Holy Homosexuals* infomercial, the Cathedral does its "great work" regardless of the attacks that keep coming from right-wing Christians. They feel themselves to be the winners of the battle over Biblical interpretation.

MANY VOICES SHOUTING IN THE WILDERNESS

Although there is a history of Christianity linked to progressive social action (the African American Civil Rights movement, Liberation theology, Quaker activism), in a contemporary climate of intense religious conservatism it is hard to remember that many Christians have been (and are) pacifists, abolitionists, feminists, and environmentalists. "Christian" and "Right" slip off the tongue effortlessly, and, consequently, queer Christians who are closeted as gay in their churches are often also closeted as Christian in the gay community. As one scholar notes,

To be queer and religious . . . means putting yourself on the margins of an already marginalized minority: as many lesbian and gay Christians have said, the one thing harder than coming our as queer in Church is coming out as religious to your fellow queers. There response is, at best, incomprehension, sometimes hostility: you are viewed as a traitor . . . these two identities are simply not supposed to exist in the same person—they should cancel each other out.[59]

The Cathedral of Hope shows unequivocally that these two identities are not incommensurate; in fact, they fit together quite neatly. "Gay fundamentalist," conversely, remains oxymoronic, in theory if not in practice.

Above and beyond illustrating that gay and Christian can be coterminous identities, the Cathedral illustrates the process of cultural negotiation between fundamentalist and postfundamentalist identities, a process whereby the old cultural affiliation is respun to accommodate new modes of Biblical interpretation and new politics. How exactly to position these "new politics" remains open to question. Gay Christians who are nervous to even label themselves "moderate" will appear "radical" to Southern Baptists, "liberal" to Southern Democrats, and "conservative" or even "right-wing" to some progressive queers in New York. Cathedral congregants are perhaps best understood not as really fitting under any one of these rubrics but rather as representing a completely unique political position.

Cultural Studies researchers often conceptualize subcultures as internally dynamic yet fixed as groups. Within this interpretive framework, slash pornography writers are not romance readers, and romance readers are not soap opera viewers. In reality, of course, we know that such identities can overlap and that our conceptual grouping of people under subcultural headings is simply pragmatic. The Cathedral illustrates one instance of overlapping multiple identity negotiation, but even this case study could be pushed farther. In identifying a group as "postfundamentalist" and "gay Christian" we run the risk of ignoring other identifications members of the Cathedral may have, as Southerners, whites, professionals, members of the middle class, and so on. The Cathedral makes the importance of considering multiple identity negotiation patently clear. Virtually everyone at this church conceives of religious belief and sexuality as interlocked dual identities, and it is *dual* identity that I have focused on here. But a glance at the Circles of Hope directory, a list of small spiritual discussion groups that many members belong to, indicates a variety of other identities. Circles include Legacy (50+), Mickey Mouse Club (kids), Parents, Twenty Something, HIV-positive, and Shouts in the Wilderness (leather gays). The Shouts in the Wilderness Circle draws inspiration from Matthew (3:1–4):

In those days came John the Baptist, preaching in the wilderness of Judea, and saying, Repent, for the dominion of Heaven is at hand . . . For this is the one that was spoken of by the prophet Isaiah, saying the voice of one shouting in the wilderness, prepare the way of the Lord, make his paths straight. John's clothing was woven from camel's hair and he wore leather; his food was locusts and wild honey.

Leather Christians take multiple identity formation and queer Biblical interpretation to a new plateau; the Bible provides inspiration to gay sadomasochist Christians who joyously proclaim that "the body of Christ, the church, welcomes and includes those creations of God that live and love in leather."[60] Locusts and wild honey have never sounded so sexy. Sadomasochism has (arguably) never sounded so sanctified. Postfundamentalist, gay, leather, and Christian have never felt so interconnected and indivisible. While the Christian Right would like to see gays and lesbians silenced—cast into the wilderness—it seems that the Cathedral of Hope has successfully staked a claim for the end of queer Christian silence.

For all its differences from conservative evangelical culture, the Cathedral, as we have seen, still shares a number of traits with Pat Robertson et al. Both camps take witnessing to be crucial to identity formation, both seek new converts to their ideas, and both make use of secular media forms. Both are subcultures, if you will, seeking to expand their ranks by taking "outsiders" and making them "insiders." Both camps, in other words, seek converts to their spiritual and political ranks. They think that media can be a helpful tool in this endeavor, but media production is only one of a number of tools that they use to accomplish their goals.

Chapters 5 and 6 will focus on Christians for whom media production is absolutely central. Specifically, these chapters will examine scientific and apocalyptic filmmakers who seek to bring about supernatural changes in viewers through their films. As with other Christian media, these films vacillate between the sacred and the profane, the emotional and the intellectual, the supernatural and the mundane. In fact, once scrutinized, such polarities quickly crumble.

COMMODIFICATION

SEXUALITY

PART THREE

FILMMAKING

CHAPTER FIVE

PUTTING GOD UNDER THE MICROSCOPE:

THE MOODY INSTITUTE OF SCIENCE'S

CINEMA OF DEVOTION

Today's evangelicals have reclaimed postwar America as a Golden Age when kids were safe in schools, families went to church, moms were happy housewives, and no-fault divorce was inconceivable (fig. 33). It is almost unthinkable that such a "perfect" world would require the ministrations of Christian media, but this halcyon image of the past is the product of selective amnesia. In reality, most Americans had not "made decisions for Christ" in the 1950s, and evangelicals then were as concerned about fighting sin and depravity as their counterparts are today. For aspiring Christian filmmakers, the burning question at the time was, what role could media play in saving people?

It is widely known that Oral Roberts, Billy Graham, and others were involved in radio and television at this time. What is less well known is that a small cadre of evangelicals was also active in the production of films. Hardly a small subcultural phenomenon, these films about science were shown to viewers largely in secular venues such as public schools and air force training camps. The military audience alone numbered in the millions: between 1945 and 1958 the air force screened these films over 200,000 times with attendance ranging from 200 to 1,500 per screening. These scientific films were ubiquitous two decades before the rise of the Christian bookstore, which provided distribution outlets for the nascent industry in religious products, and three decades before the rise of home video, which revolutionized Christian media production.

Rather than appealing to emotion or drawing on therapeutic ideas about self-improvement, as much of today's evangelical media do, these midcentury films are aggressively argumentative and rational. And unlike today's watered-down Christian pop tunes or "religious" but ecumenical video series, the evangelical films of the fifties contain a salvation message that marks them as Christian. Their messages were

FIG. 33 EVANGELICALS HAVE RE-
CLAIMED THE 1950s AS A GOLDEN
AGE OF FAMILY VALUES.

deemed "nonsectarian" at the time, though, since they were Christian but not specifically evangelical: the salvation message was interwoven with lengthy scientific exposition and the narrator mentioned the "Creator" but rarely Jesus. Many conservative evangelicals (and fundamentalists) probably considered these films to be spiritually lightweight. In sum, these films are an excellent early example of Christian media that make compromises to reach a secular audience. The final product may indeed have been diluted, yet, unlike many contemporary products, its religious intentions were unambiguous. These scientific films, produced by the Moody Institute of Science (MIS), truly succeeded in being "in but not of the world."

In its heyday, from 1945 to 1962, MIS produced thirty films, all under the supervision of maverick Christian filmmaker Irwin S. Moon. These forty-five-minute features (cut down to half-hour versions for television) were produced, distributed, and exhibited completely outside the Hollywood circuit and were never shown in conventional movie theaters. Yet millions watched them in elementary schools, foreign missions, world's fairs, and churches. Air force recruits were even *required* to see the films as part of President Truman's Character Guidance Program. Drawing on documents archived at the Moody Bible Institute, the home of MIS, this chapter charts the production and reception of MIS films from their inception in the 1940s through their television appearances in the 1950s and their use for "space-age evangelism" and missionary work in the 1960s. These films initially meshed well with the religious zeitgeist of postwar America, but by the 1960s they were considered "too religious" to appear in government-funded spaces. They simply lacked the ambiguity that currently typifies much evangelical media.

When the Moody Bible Institute was founded in Chicago in 1886, science was excluded from the curriculum. So it was a dramatic turn of events in 1945 when Moody's board of directors approved the establishment of MIS in California to produce evangelical scientific films. In fact, it took the president of the institute three years to convince the conservative trustees to form MIS. Their ultimate acquiescence should perhaps not be surprising, as the institute had long understood the power of media to speak to both saved and unsaved audiences. Dwight L. Moody himself had shocked fellow evangelicals in the 1880s by buying newspaper space to advertise his revivals, and the institute's radio station, WMBI, remains among the oldest in the country. Still, it seems that the institute was more fundamentalist than MIS. Institute students could not attend Hollywood films, drink liquor, smoke, swear, or go on unchaperoned dates. MIS films, conversely, aggressively engaged with mass culture, using a worldly form, cinema, to send an otherworldly message.

In fact, MIS emerged just as Billy Graham, Carl Henry, and Charles Fuller were spearheading a movement away from fundamentalist separatism toward evangelical worldly involvement. While avoiding politics like the neoevangelicals, MIS films sought out the unsaved and tried to convert them through logic. Finding not contradiction but confluence between science and religion, MIS argued that the existence of God was as rational as the behavior of molecules in a test tube. Through the magic of film, the "facts" of God could be empirically proven. In advancing a scientific view of Christianity, MIS rejected emotional revivalist tactics in favor of a "modern," rational evangelical strategy. As MIS founder and director Irwin S. Moon stated, "only the old-fashioned see conflict between science and God. There is not an unscientific fact in the Bible."[1] Each of Moon's films focuses on the glory of God's book of works, the natural world, before turning to his book of words, the Bible. Often, God is not mentioned until the final moments of the film. Although some Christians at the time might have seen this as a cop out, it was, apparently, effective in appealing to nonevangelical viewers.

FIG. 34 CHRISTIAN FILMMAKER
IRWIN S. MOON DEMONSTRATES
GOD'S POWER BY ALLOWING A
MILLION VOLTS OF ELECTRICITY TO
COURSE THROUGH HIS BODY AND
OUT HIS FINGERTIPS.

MIS sought publicity in both the Christian and the secular press, and the special topics of its films meant MIS could turn to nonevangelical specialty periodicals. *City of the Bees* (1962) was reviewed in a beekeepers' hobbyist magazine, *Gleanings in Bee Culture,* and promoted to the American Beekeeping Federation, the Department of Agriculture, and the 4-H Club. *Red River of Life* (1957) was written up in *Look* and *Scientific Monthly* because of its successful photography inside an artificially pumping, dead human heart. MIS even impressed the *Journal of the Society for Motion Picture and Television Engineers,* which periodically covered the technical breakthroughs of MIS productions. MIS also made occasional appearances on prime-time TV. In 1959, a Moody representative did the famous "Million Volts" presentation (allowing a million volts of electricity to course through his body) on *I've Got a Secret* (fig. 34). A television critic declared the event to be "eye-popping."[2] And in 1964 Moon was a hit on the *Steve Allen Show;* the producers asked him to return on a weekly basis.[3] In seeking secular audiences, MIS clearly stands apart from fundamentalists of the period. Fire-and-brimstone rhetoric was out, Bunsen burners and test tubes were in.

USING FILMS TO BE "IN BUT NOT OF THE WORLD"

A MIS press release explained that Moon was raised and educated in Hollywood, "whose product the clergy sometimes calls the tools of the Devil." But Moon "is using these tools to present the Gospel in entertaining style."[4] Moon proposed that film itself was not inherently satanic, that it could actually be used to fight the forces of darkness. MIS even went so far as to invite an MGM editor to analyze its first productions, *God of Creation* (1945) and *God of the Atom* (1947). The editor gave both "Creation" and "Atom" a thorough critique . . . It is a marvelous opportunity for us to get the "box office slant." . . . [T]his Godless Hollywood character says the film has a tremendous message—even saying "it touched him." Substantially, his criticism revolved about a merciless cutting of footage which will make the thread of the story "move." . . . We've stopped the printing of the film, and substantial cuts will definitely be made.[5]

Moon may have disapproved of Hollywood films, but he was not above taking advice from a "Godless character" who knew the secrets to increasing viewer interest.

Although his films were entertaining and slickly produced, Moon never "went Hollywood." When Cinerama (the IMAX of its day) asked him to produce a movie in the late forties, he refused because he knew people would go expecting thrills, not theology. A person tricked into hearing the Gospel would be turned off. For the same reason, Moon turned down an MGM offer to release MIS films in secular theaters. He also declined an offer to work on nature documentaries for Walt Disney because such commercial works would not be shown in a setting amenable to discussion. (Moon did, however, offer footage to Disney for free, and Disney later reciprocated by loaning MIS a few seconds of animation from *Fantasia* [1940] for use in *God of Creation*.) As chapter 6 will show, Moon's approach was strikingly different from that of today's Christian filmmakers, many of whom are eager to have their films shown in secular venues and are not concerned about turning off viewers who might feel they have been tricked into seeing a religious film.

By showing a wholesome commitment to evangelism and a determination to be in the world but not of the world, MIS seemed to win over many dubious evangelicals. It helped, of course, to be affiliated with the Moody Bible Institute, which had flawless conservative credentials. Like Moon, Dwight Moody had been opposed to evangelicals getting into politics. Historian George Marsden argues that "Moody, in fact, did as much as anyone to set the trend (which fit the national mood of the 1870s and 1880s) away from earlier nineteenth-century evangelical emphasis on the directly social dimensions of sin and holiness."[6] Moody focused exclusively on saving souls instead of feeding the poor, aiding prostitutes, and agitating for Prohibition. He argued that "a line should be drawn between the church and the world, and every Christian should get both feet out of the world."[7] That line did not waver for almost a century.

Like Moody, MIS eschewed politics, with one exception: its films were implicitly designed to fight "Godless materialism," that is, Communism. In fact, one of the institute's most successful films, *City of the Bees,* was overtly anti-Communist. Moon had been inspired by a Soviet film praising the cold efficiency of bees. In his own film, Moon observes that in bee society there is no unemployment, no labor-management problem, no crime, no juvenile delinquency, and no rebellion against authority. It is an efficient but utterly ruthless society in which bees are required to work themselves to death, drones are killed after the mating period, and the queen is killed if she can't lay eggs. Bees live this way by instinct, but humans must be forced to live this way. Worst of all, those who propose an apian lifestyle do not believe in the absolute standards of right and wrong spelled out in the Ten Commandments, which people obey by choice, not instinct.

Although *City of the Bees* was the only MIS film that directly addressed Communism, Moon's other films were implicitly anti-Communist by virtue of their godly emphasis. In 1948, former U.S. Air Force intelligence officer Edgar C. Bundy participated in a "Threat of Communism" lecture tour with Moon, showing *God of Creation* and other films. And in 1950 General Douglas MacArthur asked for prints of MIS films in Japanese and Korean, noting in a telegram that he was "confident these films will be [a] source of inspiration and courage to Korean people who are facing the Godless Communist aggressors."[8] *God of Creation* was subsequently "shown to Korean troops up on the 38th parallel, [and] to Communist ravaged villages in the Mount Shidi area of South Korea."[9]

Opposing Communism was a given in Cold War America. But explicitly fighting the teaching of evolution was another thing entirely. Although most MIS films were tacitly creationist, the producers were careful to avoid taking a controversial stance on evolution, and their school films were recut to reduce their religious messages. Unlike today's aggressive creationists, MIS avoided scientific debates and school politics in a conscious effort not to be excessively worldly. Thus, MIS would avoid locking horns not only with secular courts but also with their own fundamentalist brethren still stinging from the Scopes trial. MIS realized that many evangelicals did not agree on the details of the creationism question and wanted either to settle these difficulties away from the mockery of the secular world or to ignore scientific questions altogether. Many simply saw science as irreconcilable with religion. Moody president Dr. Will H. Houghton, who had been instrumental in setting up MIS under the auspices of the Bible Institute, said, "It is one thing to do a first-class laboratory job; it is another to do a job with our fellow fundamentalists, some of whom have little knowledge but deep prejudices in the realm of science . . . It is not our job to start a new reformation and move fundamentalism out of its inclination to think with its emotions."[10]

Moon believed that film was the best means to bring new souls to Christ because the "unchurched," who would never willingly attend a sermon, might watch an entertaining and informative film. MIS films took a "soft-sell" approach, asking questions that would get people thinking about the logic of science and then, by extension, the logic of God's plan for salvation. The films were a means of "low-key outreach in a secular world."[11] A McDonnell Douglas Corp. aircraft employee who had attended a MIS lunchtime screening series in 1969 observed, "These films are terrific even though they are religiously oriented. I wouldn't have continued seeing them if they had tried to ram religion down my throat, but they didn't. They make you think."[12] Moon felt only one kind of film would succeed in making viewers think this way: the nonfiction, scientific film.

Moon was adamantly opposed to dramatic Christian films, referring to them as "religious horse operas."[13] Scientific films, conversely, captured events that *really* happened in front of the camera, recording truth as it unfolded. Film's photographic technology captured truth, just as the Gospel expressed God's truth. When we are young, Moon argues in a seminar on drama in film evangelism, we soon learn that movies aren't real, and that we needn't cry when a man on screen is stabbed because "that isn't blood, it's ketchup." Moon argued that people see through Christian films as fiction rather than learning that the Gospel is fact. "If we really believe what we're talking about, and it isn't the medium that's the message, it's the message, we don't have to say, 'Don't believe it. Christ didn't really die on the cross. It isn't blood, it's ketchup.'"[14] As a counterexample to the typical Jesus biopic, Moon suggested a film on seed dispersal. He proposed a cinema of devotion that would convert viewers by presenting a careful, truthful record of the wonders of the natural world.

But why did Moon consider *science* the perfect vehicle for conveying the message of salvation? When MIS set up shop in 1945, science was considered particularly appealing to Atomic Age youth. Because, Moon reasoned, it was in college science classes that most young people lost their faith, youngsters especially needed to learn that science and the Gospel were compatible. MIS films assumed that "it is a small step from science, the study of God's handiwork, to the Gospel, God's plan for man's salvation."[15] An early MIS document argued that "honest science is an honest seeking after the truth, and that truth preaches a sermon no mortal tongue can enlarge. Truth is its own defense. It stands in no need of the smoke screen of partisan appeals to emotions or prejudice. To be believed, truth needs but to be seen."[16] The idea was to appeal to intelligence and common sense. While nonfiction film was the best medium for preaching, because it allowed a photographic record of the truth to unfold before one's eyes, science was the best means of revealing the Gospel, because Christianity was understood as a logical, scientific belief system.

RELIGION IN THE POSTWAR YEARS

Writing on Frank Capra's AT&T science films, Eric Smoodin explains that "the development of weapons of mass destruction at the end of World War II helped to create, or at least foster, a serious ethical discussion during the period about the confluences of and contradictions between modern science and Western religious sensibilities."[17] In the wake of Hiroshima and Nagasaki, a pressing question among intellectuals was how to exert moral control over science (or whether science could even be governed by morality). Theologians condemned the use of the atom bomb, and in a 1950 editorial, the *Partisan Review* noted that there was a "new turn toward religion among intellectuals . . . Many thinkers sound an insistent note of warning that Western civilization cannot hope to survive without the reanimation of religious values."[18]

MIS films must have appealed to politicians and educators in part because of this sensibility. It is stunning today that MIS films were shown to millions of air force recruits and public school children, since this violates the contemporary understanding of the separation of church and state. MIS was able to exhibit their films in government-funded spaces for two reasons. First, the films were soft-sell evangelism, rejecting the vituperative histrionics of soapbox preacher Billy Sunday in favor of the cold voice of reason to illustrate God's creation. Viewers would perceive the films as Christian but not necessarily evangelical. Second, 1950s America experienced what many historians have described as a religious revival. MIS productions were acceptable viewing in schools and the military because the films were only nominally more religious than the rest of popular culture. The existence of God was a given. This was, after all, a time when popular books included *Peace with God, A Man Called Peter, Pray Your Weight Away*, and *The Power of Prayer on Plants*. Bishop Fulton Sheen had a hit television show that held its own against Milton Berle's *Texaco Star Theater*, and Johnny Carson told children's Bible stories on his daytime program. J. Ronald Oakely even recounts that "in 1954, the Ideal Toy Company marketed a doll with flexible knees that could be made to 'kneel in a praying position,' the company's response, it said, to 'the resurgence of religious feeling and practice in America today.'"[19]

Did this era indeed see a "fourth great awakening," as one of Billy Graham's biographers has claimed?[20] It is certainly true that church attendance rose in the fifties and that church building, for all denominations, proceeded apace. Whereas $26 million had been spent on church construction in 1945, $76 million was spent in 1946, $251 million in 1948, and $409 million in 1950. By 1960, the annual expenditure for new churches passed the $1 billion mark,[21] and church membership had risen to over 114 million, up from 86.8 million in 1950.[22] Evangelicals are partially correct when they emphasize that America was "more religious" in the fifties than it is now.

But when evangelicals speak of religion in the 1950s they imply that America was dominated by born-agains, ignoring both the increased Jewish presence in the rising suburban middle class and the high visibility of Roman Catholics and mainline Protestants. Moreover, increases in church membership and attendance cannot be directly correlated with intensity of belief. As the growing white middle class bought homes in the suburbs, churchgoing became a crucial aspect of the *sociology* of the Cold War years. Church attendance went with marriage, children, upward mobility, and patriotism. One might even go to church out of sheer materialism; Norman Vincent Peale's 1952 bestseller, *The Power of Positive Thinking*, promised that faith would bring success. People may have frequently attended church in the fifties, but "polls . . . regularly revealed that most Americans were hard pressed to explain what their basic beliefs were, to distinguish between Protestantism and Catholicism, to explain or even identify the Christian trinity, to distinguish the Old Testament from the New, or even to name the first four books of the New Testament. In fact, a 1951 Gallup poll showed that 53 percent of Americans could not even name *one* of the Gospels."[23] As a skeptic in the *Nation* observed at the time, "the homogenized suburbanite likes his religion, unlike his martinis, diluted."[24]

Americans have always seen themselves as extremely religious, and it can be difficult to separate America's religious identity from its national identity.[25] Indeed, in postwar America, Judeo-Christian religious belief was widely equated with democracy. In 1952, President-elect Eisenhower proclaimed that "our form of government has no sense unless it is founded in a deeply felt religious faith, and I don't care what it is. With us of course it is the Judeo-Christian concept but it must be a religion that all men are created equal."[26] As if to seal the government's endorsement of religious belief, in 1954 the phrase "under God" was added to the Pledge of Allegiance and "In God we trust" was added to U.S. currency; in 1956 Congress declared that first- and second-class mail would be canceled with the message "Pray for peace."[27] The events of the 1960s (beginning, perhaps, with the legal elimination of mandatory public school prayer by the Supreme Court in 1962) would reveal that any national consensus on religion, morality, and politics had been short-lived. Yet in the postwar years, MIS began producing films that advocated belief in a creator, and these films seemed like a perfectly natural product of the times. Furthermore, as historian James Gilbert observes, the films were acceptable to viewers because of their glossy production values; they were "legitimate documentaries"[28] that "represented a denial of the amateurism that had betrayed Bryan"[29] at the Scopes trial. In other words, their very slickness seemed to mark them as appropriate for a wide, ecumenical audience.

Of course, since MIS films actually were the product of a conservative evangelical worldview, they avoided many of the ethical and political questions that Roman Catholics and mainline Protestants wrestled with in the postwar years. Like many other evangelical organizations, MIS and the Moody Bible Institute remained detached from the civil rights movement. And while many religious groups decried the use of nuclear weapons as a crime against both God and man, MIS films took a gee whiz approach to the wonders of atomic energy. The clearest illustration of this was in *God of the Atom* (1947), in which Moon tells viewers that man's true problem is not the atom bomb, scientists, or politicians but sin; if all of our weapons were taken away, we would destroy each other with our bare fists. As a memo from MIS to the Bible Institute's public relations department explains, the film showed that "6,000 years of human history is witness to the fact that the heart of man is deceitfully wicked; so the advent of the so-called Atomic Age has not really CREATED a problem, [but] rather REVEALED in a more graphic way the need of man for help in controlling his inherently evil nature."[30] The final moments of the film show mushroom clouds, as Moon's voice-over says, "Remember this: the God of the atom, the God of infinite power, is the God of everlasting salvation to whosoever believeth in him."[31] Moon is pessimistic about sin, not atomic energy. In fact, he seems impressed that God created something so powerful. While the film marks an obvious response to the Cold War, Moon's ultimate emphasis on individual salvation rather than politics reveals the film's roots in the conservative evangelical culture of the time. Like many of today's apolitical evangelical media producers, Moon was more interested in individual souls than right-wing propaganda.

THE MIS APPROACH TO SCIENCE AND EVOLUTION

In its awe of scientific achievement, MIS was in many ways in sync with wider popular attitudes. As Gilbert notes, "The years from the end of World War II into the early 1960s marked a high point in the prestige of science considered as a social model and a delivery system of social betterment."[32] MIS clearly hoped to tap into popular enthusiasm for science while ignoring coexisting anxiety about the dangers of science, as conveyed in dystopian science fiction films like *The Incredible Shrinking Man* (Arnold, 1957) and *The Beast of Yucca Flats* (Francis, 1961).

MIS films contended that the sheer glory of God's creation (nature) proved the existence of the Creator. The films seemed to render blind faith unnecessary, arguing that scientific tools could reveal the divinely created world: "In the laboratory, the eye of the lapse-time camera unfolds a bit of the mystery of God's miraculous plan . . . [and] that fabulous microscopic world beneath us is full of His creative plan and order revealed in a thrilling way by photomicrography."[33] Clearly this is a circular argument: God created a complex and perfect world, and when we see that the world is complex and perfect, we realize that this is proof that God created a complex and perfect world. MIS argued that "Biblical Christianity is one of the very few religions which claims to be capable of experimental verification." In a five-page response to a disgruntled, nonbelieving viewer in 1961, an MIS representative explained that salvation is an "experiment [that] has been performed many times, and has repeatedly given results which are as convincing in their area as are the results of experiments in physics or psychology . . . Get a New Testament and carefully read through the Gospel of John twice, with the attitude expressed by the prayer: 'God, if you exist, and if this is your message to me, I want to understand and to obey your commands.' After you have completed the experiment, we would welcome a report on the results. Only remember that complete honesty is as important in this experiment as it is in any other experiment."[34]

To viewers unfamiliar with the history of creationism, MIS films might resemble grade school science demonstrations with religious messages tacked on the end (fig. 35). Yet the films have their roots in natural theology, creationists' traditional approach to science. William Paley wrote the definitive book on the subject in 1802, but as far back as the late seventeenth century, Newton, Halley, Hooke, Boyle, and Ray—all theists who laid the foundations of modern science—contended that God would not permit contradiction between his works (the natural world) and his words (Scripture). God's glory could be understood through study of the world he created. A naturalist, for example, might study the complex structure of a flower not only out of scientific curiosity but also to enrich his understanding and reverence for God, who created the flower. A humble naturalist would not necessarily study the flower to disprove evolution.[35] Philosopher Michael Ruse explains that "arguments for the existence of God lie at the heart of natural theology. Some such arguments touch but slightly or not at

FIG. 35 *MOON'S FILMS DEMON-
STRATE BASIC SCIENTIFIC PHE-
NOMENON. HERE, HE SHOWS THE
EFFECT OF HELIUM ON VOCAL
CHORDS.*

all on the Darwinian system."[36] Thus, a natural theologian might contend that God caused the flower to evolve or that we can never really
know how he created the flower.

Today's creationists, by contrast, are not a humble lot and will often
speculate freely about God's intentions, arguing, for example, that in
the course of creating the world in six days he would not have made irrational or inefficient decisions. The contemporary creationist Alan
Hayward, for example, argues against the "young earth" creationists'
belief that stars only *appear* to be millions of light-years away because
the speed of light has not been constant. (The earth, according to them,
is only ten thousand years old.) Hayward argues that "this would have
involved God in changing the entire structure of the universe immediately after he had made it! *Not only does this seem unlikely,* but there is no
evidence whatever that such an enormous change has occurred."[37]
God is not only almighty, but he is also a consummate engineer, bio-
chemist, botanist, and zoologist, who would never behave whimsically.

MIS filmmakers were relatively modest, neither advancing theories
about God's motivations nor making aggressive, politically charged arguments against evolution. *Dust or Destiny* (1949) is the only MIS film
that dares, somewhat gently, to attack evolution. The film is a series of
vignettes examining different natural phenomena, ranging from the
functioning of the human ear to the life cycle of the grunion, a fish.
Moon provides commentary, concluding each segment with a dramatic question. After explaining how bat echolocation works, he asks,
"Where did the bat get such marvelous equipment? Obviously this is
part of an intelligent plan. But whose intelligence? The bat's?" This
questioning is classic creationism, less an argument than, as atheist
evolutionist Richard Dawkins puts it, "simply an affirmation of in-
credulity."[38]

The film finally cuts to Moon himself at his desk. He says, "It is evident that there is an infinite power behind the mystery of life. But is this a blind, unintelligent, impersonal force?" This was "soft-sell" evangelism, because Moon asks leading questions rather than simply supplying answers. Next, Moon moves on to the classic parable of creationism, the story of the watch and the watchmaker. Many evangelical viewers would know immediately that Moon was launching into an antievolution exegesis, but, then, this film was not really intended for people who had already "made decisions for Christ." Moon never uses pumped-up preacherly rhetoric, and an unsuspecting nonevangelical viewer would hear an antievolution message before knowing what hit him or her. The parable is worth quoting at some length to convey Moon's style:

Suppose that you've never seen and you've never heard of a watch. And then one day you find one. You're intrigued by its appearance and by that strange sound it makes. If you're anything like most of us, it isn't long before you have the back off, trying to find out what makes it tick . . . But now, you've got to explain the origin of the watch. You might develop the theory that the watch just happened. Especially if you're trying to convince yourself that nobody owned the watch! You could argue that the atoms and the molecules of the various parts just got together by accident. But the simplest kind of logic should tell you that somebody made those parts and somebody put them together for a purpose. How about that eye with its automatic focus? Or that tiny musical instrument inside the human ear? Or that heart, with its endless capacity for work? Or the bat, with its radar magic? Is all this the product of blind chance?

Moon is the consummate salesman. As he tells the story, he assumes that all viewers of *Dust or Destiny* are like him: curious, scientific, logical. A watch must have a watchmaker. There is no other explanation. God hasn't come up yet, but we have seen several shots of Moon's hand holding the watch over a Bible.

Next, Moon extends his argument. Eyes, ears, hearts, and bats are even more complex than a watch. Obviously, they too are the product of a maker. Since Moon avoids mentioning evolution or creationism by name, these arguments seem divorced from a wider political world, as if they were simply common sense.[39] Now Moon is ready to move in to make the sale:

You know, when you come right down to it, there are only two views we can take. Either all this happened by accident or it's the result of design, a plan. You might just shrug your shoulders and say, well, it's all a matter of personal opinion, and let it go at that. You might, that is, but for the fact that this is an issue which vitally affects your whole life. It's going to determine how you think and how you live. For after all, if man is just an accident, then he has no responsibility except that which he chooses to impose upon himself. There's no law but the law of convenience and desire. There's no ultimate right or wrong. And when people think and live according to that philosophy, the result is chaos. But if, on the other hand, there's a plan, then there's a planner. If there's a design, there's a designer. In other words, there's a God. You know, it isn't hard to believe in a God. It's the simplest and the most logical thing in the world.

Having shown that belief in God is a matter of common sense, Moon could end the film right here. Instead, he brings in the idea of civic responsibility to show the necessity of believing in God.

For some people the problem gets complicated when they begin to worry about who owns the watch. In other words, believing in God involves a responsibility, and they don't want that responsibility. They don't want anyone telling them what's right or wrong, or how to live or act, not even the God that made them. When you get as many people as there are in the world today living and acting as if there were no God, no wonder the world's in a mess.

This is a veiled reference to the Cold War and to Communists, who live and act "as if there were no God." Finally, the film concludes with an overt evangelical salvation message:

When we see the results of unbelief in the world today it doesn't seem at all farfetched to say that the only hope for the world as a whole or for you as an individual is faith in God. Not just belief in a supreme being or a great force, but belief in a personal God who loved you enough to provide a salvation for you. For God so loved the world, that he gave his only begotten son, so that whosoever believeth in him should not perish but have everlasting life.

Moon has been easing viewers to this moment and has finally swooped in for the kill. His approach to evangelism is aggressively modern: he uses film, scientific facts, logic, even advertising's methods of persuasion through demonstration. Undergirding it all is the natural theology position that God's glory is proved by the physical world, as well as the "logical," commonsense assumption that evolution just doesn't make any sense as a means of explaining the world.

Even though MIS films avoided the word "evolution," some viewers clearly knew that undermining this godless theory was an implicit goal. One high school teacher wrote that she was converted from belief in evolution to belief in God through watching *God of Creation*. She explained that "as a science teacher in a Staten Island high school, it was my duty to teach Evolution. I, myself, strongly believed in the theory of Evolution and regarded the Bible as one book too many on the market . . . I have now given up my teaching of Evolution and am now taking a course in Child Evangelism . . . I realize that through my teaching of Evolution, I have been leading boys and girls down the broad road that leadeth to destruction. . . ."[40] It is remarkable that this teacher understood the Christian message of *God of Creation*, since MIS films were so tempered for school screenings. They were substantially shortened, and anything overtly "sectarian" was omitted. But they still emphasized the existence of a creator or designer.

MIS associate director F. Alton Everest admitted that Christians might think the school films had a "weak message." But "to students who have previously heard only mechanistic explanations of the same phenomenon," he continued, "the effect is more like a bombshell. The repetitive impact of a continuous series of such films throughout secondary schools and universities has tremendous potential in building an atmosphere in which the knowledge of God might thrive and the further witness to His grace be allowed and encouraged."[41] Everest implied that creating this atmosphere was not only legal, since it was nonsectarian, but was actually what the government had in mind: "We feel it is providential that the launching of this educational program coincides with a noticeable swing of the pendulum back toward a realization of the need for greater 'Moral and Spiritual Values in Our Schools,' the exact title of a widely used booklet published by the National Education Association."[42]

Even in the favorable religious climate of the fifties, MIS was cautious in dealing with public schools. In a 1957 letter to the promotion department, Everest warned against promoting the general Gospel science films to the schools: "We can hope that they will be used in the schools but if we are put in the position of urging or arranging it, we are in a very vulnerable spot as far as our educational ministry is concerned. 'Schools' means public schools and the Gospel message has been deemed sectarian and thus illegal in many areas."[43] Although it was normal at the time to acknowledge the existence of God in the classroom, it was illegal to advocate for any particular faith, and an emphasis on Jesus would mark MIS films as evangelical. This restriction actually worked well with MIS's low-key evangelism, and it also served to keep other interpretations of Christianity out of the classroom. In a 1954 report to the American Scientific Affiliation, Everest wrote, "whether we like it or not, the teaching of Christ is considered sectarian . . . This sounds severe, but there is some good in it, too. If these schools were opened to the brethren of the First Baptist Church, would not the Mormons and Christian Scientists have equal right to mold our children's minds? We must therefore be careful not to criticize a ruling which protects us in this way."[44]

Wary of running afoul of the law, MIS had undertaken a preliminary study before launching the school program in 1954. It found most school superintendents were comfortable with science films that referred to God as "designer," "architect," or "creator," and 90 percent felt that saying "God" was also acceptable, provided there was no overtly sectarian message attached. By 1956, MIS films were used in 389 school systems in 46 states. In total, 1,734 prints had been purchased by U.S. schools.[45] But after the 1962 prayer ruling, even mentioning the "architect" or the "creator" was suspect. By 1963, MIS films were disappearing from public, government-funded spaces. The air force program was threatened when the ACLU began an investigation of military chaplains, challenging government expenditures for any kind of religious purpose,[46] and in 1966 the Washington State ACLU urged public school superintendents to withdraw MIS films.[47] MIS would thereafter redirect its efforts to church screenings in the United States and missionary use abroad.

VISUALIZING SALVATION

MIS films focused on the observable, avoiding the theoretical science that laypeople could never hope to penetrate. Physics, which had emerged as "the epitome of science itself" in the postwar years, was hardly accessible to the general public.[48] Gilbert contends that this inaccessibility was precisely what made nonscientists anxious:

Even the names of modern scientific theories could conjure an aura of misunderstanding and insecurity: the theory of relativity, the uncertainty principle, quantum physics, the principle of complementarity. What made these titles into potent metaphors was the implication that they described counterintuitive ideas. *They contradicted common sense*, which for most Americans was the basis of everyday scientific and technological thinking. The quality of uncertainty is exactly what the public identified with the new science. Consequently a certain portion of science—especially physics—was open only to a special few who could understand its opaque language and obscure theories.[49]

MIS would stay away from language and theories that seemed to violate common sense. This was not simply a populist strategy; it is the bedrock of creationism's argument against the theory of evolution.

Creationism emphasizes the visual and finds converts, in theory, by *showing* nonbelievers the truth. Here, of course, MIS was on the cutting edge, since their medium of expression—film—was inherently visual.

God of Creation shows beautiful time-lapse photographs of blooming flowers and cloud movements. Then the film moves to the microscopic world. As Gilbert notes, this film exhibits a "self-conscious preoccupation with using technology to enhance ordinary vision. Moon employed microscopes, unusual photographic techniques, and the telescope at Mount Palomar Observatory to increase the audience's range of sight. Armed with these augmentations, the viewer could 'see' the magnified patterns in nature. By making nature accessible in this visual fashion, Moon could reveal the concept of design and praise the works of the creator God."[50]

MIS prided itself on developing new photographic techniques that could capture previously unseen wonders, most notably the inside of an artificially beating dead heart for *Red River of Life*. After demonstrating how a heart functions with a plastic model, Moon says that "there is vital information that can be obtained only by looking directly inside an actual human heart while it is beating. Sounds impossible, doesn't it? Well, until recently, it has been impossible. But here at the Moody Institute of Science, working in cooperation with a famous heart surgeon, we have designed a means of viewing the heart under these exact conditions." He then walks over to a clear machine with a heart floating in it and says, "This is an actual human heart. Just a few hours ago it was pumping blood through the body of a living human being. Its owner willed his heart to medical science that we might study it and gain new knowledge of its living function" (fig. 36). Moon then shows us close-up shots taken on both sides of the valves. There are several moments of silence so that we can take in what we are seeing. Next, Moon changes the speed of the water pulsing through the heart, simulating high and low blood pressure and what a heart in shock looks like. This clinical torture of the specimen is rather gruesome (fig. 37). The heart reacts to Moon's manipulation exactly as one might expect. In other words, this elaborate demonstration reveals no "new knowledge." Its real importance is to show us the heart. In theory, only once we have *seen* an actual heart will we appreciate its majesty. Now Moon is ready to explicate the wonders of the red blood cell. He shows us an image generated by an IBM supercomputer of a mathematical model of the perfect blood cell. Moon displays the IBM image beside a model of an actual blood cell, and—no surprise—they are identical (fig. 38). Moon concludes once again that the visual marvels he has revealed could only be the product of "intelligent design," and he proceeds to a quick lesson about Christ's blood.

Moon's belief in the persuasive power of visual presentation had deep roots. As a young pastor in the early thirties, he had put together a demonstration called "The Microscope, the Telescope, and the Bible."

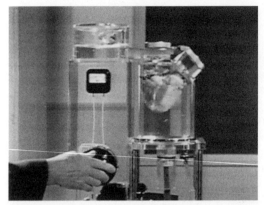

FIG. 36 THE MOODY INSTITUTE OF
SCIENCE BUILT A MACHINE TO
PUMP A DEAD HUMAN HEART.

FIG. 37 MOON DEMONSTRATES
THE EFFECTS OF HIGH BLOOD
PRESSURE ON THE HEART.

FIG. 38 MOON COMPARES A
MATHEMATICAL MODEL OF THE
PERFECT BLOOD CELL, GENER-
ATED BY AN IBM SUPER-
COMPUTER, WITH A MODEL
OF AN ACTUAL BLOOD CELL.

This would eventually be expanded into a stage show that included electronic, photographic, and stroboscopic devices, and finally refined into "Sermons from Science," a stage show he performed throughout the forties.[51] Sermons from Science provided dramatic visual presentations of God's wonders, much like MIS films did. The original title—"The Microscope, the Telescope, and the Bible"—provides a wonderful lens for bringing Moon's investment in the visual into focus. A microscope makes visible that which is too small for the naked eye to perceive; a telescope renders visible that which is too far away to perceive; and the Bible, in Moon's cosmology, reveals everything one needs to know about both the natural and the spiritual worlds. The Bible is both microscope and telescope, a tool to access answers to the most minute and the grandest questions. The Bible provided Moon with a kind of optics for his films.

Moon was not exactly consistent in his faith in the visual. He believed in vision as an ideal, while recognizing man's actual perceptual—and thus spiritual—weaknesses. While some MIS films emphasize the wonders of the eye or provide graphic images to illustrate God's salvation message (most bizarrely, Moon sending one million volts of electricity through his body), others emphasize human weakness. Weakness may function as a metaphor for sin, but Moon rarely uses that word, which again, illustrates his modern, nonfundamentalist approach. In *Windows of the Soul* (1960), Moon observes that our senses often trick us and that "the age of science was born when man quit trusting his senses and developed instruments to overcome their limitations." Thanks to the telescope, the microscope, and the Bible, man's weaknesses can be overcome. MIS's commonsense approach to science and salvation maintains that "seeing is believing" but that man cannot trust his own senses; he needs both technological and spiritual tools. *Voice of the Deep* (1956), for example, contends that just because we do not "see" God does not mean that he does not exist. Our weak human ears tell us that fish don't make noise, but special microphones prove that they do: use the Bible as your microphone!

Signposts Aloft (1967) offers a chilling illustration of Moon's interest in the frailty of human perception. Moon explains that the inner ear can provide misleading information to a pilot when he enters clouds, bad weather, or darkness and loses sight of the ground or the horizon. Moon plays a recording of a pilot flying in zero visibility, desperately beseeching aid from air traffic controllers, and finally screaming, "Help! Help! Help!" as he plummets to his death.

A pilot must have a visual reference that will override the false sensations coming from his other senses. The instrument pilot has this visual override. He can see because he has the instruments, which for him provide an even more precise reference than another pilot would have flying in clear weather . . . Before a pilot can fly solely by reference to instruments, he has to develop a unique skill that will allow the instruments to become a substitute for the normal visual reference. And he has to have a faith in those instruments that becomes a way of life.

We are now halfway into the film, and this is the first mention of "faith." Moon further emphasizes the importance of faith for the "instrument pilot": "If he feels like he's turning, and the instruments tell him he's flying straight, he believes the instruments. And then his vision overrides the false sensations, so that he isn't even conscious of them. This allows him to fly in complete safety, in conditions that would kill the noninstrument pilot." Moon then interviews astronaut John Glenn, who confirms the importance of "complete faith" in instruments. Moon illustrates this point with the story of a World War II plane that crash-landed in the Libyan desert, four hundred miles past its destination. The instruments had indicated that the plane had passed its destination hours ahead of schedule, but the seven soldiers in the plane did not believe this could be true. It turned out that the plane had been swept along in a powerful tailwind; the instruments were correct, and the seven soldiers died gruesome deaths in the desert. Moon even reads excerpts from the journals they kept as they were dying.

Having repeatedly emphasized the importance of faith in instruments, Moon is now ready in the final moments of the film to proceed to his salvation message. "On the instrument panel of every plane, and within every human heart and mind," he tells us, "these words should be deeply etched: there is a way that *seemeth* right unto a man, but the end thereof are the ways of death . . . When faced with several equally logical alternatives, we can't just trust the way we feel. At such times, man must have an accurate standard of reference." Once again, we find that science and faith are exactly the same: "This unshakable faith, that the universe is governed by unchanging laws, is the cornerstone of modern science. Now, there's just one area where man still clings to the outmoded idea that there are no absolute laws to guide him. This is the moral and spiritual, an area where man is making little if any progress, the one area where he refuses to accept a standard of reference outside himself." We cut to the tape machine playing "Help! Help! Help!" again, and Moon explains that "at that moment, the plane was being tracked on radar. All the instruments and electronic systems were working. The men on the ground were doing everything they could to help. But there was one all-important thing they could not do for the pilot. They couldn't believe for him." We do not all need to suffer this fate, however, because "God has provided a complete system for our moral and spiritual guidance. He has given us a handbook [*Moon picks up his Bible*] which describes his unchanging standards. And here, too, faith is the cornerstone of the system." The film ends with Moon and his son successfully landing their plane at night. High in the air, they trust only their instruments, but as the plane descends onto the runway, they use their eyes. That's why there are lights on the field. The vertical row of lights that Moon and his son look at as they land is cut across by a shorter horizontal line of lights about a third of the way down. The lights are in the shape of a cross. Coincidence? Nothing is coincidence in Moon's world.

Signposts Aloft teaches us that our perception is weak. Indeed, man is weak. But if we have faith our weakness will not have disastrous consequences. Even when the eye fails us, Moon's Biblical optics will save us. But were people really "saved" by watching these films? How did audiences respond?

THE AIR FORCE AUDIENCE

As of 1947, MIS films were shown under the auspices of the government's Character Guidance Program. Officially, the program was designed to develop "morality, spiritual values, and intelligent leadership in all Air Force Personnel."[52] In large part, this boiled down to an attempt to reduce venereal disease (VD) rates; while the program sought to develop character it placed "even greater emphasis on the ceaseless endeavor against promiscuity."[53] Recruits were to be given access to sports, library services, music, and other cultural activities. (After the first experimental basic training base was set up, soldiers in other units began to refer to the clean-cut recruits as "the Lace Panty Brigade."[54]) The base surgeon's duties under the Guidance Program included providing sex education and recommending condom use. Liquor consumption would be controlled, and passes would be denied to those who disregarded "accepted standards of clean living and good conduct." The surgeon was supposed to keep commanders "informed" concerning venereal disease, which presumably meant reporting men with VD so that they would be denied passes. Finally, the base would cooperate with local law enforcement agencies in suppressing prostitution. The chaplain was seen as the key moral adviser, and here is where MIS films, distributed via the chaplains' budget, came into play.

A Lackland Air Force Base chaplain's pamphlet that appears to date from the 1940s shows the centrality of the chaplain to the Character Guidance Program. The pamphlet is illustrated with a giant arrow indicating the path of the recruit. He starts at the reception center, where he is shown shaking hands with the chaplain. After basic orientation, he goes to chapel orientation. At this point, the chaplain writes a personal letter to the recruits' parents, then personally visits the recruit in the barracks. Basic training is followed by choir work, Sunday school, Bible classes, chapel services, lectures on citizenship and morality, and religious movies. Finally, the trained recruit is shipped out to his next destination, and the chaplain writes letters to the recruit's home church and to the chaplain at the next camp. Notwithstanding their concern about VD, many commanding officers probably resisted this scheme, as it would be hard to squeeze military training into a schedule already filled with choir practice and Sunday school. And it would be challenging, to say the least, for a chaplain to pull this routine off for every recruit. Screening religious movies, however, would have been easy since recruits could be shown the films en masse.

Although MIS films never actually addressed celibacy, air force chaplains testified in letters to the Institute that the films helped bring soldiers to Christ, which implied a strengthened character. It is difficult to gauge how effective the films actually were. After a 1949 series of screenings, the air force reported that chapel attendance rates went up 17.5 percent for three months. The VD rate, however, decreased a mere 0.33 percent. MIS still saw the films as a resounding success, as their own focus was on salvation. In a 1949 report, Wayne Hebert, who was traveling with the films, explained that "Being on the Air Force Character Guidance Program it is impossible to give an invitation to accept the Lord Jesus Christ as Personal Saviour. However, I was able to deliver a challenging message after each film, explaining the plan of salvation completely . . . At every service the Lord would give us greater and greater opportunities to lead the men to a saving knowledge of the Lord Jesus Christ."[55] Hebert excitedly wrote that MIS films were being screened in hospitals and military schools, and on battleships, army posts, and air force bases. He claimed that "in the Pentagon Building . . . the main conversation from Secretary of Defense Johnson down to the smallest janitor is: 'Have you seen *God of Creation, God of the Atom* and *Voice of the Deep?*'"[56] There are data on the numbers of air force viewers but not on how many soldiers made decisions for Christ, since inviting people to be saved was not permitted.

Curiously, however, we do have data on the late forties school audience. In 1947–1948, just under one million schoolchildren saw MIS films, and according to MIS records, there were 602 conversions.[57] As for television, MIS representatives could not record the conversion rate of viewers in private homes, but MIS was extremely optimistic about the potential of this new technology.

GOD OF THE CATHODE RAY TUBE

TELEVISION—soon to revolutionize the broadcasting industry . . . as well as the listening habits of the entire country. The very God who spoke and [made] the electron . . . a vital force, Whose laws enable finite Man to transmit the visual image, is the same God Whose wonders may soon be seen through the Moody Institute of Science on the magic television screen. Another 20th Century way of telling the 1st Century message![58]

After much planning, MIS began TV experiments in 1955. Evangelicals have, of course, used broadcasting since its inception. The first Christian radio broadcast was transmitted from Calvary Episcopal Church in 1921, and the Moody Bible Institute started WMBI in 1926.[59] Evangelical radio—and later TV—thrived thanks to its advocates' dogged perseverance and fundraising efforts and in spite of the roadblocks born-again broadcasters encountered in seeking access to the commercial networks. In the early 1930s, the FCC had ruled that the networks could satisfy their public service commitments through providing free airtime to religious groups. The Federal (later National) Council of Churches stepped in, distributing airtime mostly to Roman Catholic, Jewish, and mainline Protestant groups while generally denying access to evangelicals.[60] The "nonsectarian" MIS films, however, managed to get on television to satisfy public service requirements. The same soft-sell evangelistic tactics that got the films onto air force bases and into the public schools got them free TV time.

MIS films also presented themselves as a spiritual antidote to commercial TV programs, which were being singled out as causes of violence. MIS came to TV hot on the heels of the Kefauver Senate investigation of juvenile delinquency, which pointed the finger at TV and the "ideas that spring into the living room for the entertainment of the youth of America, which have to do with crime and with horror, sadism, and sex."[61] This was the perfect moment for proscience, pro-American, proreligious, sex-free, and violence-free TV. MIS was surely conscious of this when it sent a national mailing to pastors in 1955 that announced, "Here is good news for you! *Realizing the potentials of television for good,* the Moody Bible Institute is launching an eight-week series of TV programs."[62] A 1956 article in the *Chicago Tribune* quoted Moon as saying, "We hope with these films to help counteract the bad influence of so much violence and brutality seen on television."[63] Unlike later Christian groups such as the Moral Majority, or the contemporaneous Catholic Legion of Decency, MIS had never taken an interest in mainstream media. This certainly seemed to be an attempt to profit from the Kefauver climate.

In 1956, a series of 13 MIS films ran in 22 of the nation's 55 major TV markets, including the 10 largest. Because the films were broadcast during public service time on Sunday mornings, MIS evaluated their success not by the ratings but by viewer mail. They offered booklets at the end of each broadcast, and urged viewers to write letters. During the 1955 trial runs in Minnesota and Iowa, viewer response was low. A panicked Moon made a special appeal, saying, "We have no way of knowing how many are watching the program or if you feel it is of value and want it to continue . . . unless you tell us."[64] In a distraught letter to the Bible Institute, Moon wondered what factors could explain the lack of response. Could it be scheduling? Was the program a "turkey"? Or, perhaps, "the Christian public is not educated to letter response. [Or] . . . the Christian public can't or won't support a TV program."[65] In 1956, when the programs were scheduled at a better time, the letters started coming in at the rate of 1,000 per week.

Several viewers noted that the *Sermons from Science* series justified television ownership. One fan writes that "your series is the finest thing we view on television, and makes it worth having. Thank you; and we do praise God!" Another exclaims, "We were so amazed and pleased yesterday to see Dr. Moon with one of his Sermons from Science. *This is what I think television was invented for.*"[66] A third viewer goes so far as to tell Moon that "your program is the only reason we went and bought a TV set."[67] One letter writer even proposed that if *Sermons from Science* were rated by Nielsen, it would surpass the ratings of nonreligious shows: "If any program has the ability to 'buck' the *Ed Sullivan Show* and come out far on top, yours is the one."[68] In light of the positive response, MIS officials were optimistic about future television endeavors. They speculated that color TV would open another door. "Increasingly stations are setting up to transmit color programs. Many of these channels have requested color prints of *Sermons from Science*. Adjacency to network 'spectaculars' is very likely in many cases. Because of the scarcity of good color material for [free] public service time, we would most assuredly stand in an enviable position to get good, choice evening time."[69]

The *Sermons from Science* series was rerun several times in the late 1950s, but despite all their optimistic predictions for the future, MIS apparently did not reappear on U.S. TV thereafter. The reasons for the disappearance are not spelled out in any MIS archival documents, but it seems likely that the programs simply appeared dated by the 1960s, and that as production of new films dropped it was impossible to get together enough new shows for a thirteen-episode run.

Two other factors surely contributed to the demise of MIS television programs. First, in 1960, the FCC ruled that public service requirements could be satisfied with *paid* religious programs. Having been rejected by the National Council of Churches, evangelical broadcasters had spent thirty years acquiring stations and learning how to fundraise. These evangelicals could pay for time, so Jews, Roman Catholics, and mainline Protestants quickly lost their dominant position on television.[70] Ironically, now that evangelicals finally had airtime, the quietly evangelical MIS lacked the resources to compete with them financially. MIS began its gradual decline at the very moment that televangelism began its ascent.

Second, MIS lost its place on television because the American religious climate changed when the 1960s put the brakes on the postwar Judeo-Christian revival. As historians and religious studies scholars have argued, America didn't simply become "secularized" at this time. Rather, the contours of religion changed, marking the end of what Robert Wuthnow refers to as the "easy, taken-for-granted alliance between church and state."[71] Even a nonsectarian religious message would no longer fly on the TV networks.

After the 1950s, MIS films appeared on TV only outside of the United States. Details, unfortunately, are sketchy. MIS films were apparently first shown abroad in Australia in 1956. There were 3,384 MIS screenings in Australia in 1969, and the films were also shown on seventy-seven telecasts. In 1968, the Latin American television ministry was launched, and twenty-two countries saw MIS films on TV in Spanish and Portuguese. In 1970, MIS films were used in the earliest color broadcasts in Costa Rica, and around the same time, the films were televised during prime time in Jamaica, Brazil, Guatemala, Honduras, Ecuador, Peru, and Argentina. When Puerto Rico received its first TV satellite signal in 1977, the first program shown was MIS's *Dust or Destiny*. And a 1979 report noted that MIS films had also been shown on TV in Japan, Holland, Taiwan, Madagascar, and Norway. The same report explained that "behind the Iron Curtain, the films have received strong response . . . Two factors insure the increasing significance of Moody films in any global strategy for evangelism: the enormous respect for science and technology in Third World countries, and the culturally neutral content of the science films."[72] The films were, of course, far from "culturally neutral." Their proscience boosterism was born of a specific moment in postwar America, and their Christian message would certainly not appear "neutral" to Hindu or Muslim viewers.

SPACE-AGE EVANGELISM: THE SIXTIES AND BEYOND

By the early 1960s, financial difficulties forced MIS to significantly reduce film production and change its tactics. One of the most notable changes was their invention of a new distribution strategy, "space-age evangelism." There were few public school rentals or purchases of Moody films after the 1962 Supreme Court school prayer decision, which was a serious blow to MIS finances. To save money, MIS relocated from Los Angeles to Whittier, California, and revamped its distribution philosophy. Previously focused on finding unconverted audiences in schools and the military, in the 1960s MIS suddenly began to emphasize church rentals. The plan was to convince church members to show the films to unsaved friends, neighbors, and coworkers. In the 1968 annual report to the Bible Institute board of trustees, MIS explained: "We have always been concerned about the widespread emphasis in churches on the entertainment aspect of our Gospel-science films. Studying this problem in the early 1960s it was evident that emphasis on new production was a substantial part of the problem. To the churches we had been saying, 'Here is a new film Christians should *see*.' We initiated a change in emphasis, saying to Christians, 'Here are *many* films you should *use* to help you win your unsaved friends, neighbors and business associates to Christ.'"[73] Even though the unsaved had always been the most desirable target viewers, MIS films had also been shown in evangelical churches as entertainment. Now, MIS would find ways to help churches use the films for evangelistic outreach. Space-age evangelism was clearly a strategic response to the dramatic decline of the military, television, and school audiences.

Space-age evangelism, as an eponymous instructional film strip explained, encouraged evangelicals to show MIS films to unsaved friends in their backyards, in parking lots, at work, and on college campuses. The idea was that *anyone* could rent an MIS film and use it as an evangelical tool. In response, church rentals rose, 1968s figures surpassing those of 1967 by 14.5 percent, and reaching, in fact, an all-time high. But rentals were up only in churches. Although space-age evangelism was relatively cost-efficient—really just a new marketing tactic—the concomitant drive to increase international distribution included the dubbing of old MIS films into foreign languages, which was an expensive endeavor. The bottom line was that MIS's net loss for 1967 was over $70,000; they lost almost $150,000 in 1968. The glory days were over.

As sales and rentals of MIS films declined, the space-age gimmick was an attempt to appear "with it," not an unreasonable gambit given that the 1960s saw the birth of "Jesus freaks." While other hippies did drugs and protested Vietnam, the Jesus longhairs were being baptized in the Pacific Ocean. The existence of the freaks seemed to point to the possibility that Christianity and the counterculture were not utterly antithetical. Space-age evangelism would cut new production costs but also be the "key" to a new generation:

To open a locked heart and mind, a key is more effective than a sledge hammer. Christ used keys. To the woman at the well He was The Water of Life; to the hungry—The Bread; to the farmer—The Vine. He spoke to people in terms of their interests and everyday experience. If Christ were here today He would speak to men about space travel, nuclear power and go on to tell them about the power of the Gospel to transform a human life.[74]

By speaking about space travel and nuclear power and having screenings in parking lots and on the beach, space-age evangelists would bring the Gospel to people who would never set foot in a church or get dressed up for a service. As the MIS newsletter, *Reel Report,* explained in 1968, space-age evangelism might be an effective modern way to "bring hippies to Christ."[75] Space-age evangelism was not designed exclusively to speak to youth, though. Feedback from space-age evangelists indicates that middle-class, middle-aged suburbanites often showed the films to neighbors in their backyards. Corporate screenings also picked up at this time thanks to the space-age initiative. *Signposts Aloft* was shown repeatedly at a McDonnell Douglas Corporation aircraft factory in 1969,[76] and total attendance for these lunchtime screenings exceeded 20,000.[77]

MIS had managed to keep going in the 1960s by reducing production and focusing on new distribution and marketing strategies. By the 1970s, though, things were not looking good, and production slowed to a snail's pace. In 1989, the California MIS offices, laboratories, and film development facilities where shut down. The downsized MIS was relocated to Chicago and became the Moody Bible Institute's video distribution arm. MIS began to commission inspirational films to distribute. These films evoked the earlier MIS tradition only by including nature scenes. They lacked a scientific edge, and their Gospel message became more aggressive. Other popular releases included Christian self-help videos and a prolife video, *The Hidden Holocaust* (1985), featuring Chuck Colson. Today's Moody Institute of Science has been renamed "Moody Video." The old MIS headquarters were filled with incubators, test tubes, film equipment, Geiger counters, and men in lab coats. Moody Video is a large business office filled with file cabinets, ringing telephones, computers, and administrators in suits.

MIS AND THE RISE OF MODERN CREATION SCIENCE

Moon was a pioneer in evangelical film production, and he succeeded in finding a means of distributing and exhibiting his independent productions outside of conventional Hollywood channels. To some extent, then, contemporary evangelical media producers are carrying on a tradition started by Moon. On the other hand, Moon never wavered from being "in the world but not of the world." He tempered his message, but much less than many of today's Christian musicians have. And he didn't attempt to sneak his ideas into the mainstream, as chastity promoters have done by seeking federal funding for "abstinence," their secular version of chastity. Like the producers of *VeggieTales* and other apolitical Christian entertainment videos, Moon also avoided politics. In this way, he differs strikingly from the creationists producing today's Christian scientific videos. Creationist activists attack evolution and argue for "equal time" in public school curricula for "creation science," which they claim is not religious doctrine but rather a set of scientific facts supporting "intelligent design." Modern creationists invite the controversy that MIS so assiduously avoided.

But modern creationists do owe a debt to Moon and the institute. The Bible Institute's president Houghton was a founder of—and Moon was a consultant for—the American Scientific Association (ASA), a group of fifty evangelical scientists who assembled in 1941 to discuss the relationship between facts and faith. According to historian Ronald L. Numbers, the ASA was actually Moon's idea.[78] This was a novel attempt to create a place for evangelical engagement in scientific thinking. In the early twentieth century, fundamentalist preacher Billy Sunday had declared that "when the word of God says one thing and scholarship says another, scholarship can go to hell."[79] Attempting to undo the anti-intellectual legacy of Sunday and other fundamentalists, the ASA sought to forge a peaceful coexistence between evangelicalism and scholarship. F. Alton Everest, ASA president from 1941 to 1951 and associate director of MIS, explained that "the [ASA] membership shared a basic Christian faith plus a desire to seek the truth between the many conflicting scientific and scriptural interpretations."[80] Like ASA, MIS consciously avoided taking sides in the in-fighting among creationists over issues such as the age of the earth. This was also a tactical decision, as secular audiences would be unlikely to take seriously films that claimed that the earth was only 10,000 years old or that humans and dinosaurs had lived on earth at the same time. An early document explaining the MIS rationale stated that it was important "to keep the name of MBI [Moody Bible Institute] and MIS from becoming a 'laughing stock' to scientists or Christians due to unwise pronouncements in controversial fields. If wisely and conservatively handled, however, a tremendous task lies before us without the necessity of taking any sides whatsoever."[81]

As MIS began its decline in the 1960s, a group of dissident scientists broke away from the ASA to form the Creation Research Society, which sought a "fixed interpretation of science and scripture."[82] This group would become the seed of the modern American creationist movement. According to Numbers, Henry Morris, an engineer and one of the society's founders, was first convinced of "the importance of harmonizing science and the Bible" when he saw one of Moon's Sermons from Science in 1942. "From the itinerant Moody preacher he learned for the first time about the geological effects of Noah's flood and the vapor canopy that had enveloped the earth until the deluge."[83] Unlike Moon's organization, however, Morris's creationist group insisted on a rigid, literalist interpretation of the relationship between facts and the Bible. MIS's "conservative" approach of not taking sides had actually made MIS, like the ASA, too liberal for Morris's group. The Creation Research Society later became the Institute for Creation Research (ICR), which is currently a prominent creationist research laboratory, providing many of the facts that fuel modern creationism as a political movement. In a stark break from the MIS emphasis on biology and zoology, the modern antievolution argument focuses on geology. William Jennings Bryan famously declared that he was more interested in the Rock of Ages than the age of rocks.[84] Now, thanks to the ICR, the age of rocks has taken center stage in arguments against evolution.

MIS films and contemporary creation science videos do have one thing in common: an emphasis on logic and reason. Both seem to set up conversion experiences devoid of emotion. As one man who relates his engineering work to his creationist beliefs explains, "The more I understand electron theory, the more I become persuaded of an intelligence behind it. I was an electronics instructor before I was a believer. I was converted while I was in electronics . . . it reinforced my belief in an intelligent, ordered universe."[85] This discourse is dramatically different from the emotional, moral rhetoric of evangelical testimonials in chastity videos or contemporary Christian music. This convert did not appear to experience an epiphanic moment of salvation when the Holy Spirit filled his heart. On the contrary, it was his *mind* that was filled with God, in a rational manner; men who discover God through studying science are unlikely to shed tears or make other "feminine" emotional signs.[86]

As with MIS, today's creation science media emphasize common sense and visual observation. While the new creationists showed little interest in costly film production, they began to produce cheap film strips and slide shows for classrooms in the sixties. Today there are numerous creationist videos, as well as books, cassettes, pamphlets, and school supplies such as posters and overhead projector transparencies. The ICR and other groups have produced four genres of creationist videos: lectures, debates, short dramas, and nature documentaries. These materials are used primarily in four contexts: Christian home schooling, Christian schools, adult discussion groups, and, occasionally, public schools. Videos used in public schools attempt to substantiate the events of Genesis with scientific evidence, but without directly citing Scripture.[87]

As in MIS films, today's creationist media accentuate the visual. Most creationist videos promote the idea that evolution cannot be proven because it cannot be seen.[88] In particular, we cannot witness the moment when life began, whether in a primordial soup or by grace of God. In *When Two Worldviews Collide* (1995), a teenager asks a creationist geologist what he should believe about the Big Bang. The geologist tells him,

You might be surprised to know that the Big Bang idea is really just a philosophy more than a science . . . The scientific method has to do with observation. You gather your data. You collect your facts. You run your experiments. You make your measurements. Those *observations*, that's science. That happens in the present. But the Big Bang, if it happened at all, it happened in the *unobserved* past, and therefore it's not really in the same category as observational science. The Big Bang, it's primarily just a mathematical model of history. It's certainly not an observation. And that's just not empirical science. I predict it will be totally dead in a few years. Meantime, don't be intimidated by it.[89]

While MIS films verified the existence of God by emphasizing that which could be seen, this video emphasizes what cannot be seen—the Big Bang. MIS films would never have overtly attacked any theory widely accepted by secular scientists. ICR videos not only attack mainstream theories but go so far as to posit that there is a conspiracy among scientists to deceive schoolchildren by teaching them, via evolution, that there is no God. In *When Two Worldviews Collide* the geologist explains that "two worldviews are at war, two belief systems. Many leaders in education, the textbook writers and the university professors, they consider themselves to be *evangelists* for this naturalistic, humanistic religion [evolution], and they'll use any tricks at their disposal to win converts."[90] Evolutionary evangelists, according to this video and others, advocate premarital sex, physician-assisted suicide, divorce, homosexuality, and abortion. Contemporary creationist videos, in sum, seem to mirror a key change in evangelical culture since the seventies, and since the demise of MIS, the move toward increasing political engagement. Creationist media now use militaristic rhetoric, repeatedly emphasizing that creationists and evolutionists are engaged in a "battle for the mind." *When Two Worldviews Collides* concludes by telling viewers, "Arm your family and your church" by using ICR newsletters, books, videos, and seminars.

Anthropologist Christopher P. Toumey explains that creationism has undermined its potential for outreach "by being too blatantly sectarian, thereby leaving the creationists and their preachers to persuade their congregations of what they already believe."[91] The history of creationist media, then, presents an interesting paradox. From the postwar years through the 1960s, MIS films sought to save souls with science, avoiding politics altogether. Yet as evangelicals have increasingly entered the political fray, and as the Christian Right has gained political power since the seventies, creationist books, videos, and magazines are often so dogmatic they seem likely to turn off nonconverts. The staunch inerrant attitude of many of these videos seems more in line with separatism than worldly political and social engagement. Some of the videos set up a "debate" between evolution and creation, but it is clear that creation will win, and there is no room for a compromise such as the idea that God created evolutionary processes. This limits the potential of creation science to find converts, religious or political.[92] With his gently tempered approach to salvation, conversely, Moon reached out beyond his fellow believers.

Despite their stylistic difference, both past and present creationist media depend upon the Bible as a "nonfiction" text—or textbook—containing God's plan. As the next chapter will show, Christian apocalyptic media also interpret the Bible as an infallible blueprint. But whereas creationists use the Bible to explain the past, apocalyptic thinkers use it to explain the world's future. And, according to their predictions, it doesn't look good.

CHAPTER SIX

PRAYING FOR THE END OF THE WORLD:

THE PAST, PRESENT, AND FUTURE OF

CHRISTIAN APOCALYPTIC MEDIA

In the final months of 1999, Y2K anxiety reached a fever pitch in America. The nightly news gave regular updates on how to safeguard personal computers, and the Sunday *New York Times* featured articles on how the rich were hoarding canned goods to prepare gourmet dishes that did not require refrigeration. Meanwhile, in movie theaters, a few films tried to tap into the zeitgeist. The Arnold Schwarzenegger apocalyptic thriller *End of Days* (Hyams, 1999) told the story of a cop who hits the bottle after his family is gunned down. An atheist, he finds redemption by helping a virgin whom Satan intends to impregnate on New Year's Eve. Gabriel Byrne, playing Lucifer with panache, engages in a ménage à trois with his henchman's wife and daughter and blows stuff up by setting his own thick black urine on fire.

Another apocalyptic flick, *The Omega Code* (Marcarelli, 1999), was also released just before the dawn of the new millennium. In this film, Michael York portrays the Antichrist as "a fictional cross between . . . Romano Prodi, current president of the European Commission, and Rupert Murdoch."[1] He has brought about global peace, and the world is ready to worship him as the new Messiah. Our feeble hero (played by Casper Van Dien) is a New Age motivational speaker who rejected God after his mother was killed by a drunk driver. He hides Biblical decoder disks from the Antichrist and is ultimately redeemed when he asks Jesus to save him. This was the first Christian apocalyptic feature to receive a nationwide theatrical release.

Omega Code is an odd piece of the jigsaw puzzle that is American popular culture. On the one hand, it is a typical Hollywood product, an apocalyptic film with lots of action and a lost-yet-redeemable hero. On the other hand, none of the characters are truly loathsome, especially not Michael York's clean-cut villain, who has no interest in using dirty words, much less raping virgins. This PG-13 Antichrist could only (maybe) frighten a born-again Christian already versed in end-of-the-world eschatology. If you weren't already an evangelical, you probably wouldn't realize that the hero's plea—"Save me, Jesus," shouted as computer-generated demons swirl around him—is supposed to represent a born-again experience. As a number of disappointed Christian viewers have pointed out, this is the only overt mention of Jesus in the whole film.[2]

Irwin Moon's scientific films may have constituted "soft-sell" evangelism, but by the end, viewers had no doubt that these films were about salvation. By comparison, *Omega Code* is a bit fuzzy, and in this respect it is representative of a major change in Christian media as it grows beyond its small-time roots: the tempering of salvation messages. As we have already seen, some of the most profitable evangelical media products can be interpreted as Christian by believers but enjoyed simply as entertainment by nonbelievers. Today's apocalyptic filmmakers aspire to make blockbusters, but they have not struck the right balance between Biblical messages and entertainment.

The secular press panned *Omega Code*, but more for its poor script and acting than for its muted spiritual message. Journalists tended to define this film as something *outside* of popular culture that had *intruded into* the secular mainstream. While conceding that conservative Christians had carried this film to respectable box office returns, reviewers saw *The Omega Code* as a mere curiosity, not a film of potential appeal to millions of Americans fascinated by the Book of Revelation and what evangelicals call "prophecy theology."

This was a serious error. *The Omega Code* is, indeed, a snoozer, but Christian apocalyptic belief is in no way a marginal phenomenon. There are as many as sixty million born-again Christians in America; widespread interest (if not universal belief) in prophecy is a fact of American popular culture, and apocalyptic books routinely fly off the shelves of U.S. bookstores. Nor is this popularity a recent development: the "prophecy consultant" for *Omega Code* was Hal Lindsey, whose "nonfiction" classic of 1970, *The Late Great Planet Earth*, is still in print and has sold over 28 million copies.[3] Tapping into Cold War fears of nuclear annihilation, Lindsey's book "systematically went through the apocalyptic scriptures mechanically transcribing every phrase and image into the vocabulary of Pentagon strategists."[4] Lindsey found predictions of the Apocalypse throughout the Bible, though like most prophecy authors his primary sources were the Book of Revelation, Daniel, and Ezekiel.

Prophecy books continue to top the bestseller lists, although they are now usually classified as fiction rather than nonfiction. Among the "nonfiction" bestsellers was *The Bible Code* (1997), which loosely inspired *Omega Code*.[5] Tim LaHaye and Jerry Jenkins produced eight novels for their Left Behind series between 1995 and 2001; by July 2001 the series had collectively sold 28.8 million copies.[6] When the ninth book appeared, in 2002, sales for the series climbed past fifty million.[7] (The spike in sales can partly be attributed to the all-around success of prophecy books after the terrorist attacks of September 11, 2001.[8])

Like most prophecy novelists, LaHaye and Jenkins tell the story of the Rapture: saved people are suddenly removed from the earth; the Antichrist rises to power and torments newly converted Christians during seven years of "Tribulation"; and, finally, after the Battle of Armageddon, the Second Coming of Christ occurs. But instead of telling the whole story in one book, as others have done, LaHaye and Jenkins draw it out over several volumes, thereby increasing their profits. LaHaye and Jenkins sold the film rights for the first book, and pondered developing a TV series. In August 1999, book six, *Assassins,* debuted on the *New York Times* bestseller list at number two, which is all the more remarkable given that the *Times* does not even count Christian bookstore sales. In less than a week *Assassins* sold almost one million copies.[9] The seventh book, *The Indwelling,* became the first Christian novel ever to reach number one on the *Times*'s bestseller list.[10] Book eight, *The Mark,* had an initial printing of 2.5 million copies in November 2001. By then, the series had already spun off T-shirts, books-on-tape, a radio series, a board game, and a very successful children's book series, Left Behind: The Kids, which was marketed as a Christian version of *Goosebumps* (figs. 39–40). The series was supposed to conclude with volume twelve in 2003, but by 2001 LaHaye had expressed interest in developing prequels.

Apocalyptic fiction sells, in part, because it is exciting. But it also claims to dramatize Biblical truths, which are, of course, of vital interest to evangelicals, who emphasize the individual's ability to study and understand the Bible without priestly intervention. That's easier said than done. Without instruction, the Book of Revelation is quite simply indecipherable. What is one to make of verses like, "I saw a woman sit upon a scarlet-colored beast, full of names of blasphemy, having seven heads and ten horns" (Rev. 17:3 AV)? Mainline Protestants interpret Revelation symbolically,[11] but evangelicals take a more literal approach. To decipher difficult passages, they turn to their pastors, televangelists, fiction and nonfiction books, films, and videos. Apocalyptic media have three apparent goals: to show Christians, in an entertaining way, what will happen after the Rapture while also instructing them in the specifics of prophecy theology (thereby confirming Bibli-

**LEFT BEHIND™
ORANGE EARTH T-SHIRT**
You'll be prepared for the Rapture with this special T-shirt inspired by the bestselling series, *Left Behind*™! Marked with the important message "Don't Be Left Behind" on the front, and the clarion call of "The Future is Clear" on the back, this 100% preshunk cotton shirt sends a solid message of Christian vision. *Available in Black XL only.*
T-Shirt 085837 • $19.99

PEOPLE GET READY: Various Artists
Are you prepared in your heart and soul for the return of Christ? Well now you can get ready with this special musical collection inspired by the bestselling fiction series *Left Behind*™. The lineup of artists who take you on a journey through your own heart and into the Spirit of God reads like a who's who of modern Christian music: Dove Award Winner **Michael W. Smith**, young superstar **Rebecca St. James**, hit rockers **dc Talk** and **Big Tent Revival**, contemporary legends **Crystal Lewis** and **Geoff Moore**, plus a host of others. This unique CD is enhanced with features playable through your computer CD-ROM. Forefront.
CD 325597 • $15.98

Please use your Member Reply Form to order.
Music, video and merchandise offerings are a service of your book club. Please note that purchases from this brochure do not count toward your membership book commitment and cannot be combined with any other special offer. Shipping and handling will be added to your order. Supplies are limited. Book Club Service Center, 6550 E. 30th Street, P.O. Box 6325, Indianapolis, IN 46206-6325, (317) 541-8920, 8:00 AM - 6:00 PM (EST) or e-mail us at service@memberservice.com

HAVE YOU BEEN LEFT BEHIND?

Experience life after The Rapture with this unique video based on the blockbuster novel *Left Behind*™!

In their bestselling series, *Left Behind*™, authors **Tim LaHaye** and **Jerry B. Jenkins** take readers into the End Times as Jesus whisks His faithful up to Heaven. However, the good people who did not believe in Christ are not left without hope.

In *Left Behind*™, survivors of the Rapture find a video that contains instructions and encouragement for those who would stand against Satan's spreading evil. This video becomes their lifeline to Heaven, giving hope to those left behind.

Now you can see that very same video, taken directly from the pages of the novel! *Have You Been Left Behind?* speaks directly to the characters in the series, so you will get to experience what the world will be like during the Tribulation. It is filmed to capture the turmoil that the characters themselves are living through, as if they are actually holding the camera and filming their stories.

If you are a fan of **LaHaye** and **Jenkins**' masterwork or new to the Bible-based fictional series that has taken the world by storm, this video is a must-have! It is 20 minutes of gripping drama that will change your life.
VHS 273615 • $12.95

A113

FIGS. 39–40 LEFT BEHIND MERCHANDISE.

cal truth); to frighten people into conversion by showing them the bleak future that awaits the unraptured; and to convert those "left behind" after the Rapture. Some marketers advise Christians to keep copies of apocalyptic books and videos (along with the Bible) in their homes so that potential converts will discover them during the seven-year Tribulation period.

Nonevangelicals are perplexed by prophecy theology and the idea that the Antichrist is *real,* not just a villain in a secular thriller. I am less interested in the truth-value of prophetic narratives than in their role in contemporary evangelical culture and the wider media marketplace. The films seek to convert viewers, but their methods have shifted over the years. Whereas early apocalyptic films focused on personal transformation and were shown almost exclusively in churches, now films are seeking a place in multiplexes and, not surprisingly, making theological compromises along the way. This chapter charts the history of Christian feature filmmaking, examining the complicated push and pull between two objectives: making profits and saving souls. Many of today's evangelical producers—unlike earlier filmmakers such as Moon and the Rev. Billy Graham—would argue that these objectives are symbiotic: if more people watch (and pay) more will be saved. So to reach secular audiences, contemporary filmmakers have diluted their salvation messages, and the resulting films are peculiar. The producers believe that these films are palatable to a mass audience. But even though they don't mention Jesus, nonevangelical viewers easily identify and dismiss them as religious films. While Christian music and music videos, as well as series like *VeggieTales,* have succeeded in exploiting religious ambiguity to speak to evangelical and nonevangelical audiences, contemporary apocalyptic films have *attempted* but, for the most part, *failed,* to be ambiguous.

THE ROOTS OF CHRISTIAN FEATURES: WORLD WIDE PICTURES, THE CROSS AND THE SWITCHBLADE, AND A THIEF IN THE NIGHT

The maverick in early Christian film production—after Irwin Moon, of course—was Billy Graham. He formed World Wide Pictures in 1952 to produce and distribute evangelical films and television programs. By 1984, the company had produced over 125 films of various lengths (including twenty features), which were translated into seventeen languages and distributed in over one hundred countries.[12] World Wide Pictures produced the first theatrically released Christian film, *The Restless Ones* (Ross, 1965). But like most Christian films of the 50s and 60s, Graham's productions were usually shown in churches. Today, the company focuses mostly on made-for-TV movies shown on independent (usually televangelical) stations. World Wide's standard practice is to release films to churches, region by region, over a three-year period, and to promote them locally rather than nationally.[13]

Graham's movies typically present themselves as dramatic nonfiction. They often portray the life of a real Christian who has triumphed over adversity, and like Moody Institute of Science films, they take a subtle approach to their evangelism, postponing the strong salvation message until the end. *Wiretapper* (Ross, 1955) is a classic early example. This suspense film is based on the real-life story of Jim Vaus, an electronic genius who produces clever alarm systems, bugs, and wiretaps for the mob. His wife urges him to attend church with her, but he is uninterested. He finally realizes that he cannot keep his family together if he stays with the mob, but he's in too deep. His family will be killed if he tries to escape. As he desperately attempts to deliver his wife to safety, he happens to drive past a billboard advertising Billy Graham's Crusade. Jim and his wife stop, and the film here includes footage of Graham preaching at his 1949 Crusade. Needless to say, Jim is saved. *Wiretapper* is a fairly entertaining, low-budget thriller, a B-movie with a message.

Graham's two biggest hits were *Joni* (Collier, 1979) and *The Hiding Place* (Collier, 1975). Like *Wiretapper,* both films were based on the lives of real people, Joni Eareckson and Corrie Ten Boom, who had written bestselling spiritual autobiographies. Eareckson and Ten Boom were, in fact, Christian celebrities. *Joni* stars Eareckson as herself; it is the story of a courageous paraplegic's struggle with her faith. When she encounters a bitter, disabled Vietnam vet, played stiffly by a handsome man with an eye patch, Joni has her breakthrough. She declares, "I would rather be in this chair knowing Him than on my feet without Him, and I never really knew that until this moment." Echoing *Wiretapper,* Joni gives her testimony at a Billy Graham crusade, and Graham himself briefly appears. (The relentless insertion of crusade scenes in Graham's pictures irritated a *Christianity Today* critic: "There ought to be a way to present the Biblical message without the telltale 'And now a word from our sponsor.'"[14]) Near the end, Eareckson also directly addresses viewers and invites them to be saved.

The Hiding Place is about a Dutch Christian, Corrie Ten Boom (played by Jeanette Clift), who helps Jews hide from the Nazis during World War II. She and her family are finally sent to a prison camp, where Corrie struggles to keep her faith, while her sister (played by Julie Harris) preaches to other prisoners. While Ten Boom was too old to play herself, the film ends with footage of her testimony (this time without Graham). Ten Boom's presence, like Eareckson's, validates the film—and, by extension its salvation message—as indisputable nonfiction. Although the films lack scientific discourse, it almost seems that Vaus, Eareckson, and Ten Boom are held up like Moon's bats and flowers as empirical proof of the necessity of accepting Jesus as one's personal savior.[15] The film was reviewed in the secular press, and Jeanette Clift was nominated for a Golden Globe "Best Newcomer" award. There was even speculation that Clift and Harris would also receive Academy Award nominations. When they did not, the film's director "realized that being outside the major studio system, 'the club,' World Wide would never be able to play at the club's table."[16]

Though not made under the auspices of Graham's organization, *The Cross and the Switchblade* (Murray, 1970) was produced by Dick Ross, a World Wide Pictures director. Like *A Thief in the Night* (Thompson, 1972), it is widely considered a Christian film classic. The film opens with a shot of the sun setting behind the Manhattan Bridge. An authoritative voice-over intones: "If the story you are about to see were the product of a writer's imagination, you might label it unbelievable. But these events actually took place in the streets and alleys and in the tenements where we filmed them—in the shadow of the bridge." We cut to a close-up of a switchblade opening, and we see gang members brutally beat a man. The film—starring Pat Boone as Rev. Wilkerson and Eric Estrada as gang leader Nicky Cruz—dramatizes the life of a real pastor who preached to gang members and drug addicts in the inner city (fig. 41). The film is striking in its vivid depiction of sin, always a challenge for Christian media producers. Profanity is used when necessary to heighten a scene's grittiness. Moreover, we see junkies shoot up, hippies smoke pot, and even a brief make-out session. Nicky tells Rosa, a heroin addict and a "deb" who "belongs to the whole gang," that the preacher is trying to bust up the gang. If Wilkerson succeeds no one will be around to help her get her fix. "You'll have to whore for your habit," he says. Nicky sends Rosa to get rid of the preacher, and when she asks how, he responds, "Kill him, scare him, ball him. I don't care" (figs. 42–43). This is tough stuff for a Christian movie. The film contains a number of hokey moments, but it earnestly tries to show how down-and-out gang members suffer before they are saved. And by the end, of course, they are saved (fig. 44). The movie has a moderate budget, is decently acted, and contains a few stylistic flourishes. With the presence of Pat Boone and its tough portrayal of drugs and violence, *The Cross and the Switchblade* has been a hit over the years, screened around the world and translated into over twenty-five languages.

The first Christian filmmaker to turn to prophecy theology was Donald Thompson. When Thompson began making his apocalyptic pictures in the 1970s, *The Cross and the Switchblade* and Graham's productions

FIG. 41 *ERIC ESTRADA STARS AS CONFUSED GANG LEADER NICKY CRUZ IN THE CLASSIC CHRISTIAN FILM, THE CROSS AND THE SWITCHBLADE.*

FIG. 42 *THE CROSS AND THE SWITCHBLADE IS MORE GRAPHIC IN ITS PORTRAYAL OF SIN THAN MOST EVANGELICAL FILMS. HERE, ROSA HAS ACCEPTED JESUS AND KICKED HER HEROIN HABIT BUT HAS A BRIEF RELAPSE AND SHOOTS UP.*

FIG. 43 *ROSA THINKS HER HEROIN HAS BEEN CUT, BUT AC-TUALLY THE DRUG NO LONGER WORKS, SINCE NOW SHE IS FILLED WITH JESUS.*

FIG. 44 PAT BOONE, AS REV. WILKERSON, FINALLY GETS THROUGH TO THE GANG MEMBERS AT THE CLIMAX OF THE CROSS AND THE SWITCHBLADE.

were the only models for high-quality 16mm pictures. Rather than focusing on historical characters, Thompson's four prophecy films spin contemporary action-adventure stories around the apocalyptic events that many evangelicals believe are predicted in the Bible. Like Moon and Graham, Thompson emphasizes the nonfictional quality of his films. Everything he's showing will *really* happen, he contends. Although it was never released in conventional theaters, the first film in Thompson's series, *A Thief in the Night*, "has been translated into three foreign languages, subtitled in countless others, and its international distribution continues strongly . . . six or seven hundred prints now circulate, in addition to videocassettes."[17] Randall Balmer explains that,

In the United States, where distribution is limited to church groups, camps, youth organizations, and the like, it is difficult to quantify the number of people who have seen the film. When I pressed Russell Doughten [the film's coproducer] for a figure, he reluctantly estimated that one hundred million people had seen *A Thief in the Night* in the United States, a figure, he hastened to add, that would include those who had seen it more than once. Even if you slash that number in half to account for hyperbole, fifty million is still a staggering figure, a viewership that would be the envy of many Hollywood producers.[18]

But Hollywood producers would hardly approve of the usual ticket price: an optional donation. This was the norm for Christian films in the prevideo days. They were made on small budgets, distributed on 16mm, shown in churches, and usually advertised only in Christian publications. They were also unambiguously evangelical, even if the strong salvation message was deferred until the end, as in most of Graham's films. There was no need to dilute the message. After all, audience members who had not yet made a decision for Christ had at least decided to watch a movie in church: they knew what they were in for. Yet subtlety, most producers assumed, was important. A gentle film would open the hearts and minds of unsaved viewers.

Thompson dispenses with subtlety. Instead of first softening up viewers by raising moral and spiritual issues, then moving on to a more detailed Gospel message, Thompson deluges viewers with scare tactics and Biblical exegesis. The souls left on earth after evangelicals are raptured suffer tremendously. All of humanity is asked to take the Mark of the Beast, 666, imprinted as a barcode on the forehead or right hand. Without the mark you cannot buy or sell. People who accept Christ into their hearts refuse the mark and become martyred "saints." The world becomes increasingly chaotic, and even those who have taken the mark suffer. This is complicated stuff, and I present only the bare-bones version here.[19] In fact, evangelical interpretations of Biblical prophecy are so complex that several films in Thompson's series actually grind to a halt as a character uses a giant wall chart to explain the most perplexing passages from Daniel, Ezekiel, and Revelation.

The protagonist of the first two films, *A Thief in the Night* and *A Distant Thunder* (Thompson, 1978), is Patty, a nonbeliever whose husband was raptured. Patty believes in God but has not been born again. Although she will not take the Mark of the Beast, she is also reluctant to give her heart to Jesus. At the end of the second film, she is dragged screaming to a guillotine. At the beginning of the third film, *Image of the Beast* (Thompson, 1981) her head is chopped off shortly after she screams, "I want the mark!" (Figs. 45–47). Patty has finally made her choice, and she will pay the price for all eternity.

Image of the Beast introduces a new hero, a saved man who moves the series away from the horror and melodrama that drove the first two films. Although the hero has a female companion whom he tries to convert, this and the final film in the series, *The Prodigal Planet* (Thompson, 1983), do not ask audiences to identify so strongly with a struggling, unsaved protagonist. Much of the second half of the series is devoted to witnessing and Scripture-quoting, but it is done *by* instead of *to* the protagonist.

All four of Thompson's films largely ignore politics. Through his organization, UNITE, the Antichrist torments Christians and rules the world. But the Antichrist is not an important character in the four films. In fact, he only appears once in the entire series. The United Nations and other global organizations may be in cahoots with him, but Thompson's main point is that the Rapture could happen at any moment, and unimaginable suffering is in store for those who are not raptured. God's grace is the ticket to heaven. So get saved now! (figs. 48–49). This may also be the implicit message of contemporary apocalyp-

FIGS. 45–46 PATTY SEES THE FATE THAT AWAITS THOSE WHO REFUSE TO TAKE THE MARK OF THE BEAST IN THOMPSON'S SECOND PROPHESY FILM, A DISTANT THUNDER

FIG. 47 THOMPSON'S SCARE TACTICS: THE FINAL FREEZE FRAME OF A DISTANT THUNDER

FIGS. 48–49 BEFORE AND AFTER THE RAPTURE: LIKE MOST PROPHESY FILMS, A THIEF IN THE NIGHT EMPHASIZES THAT THE RAPTURE COULD HAPPEN AT ANY TIME.

tic films, but it is now sandwiched into plots that focus on action, intrigue, and global politics at least as much as on individual spiritual introspection.

It would be hard to overstate the influence of Thompson's films on evangelical culture. Today, many teen evangelicals have not seen *A Thief in the Night*, but virtually every evangelical over thirty I've talked to is familiar with it, and most have seen it. Christian viewers discussing *Left Behind: The Movie* (Sarin, 2000) in on-line discussion forums have taken *A Thief in the Night* as a touchstone. Focus on the Family film reviewer Steven Isaac, for example, says kids may be scared by *Left Behind: The Movie*, "just like *A Thief in the Night* scared the dickens out of me when I was a kid."[20] In fact, evangelicals who grew up in the 1970s and early 1980s often cite *Thief* as a source of childhood terror, in part because the film shows people who *think* they are saved but are not and are therefore not raptured with their families. Interestingly, for every person who says this film drove them away from the church for good, there is another who says he or she was saved immediately upon seeing the film. I have found that *A Thief in the Night* is the only evangelical film that viewers cite directly and repeatedly as provoking a conversion experience.

Ex-evangelicals, by contrast, sometimes take the film as a testament to the horrors of their childhood. Satanic rocker Marilyn Manson, who was raised as a conservative evangelical, reports having nightmares about the film when he was young. In one of his on-line articles about growing up as a fundamentalist, Andrew Hicks adds,

Just as most Christians have an anecdote about *A Thief in the Night*, they also have at least one about thinking they missed the Rapture. There's a little girl in the movie who comes home to an empty house and thinks the same thing. And there were a couple times after I saw *Thief* that I woke up on a Saturday morning to find a completely empty house. I was in a mad panic until I ran out to the garage and breathed a sigh of relief when I saw that the car was gone too.[21]

Kids aren't the only ones who have been traumatized by phony raptures. Hicks writes that one year on April Fool's Day at his school

the entire typing class organized a prank. . . . The teacher was called away from the room for a couple minutes while all the students except one snuck out of the room and into the library next door. When the teacher came back she asked the one student (one of the potheads) what happened and he said, in a daze, "Rapture, man . . ." She ran out of the room and down the hall to the next room, yelling to the teacher, "Was your class raptured, too?!" . . . True story.[22]

Today *Thief* and its sequels seem dated and cheap. *Thief*'s budget was about $68,000. Balmer notes how *high* this was compared with earlier features. Many church films that preceded Thompson's were poorly produced, with terrible acting. By contrast, Balmer argues, "When Thompson turned his cinematic skills to the subject, he produced a film that, despite its low budget and some infelicities in acting, combined drama, action, and suspense into a convincing portrayal of the 'end times.' It is only a slight exaggeration to say that *A Thief in the Night* affected the evangelical film industry the way that sound or color affected Hollywood."[23] By 1984, the film had grossed $4.2 million,[24] not much by Hollywood standards, but a fair sum for a film not even intended to turn a profit. Though contemporary viewers tend to laugh at some of the awkward acting—not to mention the early seventies' fashion statements—at the time *Thief* represented a major breakthrough.

For almost thirty years Thompson's films were the most widely seen prophecy films in America. They were shown on 16mm in churches, virtually always followed by an altar call where audience members would come forward to be saved. In fact, Peter Lalonde, the current impresario of prophecy films, says that he became a Christian after seeing Thompson's fourth film, *The Prodigal Planet,* in a church. As video arrived in the eighties, Thompson's films became the sine qua non of Christian bookstores. Even the smallest store was likely to have at least one of Thompson's films for sale.

SHIFTING FROM THE PERSONAL TO THE POLITICAL

In the late 1990s a new series of apocalyptic films appeared, produced by Peter and Paul Lalonde's Cloud Ten Pictures. These films have stolen Thompson's prophetic limelight with a dramatically different approach toward apocalyptic subject matter. Like Thompson, Peter Lalonde (the creative half of the pair), addresses religious issues, but his films also seek to entertain by emphasizing the power of the Antichrist, his methods of domination, and the countertactics of Christian resistance fighters. Like other Christian media products in search of a mainstream audience, Peter Lalonde's films lighten their Gospel message, deemphasizing the importance of Jesus and tempering their message to appeal to a mass market. That they have achieved little success in the secular market suggests, I think, that Lalonde does not realize how peculiar prophecy theology is to nonevangelicals.

Journalist Adam Davidson has argued that since *A Thief in the Night,* evangelical filmmakers have radically changed their representation of apocalyptic events. As he sees it,

The progression (or regression) is the move from rural towns to the halls of power. It's the expansion of the evangelical sphere of concern from the very local (my friends, my church) to the national and global (my president, my international policy). It's a move from a complex view of the individual to an oversimplification that identifies everyone as either good-believer or bad-heathen. It's also a change in sentiment toward the unbeliever from sadness, caring, and invitation to triumph, judgment, and dismissal. It's a chilling mutation, and has entrenched evangelical Christianity in an antagonism to secular America that borders, at times, on cruelty.[25]

Davidson further observes that in Thompson's films some of the Antichrist's henchmen are sympathetic. One of Patty's friends, Jerry, ends up taking the mark and working for the Antichrist. Yet when he dies in the fourth film, he is weeping. He knows he is going to Hell, and viewers are meant to feel deeply for him. (Alas, for contemporary audiences this identification may be stymied by Jerry's behemoth sideburns and the large ice cubes representing giant hailstones in this scene.) Conversely, when the Antichrist's henchmen are blown up in Lalonde's *Revelation* (Van Heerden, 1999) and *Tribulation* (Van Heerden, 2000), we are clearly supposed to cheer. There is no room for sympathy for these unrepentant, Hell-bound sinners. Notwithstanding Patty's decapitation, Thompson's films display a compassion that is largely lacking in contemporary apocalyptic films.

Davidson errs in assuming that evangelicals have lost their compassion for the unsaved, yet his reading of the changes in apocalyptic films is astute. Films like *Revelation* do feel more political and less personal than apocalyptic films used to, and one cannot help connecting this to the reemergence of evangelicals as a political force at the end of the twentieth century. The rhetoric of the Christian Right's leaders, after all, focuses more on social and political salvation than on saving individual souls. The success of *Thief* was possibly linked to the success of Hal Lindsey's political writings, *The Late Great Planet Earth* and *Satan Is Alive and Well on Planet Earth*, but *Thief* itself did not focus on political aspects of prophecy. Lalonde's first feature, *Apocalypse* (Gerretsen, 1998), as well as *Omega Code* and *Left Behind: The Movie*, are in many ways typical Hollywood films about the dilemmas of individuals, but they do point to the United Nations as evil and use peace and war in the Middle East as key plot points. In striking contrast to Thompson's series, the tone of today's apocalyptic films resonates with Christian activists like Pat Robertson who oppose disarmament, the United Nations, the World Bank, and the existence of a Palestinian state.

Left Behind: The Movie is more political than Thompson's films but less political than the book that inspired it, which is aggressive in its attacks on the United Nations. The film, by contrast, avoids catch phrases like "new world order" and "one-world religious order." Both the book and film focus on the adventures of journalist Buck Williams and airline pilot Rayford Steele, but the book also includes classic conspiracy theories about international bankers controlling the world. In keeping with the Lindsey tradition, the Russians are evil. When they want access to a miracle fertilizer, it is naturally assumed that they should not have it: better they starve than eat and gain the strength to resurrect their evil empire. In the film, Nicolae Carpathia (the Antichrist) speaks of world peace, which fools the world into thinking he is good. Carpathia is at the center of a convoluted, confusing plot to control the world's food supply and rebuild the Jewish Temple in Jerusalem. In the book, Carpathia's political machinations receive even more emphasis. He gives a speech before the United Nations, providing a lesson in the organization's history: "Our forebears were thinking globally long before I was born . . . From [the United Nation's] official birth . . . to this day, tribes and nations have come together to pledge their whole-hearted commitment to peace, brotherhood, and the global commu-nity."[26] Authors Tim LaHaye and Jerry Jenkins write that Carpathia "displayed such an intimate knowledge of the United Nations that it was as if he had invented and developed the organization itself." He also speaks disparagingly of Ronald Reagan, because during his presi-dency the U.N. "seemed a thing of the past."[27] Any reader familiar with the political applications of prophecy theology will know right away that Carpathia is the Antichrist. Compared with *The Late Great Planet Earth,* though, *Left Behind*'s politics are subtle, toned down in fa-vor of focusing on the stories of Buck and Rayford. This is conspiracy theory lite. With his solid record of promoting the full-throttle version, Tim LaHaye was perhaps the perfect candidate to produce this politi-cally tempered story.

LaHaye is today most widely known as the *Left Behind* coauthor, but he has also written numerous nonfiction books. LaHaye and his wife Beverly are known in evangelical circles as the authors of popular self-help books such as *The Act of Marriage,* a Christian sex manual.[28] They are also known among politically involved evangelicals for supporting laws that would ban pornography, homosexuality, and abortion; they would also like to establish "decency standards" for the entertainment industries.[29] A leading figure of the Moral Majority, Tim LaHaye au-thored *The Unhappy Gays,* reprinted later with the more neutral-sound-ing title, *What Everyone Should Know about Homosexuality.*[30] LaHaye is a vocal opponent of "secular humanism," and like James Dobson and other politically engaged evangelicals, bellicose rhetoric is one of his weapons. His classic attack on secular humanism is called *Battle for the Mind;*[31] more recently, he is the coauthor of *Mind Siege.* The advertising copy for the latter book explains that "the purpose of life is found in the battle for your mind. Will you live by *man's wisdom* from the likes of Marx, Darwin and Freud? Or will you choose the *wisdom of God* and those who shared it, such as Moses, Christ and the apostles?" *Mind Siege* "provides the ammunition necessary to return our families, churches, schools and country to spiritual sanity"[32] and typifies La-Haye's Manichean worldview. As he wrote in a prophecy book in 1972, "there are only two kinds of people on the earth: Christians, and unbelievers."[33] This worldview is fictionalized and sold to a mass audi-ence in today's Left Behind series. Interestingly, the "secular human-ist" press has portrayed LaHaye in fairly gentle terms. Articles on his bestselling series usually describe him simply as a Christian, not as a right-wing activist.

Televangelist Pat Robertson has also made efforts to make his ideas palatable outside of evangelical culture but has failed to soften his right-wing image. In his 1991 *New York Times* bestseller, *The New World Order,* he focuses on the political ramifications of prophecy without ever mentioning prophecy per se. Robertson explains that there has been a movement toward global unification dating back to Woodrow Wilson's League of Nations and, before that, to the Tower of Babel. The emerging new world order would entail a dissolution of national boundaries. The United States would be subservient to the United Nations, and American families would be drained by a global tax burden. Rich countries would be forced to squander money on the Third World (the book's major villain, after Satan), and Christians would be globally persecuted. He argues that "for the past two hundred years the term 'new world order' has been the code phrase of those who desired to destroy the Christian faith and what Pope Pius XI termed the 'Christian social order.' They wish to replace it with an occult-inspired world socialist dictatorship."[34] Robertson leaves out certain key points of prophecy belief: the Tribulation, the Antichrist, the Mark of the Beast, the Battle of Armageddon, and the millennial rule of Christ on earth.[35] But readers versed in prophecy can read between the lines: "occult-inspired world socialist dictatorship" refers to the impending reign of the Antichrist. By not naming the Antichrist, Robertson potentially widens his appeal to non-Bible-believing, political conservatives.

Like Hal Lindsey, Robertson has tapped into prophecy's incredible applicability to the smallest and largest political events.[36] Indeed, it is this seemingly endless potential that makes prophecy appealing. As historian Paul Boyer argues, "Prophecy belief is a way of ordering experience. It gives a grand, overarching shape to history, and thus ultimate meaning to the lives of individuals caught up in history's stream."[37] Its elasticity may lead people to mistake it for garden-variety conspiracy theory. It's hardly a surprise that like many nonevangelicals, the *Wall Street Journal* writer who reviewed *The New World Order* did not pick up on the book's prophetic underpinnings. Notwithstanding the book's references to Satan, the reviewer simply summarized the book as "a predictable compendium of the lunatic fringe's greatest hits."[38]

In a sense, LaHaye has succeeded where Robertson has failed in mainstreaming his ideas and dulling their conspiracy theory edges. Secular reviewers have not identified LaHaye as part of a "lunatic fringe." His books straddle a middle ground between Thompson's emphasis on individual introspection and salvation and Robertson's emphasis on the social and political world. As we will see, Peter Lalonde, the producer who brought *Left Behind* to the screen, also has a track record of carefully balancing the personal and the political in his representations of apocalyptic events.

PETER LALONDE'S APOCALYPTIC VISIONS

Peter Lalonde is a prolific producer. In partnership with his brother Paul, he released five apocalyptic feature films and a number of shorter videos between 1997 and 2001, including *Left Behind: The Movie*, the only one to have received wide theatrical release.[39] Lalonde's first feature, *Apocalypse*, was shot on video for $1 million, and had sold 300,000 copies by 2001. The film dramatizes the Rapture and the rise of the Antichrist through the eyes of two reporters, Bronson Pearl and Helen Hannah. Much of *Apocalypse* consists of relabeled stock news footage of disasters. Thus, footage of a real helicopter crash becomes footage of a helicopter whose pilot has been raptured. Images of women crying after natural disasters become images of women who have lost their husbands and children to the Rapture. All the stock footage has a "WNN" logo at the bottom, as though broadcast on the "World News Network," a CNN stand-in. The actor who plays the Antichrist is weak, and there are definitely moments where the film's B-movie seams show. *Apocalypse* centers on Helen's and Bronson's spiritual doubts, with a few car chases thrown in. Helen is born again fairly early in the film when she finds her raptured grandmother's clothes on the kitchen floor. Although the Rapture theoretically happens "in the twinkling of an eye," Grandma found time to leave Helen an explanatory note. Helen reads it and then watches several of her grandmother's videos of real-life televangelists Rexella and Jack Van Impe, who happen to be cosponsors (with prophecy preacher John Hagee) of Lalonde's first three films. (Jack Van Impe has been predicting the fulfillment of Biblical prophecy and a coming nuclear war for thirty years via the Trinity Broadcasting Network, as well as on almost a hundred UHF channels, forty-three radio stations, and internationally, via Trans-World Radio.[40])

In the video that Helen watches, the Van Impes explain what will happen after the Rapture. The Antichrist will rise to power, seeming like a man of peace, but things will soon take a turn for the worse. (Since peace is assumed to augur the Antichrist, prophetic televangelists tend to portray it as evil. Van Impe actually warned against attempts to moderate Cold War tensions in the 1980s.[41] He later saw glasnost as a "giant step toward . . . World War III and Armageddon."[42]) The Antichrist, Van Impe explains in *Apocalypse*, will force people to take the Mark of the Beast, damning them for eternity. This is enough for Helen; she says a tearful prayer and is saved. Bronson is not saved until he proves to himself that the Rapture took the evangelicals away: he digs up his father's grave and finds that the body is gone. Bronson is soon rounded up with other Christians who see through the Antichrist's devious plan for global domination, which only *appears* to be a plan for global peace and unity. By now, the Antichrist (a.k.a. "Franco Macalousso") has taken over WNN and has set up public viewing stations all over the globe using billboard-sized outdoor monitors to promote his New Age–sounding peace plans. Suddenly, in a climactic moment evocative of the end of John Carpenter's *They Live* (1988), a Christian terrorist jams the Antichrist's billboard broadcasts and replaces them with footage of the Antichrist showing his true colors, which is followed by footage of the Van Impes explaining the Antichrist's deception. This is a momentary victory for the Christians, although Bronson does get his head chopped off.

Lalonde's second film, *Revelation*, was budgeted at $5 million and shot on 35mm film; it had sold 375,000 copies on video by 2001. Once again, we find a hero who does not believe in God, this time played by Jeff Fahey, best known as "Jobe" (pun intended) from *Lawnmower Man* (Leonard, 1992). The film picks up three months after the Rapture. There is no recycled stock footage in this film, the special effects are better, and the Antichrist is now played by a better actor, Nick Mancuso. Most of the evil limelight, however, is taken by the Antichrist's henchman, who beats people up without swearing or doing other nasty things one might expect from a secular movie villain. He is reasonably scary, although, frankly, he struck this viewer as a diabolical Tony Randall. In this film, Helen leads a band of Christian technoterrorists who must hack into a CD that will expose the true nature of the "Day of Wonders" the Antichrist has planned. Both Thorold Stone (Fahey) and Helen's brother work for the Antichrist's organization O.N.E. (One Nation Earth), but they join up with Helen to see what secrets the CD holds. The terrorists watch informative Van Impe videos as they wait for the brother to finish hacking. The CD reveals that Macalousso is distributing virtual reality headsets to everyone for the Day of Wonders. When the sets are put on the wearer is transported to a white, empty space and offered earthly rewards by Macalousso in exchange for pledging allegiance to him and taking his 666 mark. If the wearer refuses, he or she is guillotined in virtual reality and dies in real life. Numerous plot twists later, Stone rejects Satan and accepts God, and the Antichrist's right-hand man is blown up. The Christian terrorists have won, for now.

Lalonde's third film, *Tribulation* (Van Heerden, 2000), had a budget of $9 million and stars Gary Busey, Howie Mandel, and Margot Kidder. With the addition of second-tier Hollywood stars, *Tribulation* looks like a respectable made-for-TV movie. Busey plays an atheist, and Mandel is a New Age wacko who uses a Ouija board; this is the kind of "occult" activity, along with channeling, yoga, and astrology, that LaHaye, Robertson, and others see as a sign that we are in the "End Times," a period of moral decline occurring shortly before the Rapture. Busey is in a car accident and falls into a coma. When he wakes up, the events of the first two films have already taken place. Helen Hannah is now using a mobile van for communications terrorism, interrupting the Antichrist's broadcasts with videos of the Van Impes, John Hagee, and a few seconds of a sermon by T. D. Jakes (a televangelist who came on board as a sponsor with this film).[43] Helen is arrested, taken to virtual reality to contend with the Antichrist and guillotined. Busey is born again, and Mandel's fate is left hanging.

In 2001, the Lalondes released the fourth installment, *Judgment* (Van Heerden), with Mancuso as the Antichrist again. New actors include TV's *L.A. Law* star Corbin Bernsen and Jessica Steen, who was in the mainstream apocalyptic thriller *Armageddon* (Bay, 1998). The budget for *Judgment* was $11 million. Hagee, Jakes, and Van Impe are no longer listed as sponsors and do not make cameo appearances. Thus, this film in theory moves further toward the "mainstream" not only because of its increased budget and recognizable stars but also because it has lost the televangelists' imprimatur. In practice, though, *Judgment*, like Lalonde's other productions, will not fool anyone; even with the word "Jesus" omitted, the movie is clearly religious. It had a very limited theatrical release, and the bulk of its revenue has come not from the box office but from Christian bookstores and mail-order catalogs.

Judgment is a courtroom drama. It turns out that the Antichrist saved the indomitable Helen at the last minute, preferring to humiliate her on national television before executing her. Helen is put on trial on trumped-up charges, with Mitch Kendrick (Bernsen) as her lawyer. Mitch has been set up, with his knowledge, to lose; the Antichrist has told him exactly what to say. Mitch ends up putting God on trial, with Helen testifying on His behalf. Meanwhile, Mitch and Helen privately debate the existence of God. In a side plot, a band of Christians, including a character played by Mr. T (of TV's *The A Team* and recently saved in real life), conspires to rescue Helen. Eventually, God wins the trial, Helen is rescued, and Mitch finds salvation shortly before being shot dead.

These four films demonstrate that Lalonde perceives television— and other technologies—as inherently neither good nor evil. In this, he is markedly different from the technophobic Christian conspiracy theorists who are wary of computers, credit cards, bar code scanners, and ATMs. Lalonde's Antichrist controls WNN and uses a virtual reality environment to force people to take his mark, but the Christian freedom fighters use computers, VCRs, videotapes, and televisions to inform themselves and teach new converts. Of course, the films themselves are the product of technology, and Lalonde uses as many special effects as he can afford. It is especially interesting that although television is one of the Antichrist's greatest tools of control, video remains beyond his purview. From this perspective, the films' primary distribution on home video rather than film is a good thing. If people keep the videos in their homes rather than seeing them in theaters, the videos will be easily accessible to friends and relatives left on earth after the Rapture. If this sounds farfetched, consider that Lalonde was among the first to create nondramatic videos *specifically designed* for the unraptured.

Lalonde pioneered an apocalyptic subgenre that I call the post-Rapture survival video. The content of these videos ranges from a pastor explaining what will happen after the Rapture and how to accept Jesus into your heart, to mixtures of explanation with dramatic elements, such as CNN-style newscasts showing the rise of the Antichrist. All of these videos directly address "you," the viewer, as someone who has been "left behind" by the time you watch the video. Viewers are admonished to accept Christ, reject the Antichrist, and die a martyr's death.

It is unclear how unraptured people are to find the videos. In the *Left Behind* novel, a newly born-again person offers a video to the book's hero, explaining that the pastor of his church recorded the tape and put it in the church library with instructions to "play it if most everyone seemed to have disappeared."[44] In today's unraptured world, these tapes are widely distributed via Christian book clubs and bookstores. Many small Christian stores with virtually no videos for sale will have on their shelves one post-Rapture video, one video from Thompson's prophecy series, and one Lalonde dramatic video. Lalonde's post-Rapture video *Left Behind* (no relation to the book or feature film) has sold over 200,000 copies. The front of the box bills it as "the *original* video produced especially for those who will be left behind." LaHaye and Jenkins have also produced a post-Rapture video called *Have You Been Left Behind?* which was released concurrently with the *Left Behind* book.

The cover of the Jenkins and LaHaye post-Rapture video tells viewers, "If you find this tape, play it immediately. Your future depends on it!" At the very end of the video a message reads, "Every Christian needs to keep a copy of this video accessible in his or her home for those left behind." If it's not clear how the unraptured would run across this tape, it is at least clear that Jenkins and LaHaye have hit upon a clever marketing tactic. Except for the closing message, the video is more or less an exact rendition of the video that figures in the novel. (A shortened version appears in the film, with T. D. Jakes making a cameo as the narrator.) As *Left Behind*'s hero Rayford Steele watches the tape in the book, he periodically pushes the pause button to think things over. Steele finally comes to a conclusion: "It was time to move beyond being a critic, an analyst never satisfied with the evidence. The proof was before him: the empty chairs, the lonely bed, the hole in his heart. There was only one course of action. He punched the play button."[45] A few moments later, our hero kneels in worship for the first time. No longer a doubter, he loses the need to use the pause button to allow time for reflection. "He . . . tossed the remote control aside."[46] Like Lalonde, LaHaye and Jenkins seem to see video as a very effective post-Rapture conversion tool.

The idea of being "left behind" has been around since Larry Norman's song "I Wish We'd All Been Ready," the chorus of which laments, "You've been left behind." This song opens *A Thief in the Night*. Norman was an iconic figure for Jesus freaks, and *A Thief in the Night* became strongly associated with hippie evangelism of the early seventies. Lalonde thus pushes all the right buttons in older viewers when he opens *Revelation* with "I Wish We'd All Been Ready." As prophecy videos have proliferated since the 1980s, the phrase "left behind" has become the mantra of the prophecy media industry, and novelists, filmmakers, and videomakers seem to find endless ways to work it into titles and marketing schemes. Unsaved characters in Jenkins and La-Hayes' books repeatedly use the phrase, even though they are ostensibly unfamiliar with prophecy theology. The use of "left behind" in media theoretically designed for mainstream distribution represents a failed attempt at ambiguity. Apocalyptic films and videos like Lalonde's, which attempt to speak to nonconverts but use insider language, are unlikely to succeed.

Lalonde started with short post-Rapture survival videos before he moved on to make his first straight-to-video features. All of this, though, was a build-up to his major coup, signing a deal with Namesake Pictures, a Christian production company that had secured the rights to the *Left Behind* novel. Before Lalonde could make the film, however, another evangelical film appeared in theaters across the country. *Left Behind: The Movie* would inevitably be compared with *Omega Code*.

DECIPHERING OMEGA CODE

Omega Code cost just over $7 million to produce. It took in more than $2 million its first weekend, ranking tenth in per-screen box office gross.

The film grossed $7,869 per screen, and the producers crowed that *Omega Code* had actually surpassed *Fight Club*'s per-screen box office average. The mainstream *Fight Club* (Fincher, 1999) opened the same weekend on two thousand screens, though, while the evangelical *Omega Code* was on three hundred, mostly in Bible Belt cities, but also in a number of large Midwestern cities and on the East Coast.[47] Advance tickets were sold through the national Family Christian Bookstore chain,[48] and churches in Jacksonville, Phoenix, and Oklahoma City bought out whole theaters for weekend screenings.[49] In Portland, Oregon, 1,000 advance tickets were sold, the most in local history with the exception of *The Phantom Menace*.[50] As of July 2001, *Omega Code* had grossed $12.6 million,[51] and revenue will continue to roll in with national and international television broadcasts and video sales.[52] The producers quickly put a sequel in the works, this one again starring Michael York, as well as Michael Biehn from *The Terminator* (Cameron, 1984).

Why did *Omega Code* succeed? One answer is that there are millions of evangelicals in America, so there was a ready market for the film. Eamonn Bowles, president of distribution for Manhattan's Shooting Gallery, compared the film's audience to that of *The Apostle* (Duvall, 1997), which Robert Duvall promoted by appearing on Christian radio shows and by inviting ministers to preview the film.[53] Jimmy Daddabbo, a secular producer, even compared evangelicals' support for *Omega Code* with black women's support of *Waiting to Exhale* (Whitaker, 1995).[54] Both films filled vacuums of underserved audiences.

Omega Code was financed by the Trinity Broadcasting Network (TBN), the nation's largest Christian television broadcaster. TBN, which is geared toward a charismatic and Pentecostal audience, was founded in 1973 by Paul and Jan Crouch. Paul Crouch was *Omega Code*'s executive producer; his son Matt Crouch is the film's producer. As a not-for-profit ministry, TBN cannot sell ads, but viewers donate an estimated $80 million to the network each year. TBN is a privately owned network with twelve full-power and more than three hundred low-power stations nationwide.[55] TBN also has five thousand cable outlets accessible to over seventy million households.[56] TBN received the initial exclusive rights to air *Omega Code* on television, as well as an undisclosed percentage of the box office returns.

The Crouches turned to filmmaking to counter the sex, violence, and secular messages of mainstream movies and to redeem media as a salvation tool. As Paul Crouch explains, "2,000 years ago, Jesus told His followers vivid stories and parables about life. Today we use film and television. Millions of people see Hollywood films filled with violence and sex, yet we offer an exciting movie filled with hope."[57] Like his father, Matt Crouch believes that film is not inherently sinful.

Omega Code, he explains, taps into "a market of people who for years had wanted to embrace Hollywood but couldn't."[58] True, there is no liquor, sex, or cigarettes in *Omega Code*—not to mention profanity, unless you count "Balderdash!"—but the film earned a PG-13 rating for violence. The scriptwriter retorts that "violent things happened in the Book of Revelation. There's no way to get around that."[59] Skeptics note that the Bible also includes plenty of illicit sex, which is markedly absent from this film.

Omega Code had an initial marketing budget of only $600,000, low by Hollywood standards. The secular press credits the film's success to TBN's "grassroots" strategy of soliciting volunteers to publicize the film via e-mails, posters, and word of mouth. The official *Omega Code* Web site received 12,000 hits a day in the weeks following the movie's release, and according to the distributor, Providence Entertainment, one day the site got 500,000 hits and 150,000 posters were downloaded.[60] Providence distributed "Marketing 101 kits," which included "a sample sales pitch to turn church-goers into movie-goers."[61] Interestingly, *Omega Code* has been widely compared with *The Blair Witch Project* (Myrick and Sánchez, 1999), another low-budget independent film publicized in large part via the Internet. Impact Productions, a Tulsa, Oklahoma, religious film production company, also helped market *Omega Code* by contacting 2,400 pastors around the country,[62] and Matt Crouch himself showed two-minute promotional clips of the film during worship services in Houston, Texas, five days before the national release.[63] *Omega Code* certainly owes much of its success to these tactics, but the film also received many hours of free publicity on TBN. Unlike most low-budget independent films, this one enjoyed extensive promotion on television.

Interestingly, this "first crossover Christian film" has been rejected by many Christian viewers as not Christian enough. The Web site HollywoodJesus.com, which examines "pop culture from a spiritual point of view," has an entire archive of mostly negative responses to the film.[64] One viewer writes, "I was very surprised to think that someone would come to the Church because of *The Omega Code*. When did it say anything about the story of Christ at all? That's what Christianity is about, isn't it? Isn't it?"[65] Another viewer observes, "What little scripture that was quoted was quoted out of context and applied to the wrong persons. Even someone knowing their Bible would have a problem following this film and finding Jesus in it. To bill it as a tool for salvation is a joke."[66] As we saw in chapters 1 and 2, a subtle or absent salvation message is the hallmark of much of the media that finds financial success beyond the Christian market. The wildly successful LaHaye and Jenkins books are more the exception than the rule; they are filled with evangelical fervor and are hardly subtle. *Omega Code,* conversely, is more like successful crossover CCM tunes: clean, upbeat, and Christian only by virtue of not being anti-Christian, not promoting premarital sex, swearing, drinking, or rebellion against parents. If you don't understand prophecy theology, *Omega Code* seems Christian only because it is square.

LEFT BEHIND, *THE WOULD-BE BLOCKBUSTER*

There's no denying that *Omega Code* did well for a fairly low-budget film made by televangelists and distributed to mainstream theaters. It seemed obvious, though, that *Left Behind,* with its larger and best-selling-book tie-in, would far surpass *Omega Code*'s popularity. Lalonde sees *Left Behind: The Movie* as his first true attempt to reach a mainstream, secular audience. And the key to crossover success is getting out of churches and into theaters with a film that conveys "the truth" about the world's apocalyptic future without being too preachy. In Lalonde's mind, *Left Behind: The Movie* was subtle; to nonevangelical viewers, it was clearly a religious film. Its run in secular theaters was brief, and its box office take was minuscule.

Beyond the profit motive, what exactly is the purpose of getting Christian films into secular theaters? Christian features have always been understood as having the capability of provoking a viewer to "make a decision for Christ." Crucially, however, it took more than the film alone to do this. Until the late 1980s, Christian films like Graham's and Thompson's were most often shown in churches on 16mm. Thompson's company, Mark IV Productions, published a small manual entitled *Six Steps to Successful Film Evangelism* to make such screenings productive. A key step was properly training counselors. An "invitation" to come forward would be issued after the screening, and counselors would consult with interested viewers, hopefully leading them in a prayer of salvation. A careful introduction would precede the film, and "prayer partners" would pray for viewers as they watched. Counselors had to be very familiar with the film, and they were seen as vital to the process: "You're not an add-on or an appendage; you're an ingredient of the whole ministry."[67] Often, a film worked best when it was rented repeatedly by a church. Mark IV representative Carl L. Ardsma explained that "Christians inviting their unsaved friends still works the best . . . [and] a lot of times the strongest outreach happens the second or third time a movie comes to a church. If it was a good film the first time, members are more likely to promote it when it comes around again."[68] In fact, one church in Arizona showed the same Mark IV prophecy films every year. According to a 1984 *Chris-*

tianity Today promotional article, the Arizona church members "can almost recite the script verbatim and thus are more knowledgeable for promoting the films and for counseling first-time viewers."[69] This article also explained that video was best for small group viewing, whereas film was best for large groups. As for secular theaters, the *Christianity Today* authors noted that World Wide Pictures had made use of such venues and that a theater attracts people who would not go to church. But this was only a very short section of the article, the assumption being that church screenings, with trained counselors, were really the best way to exhibit evangelical films.

Of course, video eventually more or less killed 16mm Christian film distribution. Some churches have video projection equipment, but public exhibition rights can be quite expensive. The alternative—buying a video from a store and ignoring the bright red warning at the beginning that says "Not for public exhibition"—is less than desirable for most evangelicals wishing to show Christian films in church. So these days Christian films on video or DVD are mostly watched in non-church settings by Bible study groups or simply by evangelical families looking for an alternative to Hollywood movies. This new viewing context is crucial when we consider Lalonde's adventures in theatrical distribution.

When Lalonde contends that Christian films will increasingly be distributed in secular theaters, he assumes that this is a desirable development. That is, assuming that his intentions are not purely mercenary, he presumes that this is an effective way to reach people for Christ. This represents a radical shift in how Christian filmmaking historically has been conceptualized. Until video took over, *church* was unquestionably the ideal context for viewing such films, as the altar call, counselors, and prefilm introduction were considered crucial for a film to be effective. Can a film in a secular theater present an equivalent *context* for conversions? And is the tempered spiritual message necessary for a theatrical release an acceptable tradeoff? When World Wide Pictures was approached by major Hollywood distributors interested in handling *The Hiding Place*, World Wide turned them down, because they would have been forced to cut out some of the spiritual content.[70] "Making it" in the mainstream film business was simply not a priority for them.

Like Paul Crouch, though, Lalonde seems to assume that "church movies" preach only to the converted, whereas theatrically released Christian films reach out to nonchurchgoers while also "sending a message to Hollywood" about the profitability of Christian films. On the other hand, showing a Christian film in a secular context risks alienating viewers who will feel tricked when the apocalyptic movie they wander into is not what they expected. (Recall Moon's reservations about working with Disney and Cinerama.) Since Lalonde believes in God's supernatural power, though, perhaps he reasons that viewers who buy tickets for *Left Behind* expecting a regular, secular movie will be spiritually changed when they see the *truth* that the film offers.

Ironically, Lalonde sees prophetic films as the best way to reach unsaved people. Influenced by his own strong belief in prophetic narratives, he does not realize that prophecy is in many ways a self-enclosed system that means nothing to outsiders. Chelsea Noble, who plays one of *Left Behind*'s female leads and who, like the rest of the cast, is evangelical, says that *Left Behind* "is not a *religious* film. It's a *faith-based* message in a very large and exciting story . . . it's a supernatural thriller."[71] Only someone who already believed in prophecy would consider it not "religious" but simply a truthful message. That Lalonde and his compatriots imagine their films will speak to unsaved viewers illustrates how out of touch they are with those outside of their belief system. Nonbelievers represented in these films contend, for example, that being saved is something they can't leap into "before they are ready." Of course, anyone who proclaims "I'm not ready to be saved yet" has already bought into the belief system on some level. No unsaved character in evangelical film or fiction ever resists for complicated political or theological reasons, disagreeing, for example, that the Bible condemns homosexuality or choosing a faith more compatible with feminism.

When Lalonde set out to make *Left Behind* he dreamed it would be a blockbuster. The $17.4 million budget was certainly enormous by Christian filmmaking standards; this was even a respectable sum by Hollywood standards. (As a point of comparison, Woody Allen's films are budgeted at about $25 million each.) This was, quite simply, the most expensive Christian film ever made, but $17 million still wasn't enough, for Lalonde wanted the film to open in 2,500 theaters. How could he possibly afford the marketing such an endeavor would take? Could he even afford to strike enough projection prints? His solution was to call on Christians to help out at the grassroots level. He sent a half-hour *Making of "Left Behind"* promotional video to churches around the country and sought sponsors, each of whom would loan his production company three thousand dollars to help cover the advertising and print costs of showing the film on one screen. Sponsors would be reimbursed from the film's revenue. While Lalonde did not make his 2,500 screen goal, he eventually raised enough money to open on just under 900 screens. One month later, the film remained on about one hundred screens. Like *Omega Code*, this film was advertised by word of mouth and pushed by televangelists.

But Lalonde added an extra twist: to build buzz around the film he released it on video months before it was released in theaters. Each video came with two discount tickets for the theatrical release, and if all went according to plan video owners would not only pay to see the film again on the screen but would also bring unsaved friends. Before the video was even available 1.5 million copies were presold.[72] To the despair of Christian bookstores, who had been promised exclusive rights to sell the video, Lalonde offered the video to Wal-Mart and Kmart, which of course helped sales. Lalonde pumped the revenue from video sales back into promoting the theatrical release. Ultimately, the strategy failed; video owners did not want to pay to see the film again. Yet the video pre-release gave Lalonde a lot of free publicity. National media coverage of his unorthodox marketing scheme helped increase video sales, which enabled the wide theatrical release. The film grossed $2.2 million on its opening weekend, ranking seventeenth of the forty-two films playing at the time. It was, in fact, the top-grossing independent movie that weekend.[73] But ultimately it simply could not compete in the secular marketplace; its final box office take amounted to only $4.2 million.[74]

Christian film critics have been generous with *Left Behind*. Some are probably wary of turning people away from a film that might help set them on the road to salvation. Also, so few Christian features are made that critics are loathe to attack films with good intentions. Christian viewers, conversely, have been less enthusiastic in their evaluations of *Left Behind: The Movie*. The HollywoodJesus.com Web site, for example, has an archive of over seventy responses to *Left Behind*, and while many try to be kind, the majority of the reviews are negative. The criticism comes from several angles. Some aficionados of the book feel that it is a poor adaptation. On a technical level, others attack the film as amateurish with weak acting, bad interior lighting, poor transitions between scenes, weak special effects, and slow pacing. Television actor Kirk Cameron is skewered for lacking a leading man's presence, and the Antichrist actor is ridiculed for his Romanian accent, which has an unfortunate Count Dracula quality to it. One viewer notes that "the casting is third-tier, the performances often robotic, the script bland, and the plot jumbled . . . I wish I could recommend the film to my non-Christian friends and family members, but I'm afraid seeing it would simply reinforce their dim view of 'Christian filmmaking.'"[75] Another viewer says he looked around the theater after the film started and realized that this is what the Rapture would look like: many suddenly empty seats! A number of viewers were embarrassed that the film was released on video before it was released in theaters, seeing this tactic as both foolhardy and unprofessional. And several viewers suggested that there were stronger Christian messages in better secular films such as *Chariots of Fire, The Elephant Man,* and *Return of the Jedi.* One viewer notes, "Most 'Christian' films I have seen have been of such poor quality that it has been embarrassing . . . I find more of God speaking in non-Christian films than I do in Christian films."[76]

Finally, as with *The Omega Code,* a number of viewers at Hollywood-Jesus.com criticized *Left Behind* for not having a sufficiently clear salvation message. While the film implies that the heroes are saved by showing them praying, it does not outline exactly how to repent and be saved. This is a crucial point that may be lost on nonevangelical viewers; it's not enough just to believe in God. In the book, Rayford Steele seems (to a nonevangelical reader) to be converted right after the Rapture: he suddenly believes everything that his wife told him about God, salvation, and the Rapture, and he realizes that he is a sinner. Yet more than two hundred pages elapse before he receives proper instruction on how to *really* be saved. The book emphasizes that you have to say (and believe) the right kind of prayer to be saved;[77] prayer is a performative, transformative speech act. In the film, Ray kneels with a pastor in a church, and the camera pulls back to a long shot and tilts up to the stained glass above the characters. This makes for a dramatic image, but we don't get to hear the salvation prayer. Likewise, when Buck (Cameron) is saved at the end of the film, he breaks down crying and says, "I believe . . ." Nonevangelical viewers will assume he means he believes in God, while evangelicals may fill in the blank differently: he believes that Jesus died for his sins and that God forgives him for his sins. But don't nonevangelical viewers need to hear the full message, since people who believe in God but not Jesus will not find heavenly salvation?

One disappointed HollywoodJesus.com viewer notes that *Left Behind: The Movie* "did not offer a real clear gospel message on how to repent and get saved," and he further complains that

they announced before [the video] began, "stand by for an important message from Kirk Cameron after the movie." I thought he might give a testimony or at least an invitation to accept Christ. He didn't. All he did was promote the movie—asking people to take their friends to the theaters when it debuts. So that maybe it will make it big and Hollywood would notice and want to get into the business of making more Christian films like it. That reminded me of the recent Carman flyer I received asking me to buy his latest CD so it would outsell any secular artist and Christians would "take over the music industry for Jesus"—oh, OK, as long as it's for Jesus. Give me a break.[78]

Not all viewers were so vitriolic, but many felt that the film's spiritual message could have been strengthened, and a few reacted against the prophecy genre as a whole, complaining that people should not be frightened into loving the Lord. More positive viewers said that even if the film did not mention Jesus, at least it showed the Bible as a source of truth.

Not surprisingly, no one said, "Relax! It's just a movie!" probably because they realized that the stakes with this film were high. After all, like Lalonde many Christians had expected *Left Behind* to be a blockbuster that would far surpass *Omega Code*'s success. Further, many hoped the film would have far-reaching consequences: Hollywood would understand once and for all that evangelical Christians should be valued as a demographic. As one viewer predicts, "The film makers in Hollywood will eventually see that they can keep their usual audience and gain the Christian audience by simply eliminating the profanity and sexual scenes from their formula in films."[79] One might skeptically respond that even Christian films that are fairly well-written and acted can fall flat when an angry satanic villain is limited to screaming "Stupid!" as an insult. Depicting evil (indeed, depicting *life*) in a convincing-yet-wholesome manner remains a major challenge for evangelicals; secular filmmakers would likewise have difficulty maintaining realism in films without profanity and sex.

Even without the swearing and the sex, *Left Behind* seemed to follow at least one Hollywood formula for success: it was based on a best-selling book. The film thus had a built-in viewer base in the book's fans, and it was cross-promoted with a tremendous amount of merchandise. Lalonde's film also had enormous potential for sequels, as *Left Behind* is one of a twelve-book series, all of which have been tremendously successful. These elements are all in line with Justin Wyatt's definition of "high concept."[80] Hollywood's "high concept" is exactly what the rest of us might call "low concept." High-concept films are marketed through stars, music, and merchandising and ideally are based on presold properties, books or plays that are already widely known to viewers. In terms of marketing, a high-concept film needs an easily understood image for posters and newspaper ads; the iconic images of *Jaws* (Spielberg, 1975), *Saturday Night Fever* (Badham, 1977), and *Grease* (Kleiser, 1978) are classic examples. Conversely, a conceptually dense art film without big stars, product tie-ins, and easily marketable qualities is considered low-concept.

Left Behind: The Movie faltered in fulfilling its high-concept potential, in part, because it lacked an iconic marketing image. The image used for the poster, newspaper ads, and home video reads "From the runaway bestselling novel" at the top, and, in the center, "Left Behind: The Movie," using the same colors and typeface as the book cover. So far so good. But a legal dispute between Lalonde, Jenkins, and LaHaye prevented the authors' famous names from being used. The top of the poster shows the landing gear of a plane, a crucial scene from the film, and one that readers of the book will recognize. Below the plane we see an image of a globe, which is reproduced from the cover of the book but is only legible up close; in a small black and white newspaper ad, the image would resemble the setting sun. The poster also shows a rocky terrain at night, a scene one might recognize as Israel, again, if one were familiar with the book. This would also be hard to decipher in a newspaper ad. Finally, Kirk Cameron, the film's star, fills the bottom quarter of the image. But Cameron is a TV star, not a movie star, and thus undermines the film's high-concept potential. Another lead, Brad Johnson, is best known as the Marlboro Man. Costars Clarence Gilyard and Janaya Stephens are TV actors best known for appearing on *Walker: Texas Ranger* and *Relic Hunter,* respectively. In short, these are not A-list actors, although, to be fair, their acting was not as bad as the HollywoodJesus.com reviewers made it out to be.

And, finally, this film could not fulfill its box office potential because Lalonde overestimated both his ability to promote a wide release and the fervor among Christians at the grassroots level. Like Mark IV in the prevideo days, Cloud Ten Pictures depended on word of mouth to promote *Left Behind: The Movie.* And like Mark IV, Lalonde assumed that Christians would support a film by seeing it multiple times, as they did in prevideo days. But he miscalculated that evangelicals would buy both videos and movie tickets. Numerous viewers at Hollywood-Jesus.com complained that no one would buy a ticket for a film they could already rent or which they already owned. Viewers seemed to put their sensible consumer identities ahead of their Christian identities, exactly the opposite of what Lalonde expected.

Crucially, the *Left Behind* producers could not afford saturation levels of television advertising, although the film surely received free publicity from Van Impe and perhaps from other televangelists. Wyatt observes that with a high-concept film,

the strong images and the pre-sold elements within both the film and the marketing campaigns are able to translate to the medium of television [advertising], thereby creating viewer awareness and interest. Consequently, high concept films are likely to benefit from the saturation [release] approach, whereas films dependent on audience word-of-mouth require the more traditional, tiered release and marketing approach.[81]

Now we can clearly see why *Left Behind: The Movie* could not fulfill its high-concept potential. Without TV ads, a film cannot achieve blockbuster status. And Lalonde did not use the tiered release and marketing approach, the slow-release strategy that would have been appropriate for his film. He did, of course, rely on word of mouth, an appropriate tactic for a small, independent film targeted to a specialized audience. That audience—or at least the millions of people who have purchased Jenkins and LaHaye's books—did not come through. This would-be blockbuster ended up a small independent film.

To call *Left Behind* an "independent" film certainly complicates the usual assumptions we bring to understanding independent features. Independent films tend to be "low concept" and are typically distributed to art house theaters. They are usually not action films whose directors say, as Lalonde has, that "it's not a real movie until something gets blown up."[82] As Chuck Kleinhans observes, low-budget independent films are typically "the kinds of films that cinephiles, media teachers and students, and many liberal intellectuals like to watch (at their local art house), or on PBS."[83] These exhibition outlets did not interest Lalonde.

While high-concept hits target mass audiences, low-budget, low-concept independent films will more often serve smaller identity groups such as African American women or lesbians (or African American lesbians), groups typically ignored by Hollywood. Kleinhans observes that "independence alone does not confer political, social, or aesthetic value. But there is a long-standing connection between *some* independent feature films and political advocacy or minority cultural expression," and this political advocacy most typically is leftist, or at least liberal.[84] *Left Behind* is unique, then, because it is a *conservative* independent film. Does the film constitute "minority cultural expression"? Was it just for evangelicals? And at sixty million—and counting—can we consider this a small demographic? Lalonde thought the film was for *everybody*, but that's because he urgently wants to warn people about the impending Rapture. Nonevangelicals, for the most part, think that the Rapture is baloney, and thus, by default, the audience for *Left Behind* will be mostly evangelical. In any case, the film clearly does not target cinephiles and intellectuals, and it thus presents an interesting challenge to the typical conception of the nature of independent film.

LEAVING BEHIND BOX OFFICE EMBARRASSMENT

In discussing media with evangelicals, I've heard one frustrated question over and over again: "Why can't Christians make better movies?" Conservative Christians are increasingly striving to identify themselves as a viable consumer demographic in the United States, and this means that even breakthrough low-budget films like *Omega Code* are

no longer desirable. A tacky low-budget film released in secular theaters will allow unsaved viewers to laugh at evangelicals. And even
saved viewers laughed at *Left Behind*'s marketing. As one viewer said,
"It is unfortunate that they released the film on home video first. To
send Hollywood a message . . . they should have released it just as Hollywood does. Build up to a grand opening; open on a few preview
screens the week before; then have an opening weekend with a big
push among churchgoers; then promote the next week to the remaining audience who may have heard about it."[85] This professional approach—even if the film itself was weak—would have been less
humiliating. It was *Left Behind*'s *public* box office failure that stung.

Adding further insult to injury, Tim LaHaye pursued a lawsuit
against Lalonde, charging that he and Jerry Jenkins had sold the rights
to "a movie," not "a Christian video," and that he had been promised
the film would be shot on a higher budget. In light of the suit, Jenkins
and LaHaye's names could not legally be used to promote the film.
Jenkins eventually withdrew from the suit, citing "religious reasons."
Meanwhile, Lalonde and his lawyers observed that lawsuits are constant in Hollywood—this suit showed that Christian films had finally
made it! Evangelical moviegoers were not laughing at the joke. If anything, the lawsuit put Christian filmmaking in an even worse light
than the box office failure of *Left Behind* itself did.

Lalonde will no doubt continue to make apocalyptic thrillers, but it
is doubtful that an overtly Christian version of the Apocalypse will ever
break through at the secular box office. Secular versions of the end of
the world, like *End of Days* and *Armageddon,* will, of course, continue to
appear, and if the producers go easy on the sex and violence, such films
will even find evangelical viewers. Some secular producers already
seem to be trying to cash in on the Christian audience; films like *The
Matrix* (Wachowski brothers, 1999) and *Signs* (Shyamalan, 2002) seem
tailor-made for evangelicals, without alienating those outside the belief system. *Signs* is particularly cagey. The film never overtly cites God
or Jesus. Yet it has virtually no sex, violence, or swearing; its protagonist is a lapsed minister; and the moral is that "somebody" is watching
out for us. If this "secular" film had lower production values, it would
comfortably fit in the video section of any Christian bookstore.

Christians will continue to make media, but will they only make
"Christian media"? Or does that label carry too much old-fashioned,
low-budget baggage with it? It seems that Christian media is at a cross-
roads. On the one hand, Carman, Willie Ames, chastity video producers, apocalyptic filmmakers, and others who do not mask their true
evangelical intentions will remain peripheral to the mainstream. Even
if they make concessions to mass culture by adapting its genres or its

therapeutic language, they will never find audiences outside of evangelical culture. On the other hand, media producers willing to dilute their messages so that outsiders do not even suspect that they are evangelical are likely to find nonevangelical consumers. But are heavily diluted Christian messages going to change the world in the ways that producers envision? If the future of the world looks grim according to prophecy theology, the future of Christian media may not be much brighter.

THE END IS NEAR

One of the most interesting moments I experienced while researching this book was when a very thoughtful, intelligent Christian band manager asked me what my approach in the book would be. I replied that my perspective was cultural—I wanted to understand the past, present, and future of evangelical media and its personal and cultural significance for its consumers. I added that I was not an evangelical myself and disagreed with the politics commonly associated with the evangelical Christian movement. "What are 'Christian politics'?" he asked, with a bewildered look on his face. To him, the phrase was simply oxymoronic, because for him, being a Christian was about having a personal relationship with Jesus. Nothing could have been further removed, in his mind, from the world of politics.

While it is clear that *some* Christian media encourage a patently right-wing outlook, as researchers such as Paul Apostolides and Ann Burlein have argued,[1] it is also clear that much of the media Christians consume are more "personal" than "political" and that some of it is just plain innocuous entertainment. While Focus on the Family radio programs preach against affirmative action and feminism, *Bibleman* and *VeggieTale* videos, along with most Christian music videos, are designed as escapist fun, sometimes also preaching that it is bad to be greedy or mean. Both *Bibleman* and *VeggieTales* stress the importance of God, while *Bibleman* ups the ante and also emphasizes the power of Jesus. (*Power* is key: this is, after all, a superhero show for young boys.)

This book has focused not on evangelical political action but on evangelical cultural identity. Whether you oppose "Christian politics" or are simply interested in understanding the dynamics of contemporary American popular culture, it is important to know about Christian media, a large industry whose growth shows no signs of slowing. Evangelical cultural identity is certainly not politically *neutral*, as my examination of chastity media and the evangelical anti-gay agenda has illustrated, but it is also not *exclusively* about political action. The cultural history and criticism presented here, while not a substitute for the straightforward political analysis of researchers such as Justin Watson,

Chip Berlet, Sara Diamond, and Didi Herman, is an important complement to that kind of research.

While lacking a specific political agenda, even bland, seemingly innocuous Christian media still have a political undertone. Their very success and increased visibility in nonreligious retail venues are symptoms of the growth of evangelicalism in U.S. society, and this growth has consequences for those outside of evangelical circles. For example, Wal-Mart has increasingly stocked Christian merchandise, such as the Left Behind book series and VeggieTales videos and merchandise; it has also stocked videos of films that have been reedited by the studios to meet Wal-Mart's standards (e.g., an R-rated version of *Y Tu Mamá También* to replace the unrated theatrically released version), refused to carry music with parental advisory warnings, and eliminated *Maxim* and *Stuff*, men's magazines that verge on soft-core pornography. The store also banned a Sheryl Crow album in which the singer criticized Wal-Mart for selling guns.[2] One need not be paranoid to argue that in this case, *more* evangelical media actually means *less* nonevangelical media. A journalist covering the shake-up at large chain stores observes that stores like Wal-Mart "already help determine which new works receive the most attention, with a broad effect on popular culture. 'That is our goal, to impact the culture of this country,' said Mr. Merrell of the evangelical Big Idea Productions, maker of the VeggieTales cartoons."[3] So even if milquetoast Christian easy-listening CDs do not overtly advocate right-wing politics, it is worth remembering that, as independent book and music stores continue to flounder across the country and so-called "family-friendly" chains like Wal-Mart and Sam's Club grow stronger, more and more retail shelf space is being filled by Christian media, leaving less room for other kinds of media.

What is the immediate future of Christian media? While home video keeps growing and crossover tunes keep breaking onto the charts, theatrical film exhibition seems to be the toughest market for evangelical media makers to crack. Success in mainstream theaters is the Holy Grail for many producers. Citing *Raiders of the Lost Ark* (Spielberg, 1981) and *Star Wars* (Lucas, 1977) as their earliest influences, most of today's young evangelical filmmakers want to go mainstream. They hope to increase their production values, get distributed by Hollywood companies, and of course, reap profits at the box office. Apocalyptic film producer Paul Lalonde may be thriving in straight-to-video purgatory, as we saw in chapter 6, but others are eager for theatrical salvation. "We don't want to make a film that's 'pretty good for a Christian film,'" writer-director Jon Gunn explains. "I don't even know that we want to label ourselves as 'Christian filmmakers.' We want to make high-quality films that will make our investors' money back."[4] Gunn is not alone. Many Christian filmmakers want to lose the label and just make implicitly Christian films that spread a Gospel-inspired—if not explicitly evangelical—message.

Crossover success is not an unreasonable gambit. For, as this book has shown, while evangelicals and nonevangelicals seem to be separated by vast distances, they are also connected by curious bridges. They share certain predilections (for science fiction, melodrama, etc.) even as each is often appalled by the pleasure that the other takes in particular kinds of music, films, or books. Some issues might distance some evangelicals from nonevangelicals on the political front, but notwithstanding such political differences, both groups enjoy sit-coms, rock-and-roll, cartoons, action films, music videos, fashion magazines, video games, and talk radio.

In other words, evangelicals, who strive to be "in but not of the world," have produced media that overlap in interesting ways with unabashedly "worldly" media. For nonevangelicals, Christian media are uncanny: both distant and intimate, familiar and unfamiliar in their references. When nonevangelicals, for example, encounter a Christian film with apocalyptic themes, it rings true. Sort of. It's a thriller formula we've seen a million times; as with any genre film, there are variations on plot twists that we can all spot a mile away. But this time it's a little (or a lot) cheaper than usual. The seams are showing. And then a message about God—but rarely Jesus—suddenly pops up. While the producers think they have casually slipped in a "true message," many of us feel like we've been bonked on the head by a Biblical mallet. Even as the Christian media industry has made accommodations to widen the audience for its products (most notably dropping references to Jesus), the mallet effect undeniably remains.

Even so, these message movies are theologically lightweight compared with early classics like *A Thief in the Night*. They may not be as subtle as their producers think, but they have made more accommodations to secular culture than would have been imaginable fifty years ago. Where should the line be drawn? How secular is too secular? There is no single answer; Christian media are too diverse. For producers like Carman, Focus on the Family, and Willie Ames (a.k.a. "Bibleman"), it's okay to use forms like the sit-com or the Saturday morning cartoon, as long as Jesus remains front and center. Ames may produce a show that looks like a low-budget *Mighty Morphin' Power Rangers*, but he makes no compromises with his Biblical message. Similarly, Irwin S. Moon cultivated a Christian subtext in the nature documentary genre in the 1950s, and *Brio* and *Breakaway* magazines look like contemporary secular magazines yet promote chastity and marriage. *VeggieTales*, on the other hand, promotes God but not Jesus, and crossover musicians like Creed and Sixpence None the Richer downplay their religious messages, often veiling them in metaphor.

Even Billy Graham's World Wide Pictures is attempting to mellow its salvation message, if its publicity machine is to be believed. In 2001, the company released *The Road to Redemption*, its first attempt at a "mainstream comedy with a message."[5] The film was available for sale on video or for viewing on televangelist networks. Barry Werner, the director of operations for World Wide Pictures, describes the film as "family entertainment" and hypothesizes that such a film "relaxes you and then the message gets into your subconscious mind. We keep gates on our conscious mind, particularly when we see a preacher."[6] The producer, John Shepherd, insists that the film isn't "heavy-handed, or cheesy."[7] As one reporter explains, "Shepard said people don't want the typical, 1950s movies, with grainy film, wooden actors and an altar call at the end. 'At the end, we have a short talk with either Franklin [Graham's son] or Dr. [Billy] Graham, but it's almost more like those times when Walt Disney used to wrap up a Disney TV show. We hope it's non-threatening. Besides, people can always switch channels.'" Werner adds that "We'll have a lot of people who buy this film and enjoy it and never even think that Christianity sticks out. They'll just watch it with their family and have a good laugh."[8] Werner also notes that the characters in the film move toward God, and that making this choice changes their lives. So it is not that God is absent from the film, but rather that He is theoretically unobtrusive, especially if you use the remote control as soon as Graham appears. In sum, *The Road to Redemption* sounds like an interesting new move for Graham. Leaving its hard-sell evangelical roots behind, his ministry is changing with the times and making its salvation message discrete and "non-threatening." We could easily use this film as proof that even Graham has made major accommodations to the secular marketplace. We could, that is, if it weren't for the fact that the film itself does not match its producers' own descriptions of it.

The Road to Redemption is a screwball road movie about a hapless young woman and her boyfriend who get mixed up with the mob. The humor centers around "zany" personalities, like the mob thug who likes singing along to David Cassidy 8-track tapes. The climax occurs when the heroine listens to the Billy Graham *Hour of Decision* program on the radio, gets down on her knees, says a salvation prayer, and accepts the Lord into her heart. Not heavy-handed? If anything, the film is a bit more heavy-handed than Graham's *Wiretapper* fifty years earlier. What is striking, then, is the producers' perceptions of their own film. To them, their salvation message is subtly knitted into the film's comic plot; to any nonevangelical viewer, the message is painfully un-subtle. It is strange, then, that World Wide Pictures speaks of the film as if it were a subliminal advertisement for God. It is hard to imagine that Grandpa's discussion of his "relationship with God"—sandwiched be-tween pratfalls and chase scenes—would slip into the subconscious mind of nonevangelical viewers.

In its failed attempt to be more like Sixpence None the Richer than Bibleman, *The Road to Redemption* is symbolic of the confused state of much of today's evangelical media. It aspires to a big-budget look but is actually no slicker than the average made-for-TV movie. It is produced by conservatives but avoids politics. (The gay ex-fundamentalists of the Cathedral of Hope might cringe at the idea of watching a Billy Graham production, but they would be hard-pressed to find any overt antigay sentiment in it.) Above all, the film is confused in that it wants to convert outsiders, but ultimately only preaches to the choir.

Evangelical media producers want to use their products to reach nonevangelicals, but many of them seem to have little idea of how out-siders perceive their belief system. Only a handful of crossover musi-cians, and the producers of *VeggieTales,* understand how to speak to nonbelievers. While their producers' earnest goal is to spread their sal-vation message to new listeners, the majority of evangelical media still only makes sense to people already within the fold. For all the ways that evangelicals appear to have changed as they have become produc-ers of video games, movies, cartoons, music videos, and sit-coms, at heart most of them still speak a language different from that of the sec-ular world. But they keep on trying to converse with that world, hop-ing to turn people on to the Gospel message. It does seem that the road to redemption is paved with good intentions.

INTRODUCTION

1. Richard L. Berke, "The 1994 Election: The Voters; Religious-Right Candidates Gain as G.O.P. Turnout Rises," *New York Times,* 12 November 1994, sec. 1, 10.

2. Jeff MacGregor, "And the Road Runner Fosters Disrespect for Speed Limits," *New York Times,* 13 February 1999, sec. A, 19.

3. Heather Hendershot, "Teletubby Trouble: How Justified Were Rev. Falwell's Attacks?" *Television Quarterly* 31.1 (spring 2000): 19–25.

4. Colleen McDannell, *Material Christianity: Religion and Popular Culture in America* (New Haven: Yale University Press, 1995); David Morgan, *Visual Piety: A History and Theory of Popular Religious Images* (Berkeley: University of California Press, 1998); Diane Winston, *Red-Hot and Righteous: The Urban Religion of the Salvation Army* (Cambridge: Harvard University Press, 1999); Leigh Eric Schmidt, *Consumer Rites: The Buying and Selling of American Holidays* (Princeton: Princeton University Press, 1995).

5. McDannell, *Material Christianity,* 6.

6. Randall Balmer, *Encyclopedia of Evangelicalism* (Louisville: Westminster John Knox Press, 2002), 204.

7. Christian Smith, *American Evangelicalism: Embattled and Thriving* (Chicago: University of Chicago Press, 1988), 244.

8. On evangelicals and religious labels, see Smith, *American Evangelicalism,* 242.

9. For example, Razelle Frankl, *Televangelism: The Marketing of Popular Religion* (Carbondale: Southern Illinois University Press, 1987); Ben Armstrong, *The Electric Church* (Nashville: Thomas Nelson Publishers, 1979); Mark Ward, Sr., *Air of Salvation: The Story of Christian Broadcasting* (Grand Rapids, MI: Baker Books, 1994); David Edwin Harrell, *Pat Robertson: A Personal, Religious, and Political Portrait* (San Francisco: Harper & Row, 1987); Steve Bruce, *Pray TV: Televangelism in America* (New York: Routledge, 1990); Jeffrey Hadden and Anson Shupe, *Televangelism: Power and Politics* (New York: H. Holt, 1988); and Stewart Hoover, *Mass Media Religion: The Social Sources of the Electronic Church* (Newbury Park: Sage, 1988).

10. Linda Kintz and Julia Lesage, eds., *Media, Culture, and the Religious Right* (Minneapolis: University of Minnesota Press, 1998). Communications researcher Quentin J. Schultze has also edited *American Evangelicals and the Mass Media* (Grand Rapids, MI: Zondervan, 1990). See also Bruce David Forbes and Jeffrey H. Mahan, eds., *Religion and Popular Culture in America* (Berkeley: University of California Press, 2000); and William D. Romanowski, *Pop Culture Wars: Religion and the Role of Entertainment in American Life* (Downers Grove: InterVarsity, 1996).

11. Heather Hendershot, "Onward Christian Solders?: A Review Essay," *Velvet Light Trap* 46 (fall 2000): 4–11.

215

12. Chip Berlet, *Eyes Right! Challenging the Right Wing Backlash* (Boston: South End Press, 1995); Sara Diamond, *Spiritual Warfare: The Politics of the Christian Right* (Boston: South End Press, 1989), idem, *Roads to Dominion: Right-Wing Movements and Political Power in the United States* (New York: Guilford Press, 1995), idem, *Not By Politics Alone: The Enduring Influence of the Christian Right* (New York: Guilford Press, 1998); David H. Bennett, *The Party of Fear: The American Far Right from Nativism to the Militia Movement*, rev. ed. (New York: Vintage, 1995); Didi Herman, *The Antigay Agenda: Orthodox Vision and the Christian Right* (Chicago: University of Chicago Press, 1997); Rebecca E. Klatch, *Women of the New Right* (Philadelphia: Temple University Press, 1987); Clyde Wilcox, *Onward Christian Soldiers? The Religious Right in American* Politics, 2d ed. (Boulder: Westview, 2000).

13. Quentin J.Schultze in Schultze, *American Evangelicals and the Mass Media*, 25.

14. Joel Carpenter, *Revive Us Again: The Reawakening of American Fundamentalism* (New York: Oxford University Press, 1997), 132. On evangelical use of radio, see also Dennis N. Voskuil, "The Power of the Air: Evangelicals and the Rise of Religious Broadcasting," in Schultze, *American Evangelicals and the Mass Media*.

15. The literature on secularization and evangelical accommodation includes Smith, *American Evangelicalism;* Peter L. Berger, Brigitte Berger, and Hansfried Kellner, *The Homeless Mind: Modernization and Consciousness* (New York: Vintage Books, 1973); Peter L. Berger, *The Sacred Canopy* (Garden City, NY: Doubleday, 1967); Robert N. Bellah, *Beyond Belief* (New York: Harper & Row, 1970); James Davison Hunter, *American Evangelicalism: Conservative Religion and the Quandary of Modernity* (New Brunswick: Rutgers University Press, 1983); Thomas Luckmann, *The Invisible Religion* (London: Macmillan, 1966). Robert Wuthnow and Matthew P. Lawson offer a helpful critique of modernization theory and social movement theory in "Sources of Christian Fundamentalism in the United States," in *Accounting for Fundamentalisms: The Dynamic Character of Movements*, ed. Martin E. Marty and R. Scott Appleby (Chicago: University of Chicago Press, 1994), 18–56.

16. Carpenter, *Revive Us Again*, 234.

17. See especially Morgan's chapter 6, "Memory and the Sacred."

18. See Ioannis Mookis, "Faultlines: Homophobic Innovation in *Gay Rights/Special Rights*" (345–361); and Lesage, "Christian Coalition Leadership Training" (295–325) in Kintz and Lesage, *Media, Culture, and the Religious Right.*

19. To "witness" is to give one's personal testimony (story) of salvation, often in hopes of converting listeners. In *American Evangelicalism*, Smith argues that evangelicals are more committed to social activism than other groups surveyed in his study. His subjects were evangelicals, fundamentalists, mainline Protestants, liberals (no religious affiliation), and Catholics. In attitude, it is clear that the evangelicals felt a more pressing need to improve the world than did other groups. Evangelicals engaged more in "religious activism;" they "worked hard to set a Christian example" and "told others about how to become a Christian" (40). In terms of "social and political activism," however, evangelicals did not differ substantially from other groups when asked about their activities in the preceding two years. One percent of evangelicals, 0 percent of mainliners, and 1 percent of liberals reported participating "a lot" in political protests or demonstrations. Thirteen percent of evangelicals, 6 percent of mainliners, and 12 percent of liberals reported participating "some," and 86 percent of evangelicals, 94 percent of mainliners, and 87 percent of liberals reported participating "none" (42). If we measure activism by attitude, or by amount of praying, evangelicals are more engaged than many others, but if we look at more tangible political action, they are basically in line with other Americans.

20. "Christian Right" is a tidy shorthand way to refer to arch-conservative evangelical voters and activists, but the Christian Right is not a single unified political party or movement, as the label mistakenly implies. See Steven Gardiner, "Through the Looking Glass

and What the Christian Right Found There," in Kintz and Lesage, *Media, Culture, and the Religious Right,* 141–158.

21. Brenda E. Brasher, "Promise Keepers," in *Encyclopedia of Fundamentalism,* ed. Brenda E. Brasher (New York: Routledge, 2001), 392.

22. Further, the evangelical media that is overtly political will offend many people of color by its dogged refusal to address racism through public policy. Paul Apostolidis provides an apt analysis of Focus on the Family's radio programs in which "the solution to racism is unremittently [*sic*] individualistic, depending on private legal action and . . . private charity. . . ." (181). See chapter 5, "Christian Victims in the Backlash Society," in *Stations of the Cross: Adorno and Christian Right Radio* (Durham: Duke University Press, 2000).

23. For example, the 361 self-identified evangelicals in one of Smith's surveys included people from many denominations. The highest number (66) came from Southern Baptists. Thirty-four were grouped as "miscellaneous Pentecostals," and the same number was grouped as members of Assemblies of God congregations. Forty-four were non-denominational, and an additional nine people referred to themselves as "just a Christian." Smaller numbers were spread out across an additional twenty-two denominations. Smith, *American Evangelicalism,* 241.

24. Evangelicals are about as likely as other Americans to have disposable income. Smith compared evangelicals' income and education levels with the income and education levels of people of other religious affiliations, and with those who identified as "nonreligious." Of the evangelicals he surveyed, 35 percent earned between $40,000 and $79,000 annually. The figure for mainline Protestants was 38 percent, for Roman Catholics it was 32 percent, and for nonreligious people it was 30 percent (78). Of all groups surveyed, "evangelicals are least likely to have only a high-school education or less; the nonreligious are the most likely. Furthermore, higher proportions of evangelicals have studied at the graduate school level than have fundamentalists, liberals, or the nonreligious . . . In addition, evangelicals above all groups have made the greatest gains in intergenerational educational mobility" (76). Such data fly in the face of the common stereotype of poor, ignorant born-again Christians.

25. See Justin Watson, *The Christian Coalition: Dreams of Restoration, Demands for Recognition* (New York: St. Martin's, 1997).

26. Michel de Certeau, *The Practice of Everyday Life,* trans. Steven Rendell (Berkeley: University of California Press, 1988); John Fiske, *Television Culture* (New York: Methuen, 1987); Dick Hebdige, *Subculture: The Meaning of Style* (London: Routledge, 1988); and Henry Jenkins, *Textual Poachers: Television Fans and Participatory Culture* (New York: Routledge, 1992).

27. An exception is Apostolidis, *Stations of the Cross.*

CHAPTER ONE

1. See www.livingepistles.com.

2. Posting to rec.music.christian electronic mailing list, 19 April 1996.

3. McDannell, *Material Christianity,* 227.

4. McDannell, *Material Christianity,* 228.

5. McDannell, *Material Christianity,* 229.

6. Cited in McDannell, *Material Christianity,* 239.

7. McDannell, *Material Christianity,* 246.

8. McDannell, *Material Christianity,* 251.

9. Bob Siemon cited in McDannell, *Material Christianity,* 254.

10. Joe Dziemianowicz, "The Lord's Wares: Merchandising the Man Is Booming Business," *New York Daily News,* 5 August 2001, Lifeline sec., 13.

11. William D. Romanowski, "Contemporary Christian Music: The Business of Music Ministry," in Schultze, *American Evangelicals and the Mass Media,* 143–169.

12. John Styll, "Keith Green—A Non-Profit Prophet?" in *The Heart of the Matter: The Best of CCM Interviews, Vol. 1,* ed. John Styll (Nashville: Star Song, 1991), 68.

13. Cited in Susan Hogan-Albach, "High Fidelity Faith: Contemporary Christian Music and Its Accent on Celebrity," *Sojourners Online,* vol. 28, no. 1 (January–February 1999), 50–51, 53, quotation on 50.

14. Nicholas Dawidoff, "No Sex. No Drugs. But Rock 'n' Roll (Kind of)," *New York Times Magazine,* 5 February 1995, 68.

15. Susan Friend Harding, *The Book of Jerry Falwell: Fundamentalist Language and Politics* (Princeton: Princeton University Press, 2000), ix.

16. Smith, *American Evangelicalism,* 89.

17. The United States is full of religious people who are not evangelicals, so "secular" is a tricky word to use here. From the evangelical perspective, those outside of the fold are lost. The "secular" world is full of people who either have no religion or who have devoted themselves to tragically invalid belief systems. So in using the word "secular" here, I am mirroring the evangelical perspective. Speaking from a nonevangelical perspective, though, it is reasonable to refer to "secular culture" in the United States, as I do frequently throughout the book. Notwithstanding the therapeutic, New Age ethos infusing much of contemporary popular culture, the vast majority of films, magazines, television shows, video games, and newspapers produced in the United States are secular in that they do not, from the nonevangelical perspective, reflect a specifically religious or spiritual perspective.

18. Edward J. Larson, *Summer for the Gods: The Scopes Trial and America's Continuing Debate over Science and Religion* (New York: Basic Books, 1997), 71.

19. See Carpenter, *Revive Us Again.*

20. Carpenter, *Revive Us Again,* 197.

21. Carpenter, *Revive Us Again,* 198.

22. Carpenter, *Revive Us Again,* 202.

23. Fuller Seminary was another key player in the neoevangelical movement. See George Marsden, *Reforming Fundamentalism: Fuller Seminary and the New Evangelicalism* (Grand Rapids: William B. Eerdmans, 1987).

24. Carpenter, *Revive Us Again,* 161.

25. Carpenter, *Revive Us Again,* 162.

26. Randall Balmer, *Mine Eyes Have Seen the Glory: A Journey into the Evangelical Subculture in America* (New York: Oxford University Press, 1993), 250.

27. Harding, *The Book of Jerry Falwell,* 150.

28. Harding, *The Book of Jerry Falwell,* 78–79.

29. Harding, *The Book of Jerry Falwell,* 151.

30. Although the nature of the fears are different, nonevangelicals often exhibit a similar ambivalence. Howard Rheingold, for example, is generally optimistic about the democratic potential of electronic culture, but he also expresses anxiety about technologically mediated consumer surveillance, and his "Big Brother" sounds a bit like a secular version of the Antichrist. See *The Virtual Community: Homesteading on the Electronic Frontier,* rev. ed.(Cambridge: MIT Press, 2000).

31. Evangelicals Christianize secular forms not only by producing their own alternative media but also by deciphering secular media from a Christian perspective. For example, in an on-line zine an evangelical recounts how once on *Star Trek: The Next Generation,*

Two of the crew members . . . "ceased to exist" in the normal sense of the word. They were declared dead, but they were actually there on the ship . . . No one could see

them, and since they could pass right through physical objects they could not affect the "real" world . . . [W]hat made them alive during the time that their bodies did not exist? You can rule out "soul" because most network programming precludes that possibility. Consciousness, potential to become embodied, personhood, or individual will are all reasons that come to mind. These issues also play an important part in deciding exactly what we have discarded when we remove and destroy fetal tissue from a pregnant woman. (*Sackcloth and Ashes,* no. 2 (1995), http://www.sackclothandashes .org [accessed March 17, 1996])
This viewer deliberately reads the show against the grain to open up philosophical questions about abortion, all the while knowing that the show is not "really" about abortion. Such evangelical negotiation of secular culture would seem to offer a clear example of how many cultural studies scholars describe popular resistance where readers decipher popular culture texts through a process of "poaching" on the terrain of mass culture and taking what they want, "making do," as theorist Michel de Certeau puts it. See also Jenkins, *Textual Poachers.* Evangelical negotiation of popular culture points to the fact that an "oppositional" reading, to use Stuart Hall's language, can operate on a text of any ideological persuasion. Stuart Hall, "Encoding/Decoding," in *Culture, Media, Language,* ed. Stuart Hall, Dorothy Hobson, Andrew Lowe, and Paul Willis, 128–39 (London: Hutchinson, 1980).

32. See Randall Balmer, *Blessed Assurance: A History of Evangelicalism in America* (Boston: Beacon Press, 1999), 31–43; and Marsha G. Witten, *All Is Forgiven: The Secular Message in American Protestantism* (Princeton: Princeton University Press, 1993), 21–22. Here, Witten draws in particular on Berger, *The Sacred Canopy;* Hoover, *Mass Media Religion;* and Robert Wuthnow, *The Restructuring of American Religion* (Princeton: Princeton University Press, 1988).

33. R. Laurence Moore, *Selling God: American Religion in the Marketplace of Culture* (New York: Oxford University Press, 1994), 6.

34. Moore, *Selling God,* 264 (emphasis added).

35. As membership in mainline Protestant churches has steadily declined, it has concomitantly increased in evangelical congregations. See Randall Balmer, *Grant Us Courage: Travels Along the Mainline of American Protestantism* (New York: Oxford, 1996). New Agers, however, present ample competition with evangelicals both for converts and for dollars. On New Age as a satanic cult, see the popular evangelical novel *This Present Darkness* (Westchester, IL: Crossway Books, 1986) by Frank E. Peretti, the Stephen King of evangelical culture. See also Irving Hexham, "The Evangelical Response to the New Age," in *Perspectives on the New Age,* ed. James R. Lewis and J. Gordon Melton (Albany: State University of New York Press, 1992), 152–163; and, on New Age commercialism, Kimberly J. Lau, *New Age Capitalism: Making Money East of Eden* (Philadelphia: University of Pennsylvania Press, 2000). Scientology is another belief system that clearly illustrates the profit motive at play in American religion. See Stewart Lamont, *Religion Inc.: The Church of Scientology* (London: Harrap, 1986).

36. Ralph Reed, Jr., introduction to Christian Coalition, *Contract with the American Family* (New York: Moorings, 1995), ix.

37. Benjamin Svetkey, "Is Your TV Set Gay?" *Entertainment Weekly,* 6 October 2000, 24–28, quotation on 28.

38. Conservative Jewish film critic Michael Medved observes that it is not unusual for secular "special interest groups" to be consulted in the course of film production, but that members of religious groups are less frequently consulted. Medved, *Hollywood vs. America: Popular Culture and the War on Traditional Values* (New York: Harper Collins, 1992). Medved has also produced a video based on the book.

39. The videos' distributor is Word, Inc. They are Focus on the Family productions, and they can be bought via mail order from Focus or in Christian bookstores. *Adventures in Odyssey* is based on Focus's successful radio show of the same title, and cassettes of the show are also available from Focus and in Christian bookstores.

40. These Christian cartoons are actually similar to secular cartoons in that both are persistently didactic and contain "prosocial messages." In addition to the Biblical messages and an emphasis on adult authority, one of the biggest differences between *Adventures in Odyssey* and secular cartoons is that *Odyssey* contains acts of violence that TV censors would find unacceptable. In one episode, a dog is almost drowned, there is a fight with swords, hatchets, and a mace, and a man is knocked unconscious. See Hendershot, *Saturday Morning Censors* (Durham, NC: Duke University Press, 1998), chapter 2.

41. Smith, *American Evangelicalism*, 77–78. For details, see introduction, note 24 above.

42. Carol Flake, *Redemptorama: Culture, Politics, and the New Evangelicalism* (Garden City, NY: Anchor Press, 1984), 153.

43. Flake, *Redemptorama*, 165.

44. Flake, *Redemptorama*, 166 (ellipsis in original).

45. Even the evangelical label itself helps raise the class image of Bible-believers since, as Ellen Seiter observes, "fundamentalism is a label rejected by many conservative Christians because of its perceived lack of middle-class respectability." *Television and New Media Audiences* (New York: Oxford University Press, 1999), 96.

46. Julia Lesage also points to the class dimensions of Christian cultural products in her analysis of how Christian Coalition leadership videos foster a kind of "embourgeoisement." Lesage, "Christian Coalition Leadership Training," in Kintz and Lesage, *Media, Culture, and the Religious Right*, 295–325.

47. See Kathryn Montgomery, *Target: Prime Time* (New York: Oxford University Press, 1989); and Hendershot, *Saturday Morning Censors*, chapter 3.

48. Gustav Niebuhr, "Number of Religious Broadcasters Continues to Grow," *New York Times*, 12 February 1996, sec. D, 9.

49. "One of the ways [Dobson] benefits financially from Focus on the Family is the relationship he has established between the ministry and his private for-profit corporation, JDI, or James Dobson, Incorporated. For example, JDI owns the copyright to all 'Focus on the Family' [radio] broadcasts as intellectual property. Then Jim donates them back to Focus on the Family for a tax deduction. Dobson [also] uses program material developed for the Focus broadcast for the production of his own products, such as books, cassettes, videos and films." Gil Alexander-Moegerle, *James Dobson's War on America* (Amherst, New York: Prometheus Books, 1997), 121.

50. Eithne Johnson, "The Emergence of Christian Video and the Cultivation of Videovangelism," in Kintz and Lesage, *Media, Culture, and the Religious Right*, 192.

51. "20 Million Cassettes Later," *Focus on the Family* (March 2000), 19.

52. Cited in L. A. Kauffman, "220,000 Jesus Fans Can't Be Wrong: Praise the Lord and Mammon," *Nation*, 26 September 1994, 308.

53. Flake, *Redemptorama*, 13.

54. James C. Dobson, "Dr. Dobson Answers Your Questions" *Focus on the Family*, January 1994, 5.

55. Martha Wolfenstein, "Fun Morality: An Analysis of Recent American Child-Training Literature," in *The Children's Culture Reader*, ed. Henry Jenkins (New York: New York University Press, 1998), 199–208, quotation on 200.

56. Wolfenstein, "Fun Morality," 205.

57. Paul O'Donnell with Amy Eskind, "God and the Music Biz," *Newsweek*, 30 May 1994, 62–63.

58. Allison James, "Confections, Concoctions, and Conceptions," in *Popular Culture: Past and Present*, ed. B. Waites, T. Bennett, and G. Martins (London: Croom Helm/Open University Press, 1982), 294–307; Jenkins, "'Going Bonkers!': Children, Play, and Pee-wee," *Camera Obscura* 17 (May 1988): 169–193; Jenkins, "'x Logic': Repositioning Nintendo in Children's Lives," *Quarterly Review of Film and Video* 14, no. 4 (1993): 55–70; Ellen Seiter, *Sold Separately: Parents and Children in Consumer Culture* (New Brunswick: Rutgers, 1993).

59. Styll, "Jimmy Swaggart—*Christian Rock Wars*," in Styll, *The Best of CCM Interviews*, 137–138.

60. Bob Smithhouser, "High Voltage," *Brio* (February 1995): 30.

61. Cited in Dawidoff, "No Sex. No Drugs," 44.

62. Teenage CCM fan cited in Hogan-Albach, "High Fidelity Faith," 51.

63. See Susan McClary, "Same as It Ever Was: Youth Culture and Music," in *Microphone Fiends: Youth Music and Culture*, ed. Andrew Ross and Tricia Rose (New York: Routledge, 1994), 29–40.

64. Seiter, *Television and New Media Audiences*, 109.

65. Big Idea, the *VeggieTales* production company, says "we do not have age recommendations on our videos. The approximate age range that we aim for with *VeggieTales* is about three to ten years, but we do hear from fans that are much younger and much, much older. In fact, we hear from quite a few teenagers as well as college age students." E-mail communication with the author, 16 November 2000.

66. Seiter, *Sold Separately*, 115.

67. Jeff Jensen and Gillian Flynn, "The Next Temptation," *Entertainment Weekly*, 10 December 1999, 43–48.

68. Ibid.

69. Interview with Cindy Montano, 2 November 2000.

70. Jensen and Flynn, "The Next Temptation," 48.

71. The videos emphasize individual spiritual crises rather than larger political issues. A segment on school prayer, for example, shows kids meeting to pray around a school flagpole. No argument is made about school prayer as a legal issue. Rather, the kids discuss how excited they were to realize that there were other Christians at their school and that they didn't need to feel like isolated outsiders. They also say that prayer is powerful and that it will help their schools.

72. Postwar cookbooks recommended dying mashed potatoes and other techniques for making food fun for kids. Such permissive approaches to child rearing did have prewar antecedents. See "Selling Food to Children," in Jenkins, *The Children's Culture Reader*, 463–467.

73. *Bibleman* data come from Simon Ashdown, "Christian Kidvid Converts More Consumers," *Kidscreen*, 1 July 2001, 36.

CHAPTER TWO

1. Alan Light, "About a Salary or Reality? Rap's Recurrent Conflict," *South Atlantic Quarterly* 90, no. 4 (fall 1991): 857–858.

2. Interview with Robert Deaton and George Flanigan, 1 November 2000.

3. Cecilia Tichi, "Consider the Alternative: Alt-Country Musicians Transcend Country Music Stereotypes," *Women's Review of Books* 18, no. 3 (December 2000): 14.

4. Tichi, "Consider the Alternative," 14.

5. *Edge TV*, no. 36.

6. Flake, *Redemptorama*, 171.

7. Flake, *Redemptorama*, 172.

8. Flake, *Redemptorama*, 173.

9. Flake, *Redemptorama*, 176.

10. *Edge TV*, no. 31.

11. On differences between Bob Jones University and Liberty University, see Quentin Schultze, "The Two Faces of Fundamentalist Higher Education," in *Fundamentalisms and Society: Reclaiming the Sciences, the Family, and Education*, ed. Martin E. Marty and R. Scott Appleby (Chicago: University of Chicago Press, 1993), 490–535.

12. Perhaps the ultimate acceptance of contemporary Christian music by the old guard should not be surprising, in light of evangelical history. Traditionalists were scandalized when Dwight Moody and Ira Sankey replaced the old standards with new popular hymns. An elderly Scottish deacon complained that Sankey's organ was "a devilish pump machine that wheezes out blasphemously." Cited in Steve Miller, *The Contemporary Christian Music Debate: Worldly Compromise or Agent of Renewal* (Wheaton, IL: Tyndale House, 1993), 133. Evangelicals eventually realized that if new songs were necessary to compete with amusements such as drinking and gambling, then so be it. On Sankey, see Sandra Sizer Frankiel, *Gospel Hymns and Social Religion: The Rhetoric of Nineteenth-Century Revivalism* (Philadelphia: Temple University Press, 1978).

13. Flake, *Redemptorama*, 175.

14. William D. Romanowski, "Evangelicals and Popular Music: The Contemporary Christian Music Industry," in Forbes and Mahan, *Religion and Popular Culture in America*, 111.

15. Dawidoff, "No Sex. No Drugs," 42.

16. Deborah Evans Price, "Shake-Ups Hit Christian Labels," *Billboard*, 7 March 1999.

17. Price, "Shake-Ups Hit Christian Labels."

18. Daniel Fierman and Gillian Flynn, "The Greatest Story Ever Sold," *Entertainment Weekly*, 3 December 1999, 55–64, quotation on 59.

19. Lorraine Ali, "The Glorious Rise of Christian Pop," *Newsweek*, 16 July 2001, 38–48, quotation on 41.

20. Razelle Frankl, "Transformation of Televangelism: Repackaging Christian Family Values," in Kintz and Lesage, *Media, Culture, and the Religious Right*, 168.

21. Meryem Ersoz, "Gimme That Old-Time Religion in a Postmodern Age: Semiotics of Christian Radio," in Kintz and Lesage, *Media, Culture, and the Religious Right*, 212.

22. Romanowski, "Evangelicals and Popular Music," 117.

23. Dawidoff, "No Sex. No Drugs," 43.

24. Fierman and Flynn, "The Greatest Story Ever Sold," 59, 61.

25. Interview with Scott Brickell, November 3, 2000.

26. Cited in Steve Rabey, "Of Concerts and Concerns," *Christianity Today*, 19 September 1986, 42.

27. Songwriter Jimmy Owens quoted in Rabey, "Of Concerts and Concerns," 42.

28. Fierman and Flynn, "The Greatest Story Ever Sold," 59, 61.

29. Answer to FAQ (Is Creed a Christian band?) on Creed Web site, http://www.creed.com/.

30. *Edge TV*, no. 36 (emphasis in the original).

31. Romanowski, "Evangelicals and Popular Music," 108–109. There have been punk and hard-core Christian bands since the eighties, creating aggressive music that avoids the soft, "confessional" mode. Bands such as Lust Control have remained underground, with no prospects in the secular market.

32. Cited in Romanowski, "Evangelicals and Popular Music," 115.

33. Quoted in Fierman and Flynn, "The Greatest Story Ever Sold," 59.

34. Fierman and Flynn, "The Greatest Story Ever Sold," 59.

35. Cited in Rafer Guzman, "Praying for a Crossover Hit," *Wall Street Journal*, 7 October 1997, sec. A, 20.

36. Interview with Jonathan Richter, 3 November 2000.

37. On therapeutic discourse in evangelical culture, see R. Marie Griffith, *God's Daughters: Evangelical Women and the Power of Submission* (Berkeley: University of California Press, 1997); Witten, *All Is Forgiven;* and David Harrington Watt, *A Transforming Faith: Explorations of Twentieth-Century American Evangelicalism* (New Brunswick: Rutgers University Press, 1991), chapter 7.

38. Cited in Guzman, "Praying for a Crossover Hit," 20.

39. Interview with Cindy Montano, 2 November 2000.

40. Interview with Montano.

41. Interview with Montano.

42. Harding, *The Book of Jerry Falwell*, 60, see also 46–47.

43. Harding, *The Book of Jerry Falwell*, 57.

44. Interview with Stephen Yake, 2 November 2000.

45. Interview with Montano.

46. This taxonomy comes from Steve Brickell, but it was confirmed in my discussion with others in the business.

47. Interview with Ben Pearson, 3 November 2000.

48. E-mail communication to the author from Eric Welch, 14 December 2000.

49. Welch, e-mail communication.

50. Interview with Brickell.

51. Interview with Pearson.

52. Interview with Pearson.

53. Interview with Pearson.

54. Welch, e-mail communication.

55. Welch, e-mail communication.

56. Romanowski, "Evangelicals and Popular Music," 111.

57. One study has found that about 30 percent of third and fourth graders usually listen to music alone. The percentage goes up to 70 percent among fifth and sixth graders, and goes up even more in middle and late adolescence. Study cited in Donald F. Roberts and Peter G. Christenson, "Popular Music in Childhood and Adolescence," in *Handbook of Children and Media*, ed. Dorothy G. Singer and Jerome L. Singer (Thousand Oaks, CA: Sage, 2001), 399. Romanowski has argued that "the merchandising of contemporary Christian music shifted 'ministry' from collective spiritual matters to personal consumer habits, concentrating the practice of faith on the individual instead of the larger religious community" ("Evangelicals and Popular Music," 109).

58. Roberts and Christenson, "Popular Music in Childhood and Adolescence," 405.

59. Ibid.

60. Ibid, 408.

61. Quoted in Dave Shiflett, "Lambs with Chops," *Wall Street Journal*, 3 November 2000, sec. W, 18.

62. See www.dctalk.com/about.htm.

63. The popular Gospel song innovator Fanny J. Crosby is an interesting predecessor to DC Talk in terms of making passionate holy music. As George Marsden explains, by 1870 the new "hymns, especially those by women, were filled with themes of total surrender and being overwhelmed by the love of Jesus and the cleansing tide of his spirit." In *Fundamentalism and American Culture: The Shaping of Twentieth-Century Evangelicalism, 1870–1925* (New York: Oxford University Press, 1980), 75–77.

64. Http://www.dctalk.com/about.htm, accessed 7 December 2000.

65. Http://www.dctalk.com/about.htm, accessed 7 December 2000. The Web site also noted that the group met "while attending college in Virginia," neatly sidestepping their evangelical roots—they met at Jerry Falwell's Liberty University.

66. Interview with Richter.

67. Victoria E. Johnson, "Welcome Home?: CBS, PAX-TV, and 'Heartland' Values in a Neo-Network Era," *Velvet Light Trap* 46 (fall 2000): 40–55.

68. Interview with Deaton and Flanigan.

69. Interview with Brickell.

70. Interview with Montano.

71. Interview with Eddie DeGarmo, 2 November 2000.

72. Interview with Yake.

73. Interview with Richter.

74. Interview with Montano.

75. See http://www.carman.org.

76. Interview with Yake.

77. Welch, e-mail communication.

78. Interview with Deaton and Flanigan.

79. Of course, in the context of the Nashville music industry, it may be difficult to simply peg someone anxious to break into country as "not Christian." Not surprisingly, as both groups have their roots in the Bible belt, most people in both country music and Christian music grew up in Protestant evangelical churches. Flanigan explains, "We were never Christian filmmakers. We were filmmakers who happened to be Christians. There's a big difference . . . Our intent was never to become the top Christian producers" (interview with Deaton and Flanigan). Like Deaton and Flanigan, many people in the country industry identify as Christians, it just isn't their preferred market niche.

80. Sherry Milner, "Bargain Media," in *Roar! The Paper Tiger Television Guide to Media Activism*, ed. Daniel Marcus (New York: Paper Tiger Television, 1991), 17.

81. Interview with Montano.

CHAPTER THREE

1. Mimi White, *Tele-Advising: Therapeutic Discourse in American Television* (Chapel Hill: University of North Carolina Press, 1992), 177.

2. See "Religion," in Robert N. Bellah, Richard Madsen, William M. Sullivan, Ann Swidler, and Steven M. Tipton, *Habits of the Heart: Individualism and Commitment in American Life* (Berkeley: University of California Press, 1985).

3. Watt, *A Transforming Faith*, 138.

4. Hunter, *American Evangelicalism*, 93; Watt, *A Transforming Faith*, 150.

5. Hunter, *American Evangelicalism*, 95.

6. As Sara Wuthnow observes, "for many today, 'sin' is an old-fashioned word that makes them uncomfortable." "Working the ACOA Program: A Spiritual Journey," in *"I Come Away Stronger": How Small Groups Are Shaping American Religion*, ed. Robert Wuthnow (Grand Rapids, MI: William B. Eerdmans, 1994), 179–204, quotation on 184.

7. In her study of Southern Baptist and Presbyterian sermons, Marsha G. Witten notes an emphasis on "God's inner psychological states, especially on his feelings, which, in part, serve to render him familiarly human." God's love, Witten explains, has been "domesticated into human categories of usefulness." Witten identified several categories of speech in the sermons: God as daddy, God as sufferer, and God as extravagant lover. Witten, *All Is Forgiven*, 35, 48. On God as father and lover, see also Griffith, *God's Daughters*, and idem, *Born Again Bodies: Flesh and Spirit in American Christianity* (Berkeley: University of California Press, forthcoming).

8. Hunter, *American Evangelicalism,* 99.

9. Katherine G. Bond, "Abstinence Education: How Parents Are Making It Happen," *Focus on the Family,* September 1998, 12–13, quotation on 13.

10. Sharon Lerner, "Abstinence Scofflaws," *Village Voice,* 21–27 August 2002, 64.

11. Amy Stephens, "Trust Your Kids, Not Condoms," *Focus on the Family,* March 1998, 12–13, quotation on 13.

12. Kauffman, "220,000 Jesus Fans Can't Be Wrong."

13. Johnson left the *Breakaway* editorial staff in 1995 but continued to write Focus on the Family books.

14. "Dear Susie," *Brio,* April 1995, 5 (emphasis in the original). One of the most pessimistic books about dating and male-female relationships is Joshua Harris's *I Kissed Dating Goodbye* (Sisters, OR: Multnomah, 1997), which in 2001 had sold over 800,000 copies. Evangelical Jeramy Clark wrote *I Gave Dating a Chance* (Colorado Springs, CO: Water-Brook Press, 2000) as a rebuttal to Harris's book. See Laurie Goodstein, "New Christian Take on the Old Dating Ritual," *New York Times,* 9 September 2001, 1, 38.

15. *The Teen Study Bible: New International Version* (Grand Rapids, MI: Zondervan, 1993) says that girls are not at fault for being raped and refers readers to a passage from Deuteronomy (22:25–27) that confirms this. However, the passage directly preceding this one says that girls who are raped in the city should be stoned to death along with their rapists, since they did not cry out so that someone could rescue them. Only girls raped in the country, where no one is around, are not at fault.

16. Griffith, *God's Daughters,* 179.

17. Griffith, *God's Daughters,* 185.

18. This tactic is not restricted to Focus on the Family literature. See LaDawn Prieto, "An Urban Mosaic in Shangri-La," *GenX Religion,* ed. Richard W. Flory and Donald E. Miller (New York: Routledge, 2000), 57–73, in particular, 69–70. Evangelicals have taken to organizing father-daughter dances, where fathers "set a dating standard by showing the girls what being a real gentleman is like." See Jim Massery, "Finding Love in All the Right Places: Fathers and Daughters Dance the Night Away," *Focus on the Family Magazine,* February 2000, 22.

19. The purity ring first emerged in the late 1990s. The ring represents a holy pact with the girl's earthly father, her heavenly Father (God), and her future husband. See Michael Hayes and Judith Hayes, "The Purity Ring," *Focus on the Family Magazine,* May 2000, 16–17, quotation on 16. This object, which is intended simply as a *reminder* of a commitment to chastity, may become a potent sacred symbol in and of itself. On sacred images as memory aids, see Morgan, *Visual Piety,* chapter 6, "Memory and the Sacred."

20. Susie Shellenberger, *Guys and a Whole Lot More: Advice for Teen Girls on Almost Everything* (Grand Rapids, MI: Fleming H. Revell, 1994), 160.

21. See chapter 5, "Freud vs. Women: The Popularization of Therapy on Daytime Talk Shows," in Jane M. Shattuc, *The Talking Cure: TV, Talk Shows and Women* (New York: Routledge, 1997).

22. Michel Foucault, *The History of Sexuality, Vol. 1: An Introduction* (New York: Vintage Books, 1980), 21.

23. Wayne C. Booth, "The Rhetoric of Fundamentalist Conversion Narratives," *Fundamentalisms Comprehended* (Chicago: University of Chicago Press, 1995), 367–395, quotation on 390.

24. Booth, "The Rhetoric of Fundamentalist Conversion Narratives," 372–373.

25. Susan Jeffords, "The Big Switch: Hollywood Masculinity in the Nineties," *Film Theory Goes to the Movies,* ed. Jim Collins, Hilary Radner, and Ava Preacher Collins (New York: Routledge, 1993), 196–208.

26. *Good Sex,* videocassette, distributed by Zondervan, 2000.

27. Hendershot, "Shake, Rattle and Roll."

28. Susie Shellenberger and Greg Johnson, *258 Great Dates While You Wait* (Nashville: Broadman and Holman Publishers, 1995).

29. Shellenberger, "What Is Sexual Purity?" *Brio,* October 1995, 26.

30. Shellenberger, *Guys and a Whole Lot More,* 154.

31. "Dear Susie," *Brio,* April 1995, 5.

32. "Dear Susie," *Brio,* March 1995, 6. Shellenberger responds, "No one knows the time or date of Christ's return. He may come back before you receive your next issue of *Brio,* and if He does, sex won't be the ONLY thing you'll miss out on. What about college life, grad school or giving birth? Heaven is going to be so TERRIFIC that none of the things of seeming importance *now* will matter when we're standing right next to Jesus Christ."

33. Shellenberger, *Guys and a Whole Lot More,* 155.

34. "Guys Gab about Going Out," *Breakaway,* February 1996, 28 (emphasis added).

35. "Yo Duffy!" *Breakaway,* February 1996, 16.

36. This incident is recounted in Nancy Tatom Ammerman, *Bible Believers: Fundamentalists in the Modern World* (1987; New Brunswick: Rutgers University Press, 1993), 181.

37. *Teen Study Bible,* 816.

38. On the development of the evangelical antiabortion platform, see Susan Harding, "If I Should Die Before I Wake: Jerry Falwell's Pro-life Gospel," *Uncertain Terms: Negotiating Gender in American Culture* ed. Faye Ginsburg and Anna Lowenhaupt Tsing (Boston: Beacon, 1990), 76–97.

39. Cited in Joey O'Connor, "Eating Disorders: Starving for Attention," in *Hot Buttons II,* ed. Annette Parrish (Ventura, CA: Regal Books, 1987), 102. In this passage, Paul condemns fornication with prostitutes. O'Connor uses the passage to discourage eating disorders.

40. Federally funded abstinence programs share this point of view. "The law requires that programs that receive abstinence grants discuss contraception only in terms of its flaws." Lerner, "Abstinence Scofflaws."

41. *Breakaway,* June 1995, back cover.

42. Laura Kipnis, "(Male) Desire and (Female) Disgust: Reading *Hustler,*" in *Cultural Studies,* ed. Lawrence Grossberg, Cary Nelson, and Paula Treichler (New York: Routledge, 1992), 373–391, quotation on 375–376 (emphasis in the original).

43. Kipnis, "(Male) Desire and (Female) Disgust," 379.

44. Manny Koehler, "Don't Gag at the Bench Press," *Breakaway,* March 1995, 8.

45. Edward N. McNulty, *Hazardous to Your Health: AIDS, Steroids & Eating Disorders* (Loveland, CO: Group, 1994), 27.

46. There is a historical precedent for this use of sports to curb lustful activity in boys: the muscular Christianity movement of the turn of the century. With roots in the English public schools, the idea behind muscular Christianity was that "Christian virtues, morality, manliness, and patriotism can be engendered through physical activity, recreation, and sports." James A. Mathisen, "I'm Majoring in Sport Ministry: Religion and Sport in Christian Colleges," *Christianity Today,* May–June 1998, 24–28, quotation on 24. Muscular Christianity came to the U.S. in the 1860s, where it flowered in private high schools before being recognized by the YMCA as a way to evangelize to lower-class urban youth. Evangelist Dwight L. Moody should probably receive the greatest credit, however, for popularizing muscular Christianity in the 1880s. The movement had died out by the 1920s. For a contemporary example of the use of sports to evangelize, see Sharon Mazer, "The Power Team: Muscular Christianity and the Spectacle of Conversion," *Drama Review* 38, no. 4 (winter 1994): 162–188.

47. Shellenberger *Guys and a Whole Lot More* 156.

48. On Christian tattooing, see Lori Jensen, Richard W. Flory, and Donald E. Miller, "Marked for Jesus: Sacred Tattooing among Evangelical GenXers," in Flory and Miller, *GenX Religion*, 15–30.

49. Mab Graff Hoover, *God Even Likes My Pantry: Meditations for Munchers* (Grand Rapids, MI: Zondervan, 1983), 95.

50. Griffith, *Born Again Bodies*.

51. Shellenberger and Johnson, *258 Great Dates While You Wait*, 83.

52. *Breakaway,* June 1995, back cover.

53. Andy Fletcher, "More Thanksgiving Maggot, Anyone?" *Breakaway,* November 1995, 22–23. This article marvels at "repulsive" non-American food traditions (fried scorpions, monkey brains), an insect dinner hosted by the New York Entomological society, and a World War II menu from a Paris restaurant that offered kabobs of dog's liver with herbed butter and cats garnished with rats.

54. Focus on the Family, *Eating Disorders,* narrated by Jackie Barrille, 1982.

55. Cherry Boone O'Neill, *Starving for Attention: A Young Woman's Struggle and Triumph over Anorexia Nervosa* (Minneapolis: CompCare, 1991), 5.

56. Michelle M. Lelwica, "Losing Their Way to Salvation: Women, Weight Loss, and the Salvation Myth of Culture Lite," in Forbes and Mahan, *Religion and Popular Culture in America,* 180–200, quotation on 181.

57. Lelwica, "Losing Their Way to Salvation," 195.

58. Joan Jacobs Brumberg, *Fasting Girls: The Emergence of Anorexia Nervosa as a Modern Disease* (Cambridge: Harvard University Press, 1988), 46.

59. Medieval religious fasters engaged in a number of practices that definitively distance them from modern sufferers from eating disorders: "Angela of Fogligno, for example, who drank pus from sores and ate scabs and lice from the bodies of the sick, spoke of the pus as being 'as sweet as the Eucharist.' . . . The bodies of women were also a source of food: mystical women exuded oil from their fingertips, lactated even though they were virgins, and cured disease with the touch of their saliva." Brumberg, *Fasting Girls,* 45.

60. Brumberg, *Fasting Girls,* 7 (emphasis added).

61. Ammerman, *Bible Believers,* 184. Ammerman notes that the General Social Survey—the source of her data—defines "sectarian" in a way that is "less-than-ideal." In the survey, "groups are categorized as 'sects' based on their small membership and deviance from the American norm, but this category may include everything from Jehovah's Witnesses to the Unification Church" (30).

62. Ammerman, *Bible Believers,* 186.

63. Richard W. Flory, "Conclusion: Toward a Theory of GenerationX Religion," in Flory and Miller, *GenX Religion,* 239.

CHAPTER FOUR

1. Interview with Rev. Dr. Mona West, 22 June 1998.

2. Founded in 1976, Exodus is the world's largest evangelical ex-gay ministry. The group has expanded to seventeen countries outside of North America. See http://www .exodus-international.org.

3. See Janet E. Halley, "The Construction of Heterosexuality," in *Fear of a Queer Planet,* ed. Michael Warner (Minneapolis: Minnesota University Press, 1993), 82–102.

4. Throughout I have avoided the term "fundamentalist,' which many conservative evangelicals see as an insult and which, further, is technically a word that is best used to describe separtist born-agains, not politically and/or culturally engaged born-agains. Throughout this chapter, though, Cathedral of Hope congregants generally refer to con-

servative evangelicals as "fundamentalists" or as the "Christian Right." I thus echo their language to reflect their point of view.

5. In addition to 3,200 local members, in 2003 the Cathedral also had one thousand national members. National members live beyond north Texas and do not attend services.

6. Interview with Lisa Carver, 24 June 1998.

7. Rev. Troy D. Perry with Thomas L. P. Swicegood, *Don't Be Afraid Anymore* (New York: St. Martin's, 1990), 307.

8. Interview with Rev. Michael Piazza, 23 June 1998.

9. Ibid.

10. Of course, this sentiment is not unique to the U.S. South. See Laurie Schulze and Frances Guilfoyle, "Facts Don't Hate; They Just Are," in Kintz and Lesage, *Media, Culture, and the Religious Right,* 337.

11. West interview.

12. For example, Richard Elliott Friedman, *Who Wrote the Bible?* (New York: Harper-Collins, 1997).

13. Piazza interview (emphasis in the original).

14. "Bible-believing" is sometimes used synonymously with "saved" or "born-again." Some people whom the "unsaved" would label "fundamentalist" prefer the less politically charged and more spiritually evocative "Bible-believing." See Ammerman, *Bible Believers.* I use the phrase here because it serves as a nice conceptual bridge across fundamentalism to postfundamentalism. Belief in the Bible *changes* as one crosses this bridge, but it does not go away.

15. Piazza interview (emphasis in the original).

16. Robyn R. Warhol and Helena Michie, "Twelve-Step Teleology: Narratives of Recovery / Recovery as Narrative," in *Getting a Life: Everyday Uses of Autobiography,* ed. Sidonie Smith and Julia Watson (Minneapolis: University of Minnesota Press, 1996), 328. Warhol and Michie's analysis of the conventions of Alcoholic's Anonymous codes for self-narration is surprisingly helpful for understanding the formulaic nature of evangelical witnessing. Being born again, like "living sober," "means continuously telling, retelling, hearing, and revising the story of recovery [rebirth], a recovery [rebirth] that can exist only in and through the power of narrative," 349.

17. Piazza interview (emphasis in the original).

18. Ibid.

19. Balmer, *Mine Eyes,* 117.

20. Balmer, *Mine Eyes,* 8.

21. Piazza interview.

22. Quoted in Peter Sweasey, *From Queer to Eternity: Spirituality in the Lives of Lesbian, Gay and Bisexual People* (Washington: Cassell, 1997), 9.

23. Rev. Michael S. Piazza, *Holy Homosexuals* (Dallas: Sources of Hope, 1997), 35.

24. Interview with John Wimberly, 20 June 1998.

25. Piazza, *Holy Homosexuals* 30–31.

26. Piazza, *Holy Homosexuals* 31. This Biblical interpretive strategy, obviously, offers little to observant gay and lesbian Jews. On gay and lesbian Jews, see *Trembling before God,* film, dir. Sandi Dubowski, 2001.

27. Ibid.

28. Piazza interview.

29. Tom Horner, *Jonathan Loved David* (Philadelphia: Westminster, 1978).

30. In *The Living Bible*'s restrained translation, Jonathan does not fall to the ground, and "they sadly shook hands, tears running down their cheeks."

31. Mona West, "The Book of Ruth: An Example of Procreative Strategies for Queers," in *Our Families, Our Values: Snapshots of Queer Kinship*, ed. Robert E. Goss and Amy Adams Squire Strongheart (New York: Harrington Park, 1997), 53.

32. Ibid.

33. See Nancy Wilson, *Our Tribe: Queer Folks, God, Jesus, and the Bible* (San Francisco: Harper, 1995).

34. This eventually became such a problem that the Roman Catholic Church decided to excommunicate self-castrators. See Victoria S. Kolakowski, "The Concubine and the Eunuch: Queering up the Breeder's Bible," in *Our Families, Our Values*, 43. Although the book says little about eunuchs per se, Uta Ranke-Heinemann, *Eunuchs for the Kingdom of Heaven* (New York: Doubleday, 1990) offers an in-depth investigation of Roman Catholic regulation of the minutiae of sexuality.

35. See John J. McNeill, *The Church and the Homosexual*, 4th ed. (Boston: Beacon Press, 1993), 65.

36. Kolakowski, "The Concubine and the Eunuch," 44–45.

37. Kolakowski, "The Concubine and the Eunuch," 49.

38. Interview with Marty Ruggles, 25 June 1998.

39. Lott said homosexuality should be treated like alcoholism, sex addiction, and kleptomania. Armey had received previous notoriety for referring to gay House representative Barney Frank (D-Mass) as "Barney Fag." Lott and Armey's 1998 comments came only a few weeks after James Dobson had made a pilgrimage to Washington to scold Republicans for not being more active in pursuing a conservative social agenda. See Michael Piazza, "Politics Prod Lott, Armey to Bash Gays," *Dallas Morning News*, 16 June 1998, sec. A, 11; and Vikas Bajaj, "Lott, Armey Not Likely to Accept Invitations from Gay Church," *Dallas Morning News*, 20 June 1998, sec. A, 33.

40. Carver interview.

41. Piazza interview (emphasis in the original).

42. Public access gives U.S. citizens access to one or more cable channels (as well as studio space and equipment) set aside for this purpose by the terms of the contract negotiated between the city and the local cable franchise. Public access programs are generally understood to be local and noncommercial. There is great stylistic variation among programs, with some shows embracing a cheap aesthetic and others mimicking the slick conventions of national television.

43. Interview with Paul Taylor, 24 June 1998. Taylor is the director of COH-TV.

44. As Sedgwick succinctly notes in her essay on methods for "curing" gay children, "It's always open season on gay kids." "How to Bring Your Kids Up Gay," 69.

45. See Pat Califia, "Feminism, Pedophilia, and Children's Rights," in *Public Sex: The Culture of Radical Sex* (San Francisco: Cleiss, 1994), 135–147.

46. "Once We Were Not a People," lyrics by J. Thomas Sopko, 1987, in *The Hymnal Project* (San Francisco: MCC, 1989).

47. Cathedral of Hope, e-mail press release, 27 March 1999.

48. Pam Belluck, "Gay Church Sues TV Station for Rejecting an Infomercial," *New York Times*, 28 October 1998, sec. A, 16.

49. Cited in Belluck, "Gay Church Sues TV Station for Rejecting an Infomercial."

50. West interview.

51. Rev. Michael S. Piazza, *Rainbow Family Values: Relationship Skills for Lesbian and Gay Couples* (Dallas: Sources of Hope, 1995).

52. Piazza, *Rainbow Family Values*, 35.

53. On the use of children to advance adult policy goals, see Hendershot, *Saturday Morning Censors*.

54. Schulze and Guilfoyle, "Facts Don't Hate," 332.

55. Taylor interview.

56. Carver interview.

57. Taylor interview.

58. Piazza interview (emphasis in the original).

59. Sweasey, *From Queer to Eternity*, 5.

60. Pamphlet, *Shouts in the Wilderness: Leather Interest Circle of Hope* ([Dallas]: Cathedral of Hope).

CHAPTER FIVE

1. Quoted in J. W. Haas, Jr., "Irwin A. Moon, F. Alton Everest and Will H. Houghton: Early Links between the Moody Bible Institute and the American Scientific Affiliation," *Perspectives on Science and Christian Faith* 43, no. 4 (December 1991): 249–258, quotation on 251.

2. Harriet Van Horne, "Television Gets a Big Charge," *World-Telegram and Sun*, 23 July 1959, MIS archive.

3. Letter from F. Alton Everest to Jack Houston, 28 February 1964, MIS General Correspondence folder, MIS archive. It is unclear how long this arrangement continued.

4. Grady Johnson and Gordon L'Allemand, press release, "A Revolution in Religion," 1950, MIS Archive.

5. Interoffice memo, 30 July 1947, MIS Archive.

6. Marsden, *Fundamentalism and American Culture*, 36.

7. Ibid.

8. Western Union radiogram from General Douglas MacArthur, 30 December 1950, MIS Archive.

9. Letter from Yun Chi Dong to R. L. Constable, 27 May 1950, MIS Archive.

10. Cited in Haas, "Irwin A. Moon, F. Alton Everest and Will H. Houghton," 253–254.

11. Robert G. Flood and Jerry B. Jenkins, *Teaching the Word, Reaching the World* (Chicago: Moody Press, 1985), 206.

12. *Reel Reports*, no. 6 (1969).

13. Videotape no. 184, "Drama in Film Evangelism," MBI video collection [1978].

14. Ibid.

15. Letter from Jack Houston, MIS publicity manager, to S. S. McGregor, U.S. Dept. of Agriculture, 7 December 1964, MIS Archive.

16. "Preface to Sermons from Science Outlines," undated document from the late forties, MIS Archive.

17. Eric Smoodin, "Who Was the Sponsor of *Our Mr. Sun?* Frank Capra, the Television Audience, and Science in the 1950s," paper presented at Society for Cinema Studies conference, Dallas 1996, 5.

18. Quoted in Mark Silk, *Spiritual Politics: Religion and America since World War II* (New York: Simon and Schuster, 1988), 31.

19. J. Ronald Oakley, *God's Country: America in the Fifties* (New York: Dembner Books, 1986), 320.

20. William G. McLoughlin, Jr., *Billy Graham: Revivalist in a Secular Age* (New York, 1960), 22.

21. Silk, *Spiritual Politics*, 38.

22. Oakley, *God's Country*, 319.

23. Oakley, *God's Country*, 325 (emphasis in the original).

24. Stanley Rowland cited in Oakley, *God's Country*, 326.

25. Balmer notes that "today in the United States, still among the most modern and

industrialized of nations, religion both informs public discourse and, for many Americans, lies at the heart of personal identity. Gallup poll data [from 1985] are staggering: 94 percent of Americans believe in God or some supreme being, as compared with 76 percent of the British, 62 percent of the French, and 52 percent of Swedes. More than 90 percent of Americans say they pray at least once a week. In addition, 56 percent claim membership in a church or synagogue, and 40 percent say they attend church, mosque, or synagogue at least once in an average week, compared with 14 percent in Great Britain and 12 percent in France. While those numbers say nothing about the *quality* of religious life in the United States, it is clear that Americans think of themselves as religious." *Blessed Assurance*, 2 (emphasis in the original).

26. Quoted in Silk, *Spiritual Politics*, 40.

27. Silk, *Spiritual Politics*, 96, 99, 100.

28. James Gilbert, *Redeeming Culture: American Religion in an Age of Science* (Chicago: Chicago University Press, 1997), 129.

29. Gilbert, *Redeeming Culture*, 131.

30. Memo, dated "Friday the Thirteenth," MIS Archive.

31. Contrast this to Frank Capra's 1957 AT&T television program *The Strange Case of the Cosmic Rays*, which ends by praising a career in science as "a glorious opportunity to add to man's history . . . to harness these NUCLEAR fires for man's use! . . . To accept the challenge of Creation . . . and to use the gifts God gave us to explore the grandest of all frontiers . . . the Universe! For the more we know of Creation, the closer we get to the Creator." Cited in Gilbert, *Redeeming Culture*, 221.

32. Gilbert, *Redeeming Culture*, 5.

33. MIS introductory film shooting script, undated document apparently from the late forties, MIS Archive.

34. Letter from David F. Siemens, Jr., to Richard Stern, 25 May 1961, MIS Archive.

35. John Polkinghorne, a theologian who does not reject evolution, describes a contemporary version of natural theology as "theological metaphysics": "The wonderful order of the world is perceived by it [theological metaphysics] as being a reflection of the Mind of the Creator, and the universe's finely tuned aptness to the evolution of life is perceived as an expression of the Creator's fruitful intent." *Faith, Science and Understanding* (New Haven: Yale University Press, 2000), 22.

36. Michael Ruse, *Can a Darwinian Be a Christian?* (Cambridge: Cambridge University Press, 2000), 111.

37. Alan Hayward, *Creation and Evolution* (Minneapolis: Bethany House, 1995), 100 (emphasis added).

38. Richard Dawkins, *The Blind Watchmaker: Why the Evidence of Evolution Reveals a Universe without Design* (New York: W. W. Norton, 1987), 39.

39. William Paley, the theologian who first used the parable of the watch, used similar rhetorical tactics in *Natural Theology:* "There is precisely the same proof that the eye was made [designed by God] for vision, as there is that the telescope was made for assisting it." Paley cited in Dawkins, *The Blind Watchmaker*, 5. In refuting Paley, Dawkins reverses his visual metaphors: "Natural selection, the *blind*, unconscious, automatic process which Darwin discovered, and which we now know is the explanation for the existence and apparently purposeful form of all life, has no purpose in mind. It has no mind and *no mind's eye*" (5, emphasis added).

40. Letter from Edith Dallin to "Mr. Wyrtzen," 10 February 1946, MIS Archive.

41. F. Alton Everest, "Moody Institute of Science Educational Film Program," presentation to the American Scientific Affiliation Convention, 24–26 August 1954, MIS Archive.

42. Everest, "Moody Institute of Science Educational Film Program."

43. Memo from F. Alton Everest to Milton Regier, promotion department, Moody Bible Institute, 25 November 1957, MIS Archive.

44. Everest, "Moody Institute of Science Educational Film Program."

45. Paul W. Schwepker, distribution department report, 1956, MIS Archive.

46. Gilbert, *Redeeming Culture,* 142–143.

47. Carin Morhead, "Moody Institute of Science: Historical Time Line—1907–1994," 1994, MIS Archive.

48. Gilbert, *Redeeming Culture,* 5.

49. Gilbert, *Redeeming Culture,* 7 (emphasis added).

50. Gilbert, *Redeeming Culture,* 131.

51. To this day, the Sermons from Science programs continue to be presented at schools, civic centers, and military bases. In 1990, Sermons from Science presented 26 programs attended by 54,227 people. Between 1949 and 1990, Sermons from Science performed 399 programs on military bases and 576 programs before civilian audiences. *Sermons from Science News* 2, no. 2 (fall 1991). In 2000, the Moody Bible Institute ended its sponsorship of Sermons from Science, and the program was relocated to Whittier Christian schools in California.

52. Air Force Regulation no. 35–31, MIS Archive.

53. Ibid.

54. Gilbert, *Redeeming Culture,* 105.

55. Report to Robert Constable from Wayne A. Hebert, September 22, 1949, MIS Archive.

56. Report to Constable. The films had at least one fan in state government; South Carolina governor Strom Thurmond wrote in an appreciative letter that "each of these pictures is worth while and emphasizes to me the wonders of creation and man's dependence on God." Strom Thurmond to Dr. H. H. Newell, August 9, 1949, MIS Archive.

57. "Film Showings (January 1947 through October 1948)," MIS Archive. This document also notes church screenings and conversions for the same period. Not surprisingly, conversion rates in churches were higher. Of 1.5 million viewers, there were 3,347 conversions reported.

58. Moody Institute of Science introductory film shooting script, undated, 4–5, MIS Archive.

59. Diamond, *Spiritual Warfare,* 2–3.

60. See Tona J. Hangen, *Redeeming the Dial: Radio, Religion, and Popular Culture in America* (Chapel Hill: University of North Carolina Press, 2002).

61. Chairman Robert C. Hendrickson, cited in Lynn Spigel, *Make Room for TV: Television and the Family Ideal in Postwar America* (Chicago: Chicago University Press, 1992), 55. Democratic senator Estes Kefauver led the Senate Subcommittee on Juvenile Delinquency in 1955–56. The hearings "elicited from network witnesses both promises of increased sensitivity to 'responsible' programming and disclaimers of social scientific proof of any deleterious social effects of violent television programs." William Boddy, "Senator Dodd Goes to Hollywood: Investigating Video Violence," in *The Revolution Wasn't Televised: Sixties Television and Social Conflict,* ed. Lynn Spigel and Michael Curtin (New York: Routledge, 1997), 161–83, quotation on 163–64.

62. Letter dated 17 November 1955, MIS Archive (emphasis added).

63. *Chicago Daily Tribune,* clipping, 21 June 1956, MIS Archive.

64. "Minneapolis Appeal," 31 December 1955, MIS Archive.

65. Letter from Irwin Moon to John Raymond, 1 January 1956, MIS Archive.

66. Cited in John Raymond, television report, 10 November 1956, MIS Archive (emphasis in the original).

67. Cited in "Promotion Dept. Analysis TV Test," 1 February 1956, MIS Archive.

68. Cited in Raymond, television report.

69. Raymond, television report.

70. See Jeffrey K. Hadden, "Religious Broadcasting and the Mobilization of the New Christian Right," in *Fundamentalism and Evangelicalism*, ed. Martin E. Marty (Munich and New York: K. G. Saur, 1993), 310–311.

71. Wuthnow, *The Restructuring of American Religion*, 5.

72. Moody Institute of Science annual report, 1979, MIS Archive.

73. Moody Institute of Science annual report, 1968, MIS Archive (emphasis in the original).

74. Ibid.

75. *Reel Reports*, no. 4 (1968), MIS Archive

76. MIS films had been shown in factories before. They were shown in McDonnell Douglas plants in 1962, and as early as 1951 the Kiwanis International was urging the use of MIS films for assembly-line workers. Gilbert, *Redeeming Culture* 350, n. 26.

77. *Reel Reports*, no. 6 (1969), MIS Archive.

78. Ronald L. Numbers, *The Creationists* (New York: Alfred A. Knopf, 1992), 159.

79. Cited in Christopher P. Toumey, *God's Own Scientists: Creationists in a Secular World* (New Brunswick: Rutgers University Press, 1994), 22.

80. Haas, "Irwin A. Moon, F. Alton Everest and Will H. Houghton," 252.

81. F. A. Everest, interoffice memo in bound manuscript, "Correspondence (1939–1946) Having to Do with the Founding of MIS," October 16, 1946, MIS Archive.

82. Cited in Haas, "Irwin A. Moon, F. Alton Everest and Will H. Houghton," 252.

83. Numbers, *The Creationists*, 193.

84. Toumey, *God's Own Scientists*, 22.

85. Toumey, *God's Own Scientists*, 232–233.

86. For the women in R. Marie Griffith's study, by contrast, total surrender to God meant valuing "the heart" over "the head." One woman said, for example, that "her intelligence interfered with her spiritual growth" (*God's Daughters*, 63). Griffith notes that weeping has particular symbolic significance for members of Women's Aglow: "Weeping acts as a crucial sign of sincerity, if not its sine qua non . . . Closely associated . . . with notions of traditional femininity, tears elaborate and refine the possibilities of healing and transformation for spirit-filled women, in part by enabling them to enter more fully into a distinctively 'female' practice that makes them feel 'real'" (*God's Daughters*, 122–123).

87. The ICR has produced a video, *Origins: Creation or Evolution*, that explains both evolution and creation science in an apparently "objective" manner. Even though the courts have ruled against state equal-time laws, declaring that these laws violate the establishment principle of the First Amendment, this "balance" makes the video conceivably usable in public schools, especially in areas where school boards are dominated by Christians.

88. There is an enormous literature on creationism. The classic text is Numbers, *The Creationists*. Other useful texts include Numbers, *Darwinism Comes to America* (Cambridge: Harvard University Press, 1998); David B. Wilson, ed., *Did the Devil Make Darwin Do It? Modern Perspectives on the Creation-Evolution Controversy* (Ames: Iowa State University Press, 1996); Ashley Montagu, ed., *Science and Creationism* (Oxford: Oxford University Press, 1984); Stephen Jay Gould, *Rock of Ages: Science and Religion in the Fullness of Life* (New York: Ballantine, 1999); Niles Eldredge, *The Triumph of Evolution and the Failure of Creationism* (New York: W.H. Freeman, 2000); Raymond A. Eve and Francis B. Harrold, *The Creationist Movement in Modern America* (Boston: G.K. Hall, 1991); and Laurie R. Godfrey, ed., *Scientists Confront Creationism* (New York: W.W. Norton, 1983).

89. Emphasis in the original.

90. Emphasis in the original.

91. Toumey, *God's Own Scientists*, 263.

92. By virtue of their dogmatism and inflexiblity, many creationists seem to be out of step with the new Christian Right. The Christian Coalition, conversely, has made political inroads in large part by presenting Christians as nonextremists. See Gardiner, "Through the Looking Glass and What the Christian Right Found There," 151.

CHAPTER SIX

1. Phil Miller, "Christian Thriller Has Fans Flocking to Cinema Aisles," *Scotsman*, 27 October 1999, 11.

2. Scott Martelle and Megan Garvey, "A Film Christians Believe In," *Los Angeles Times*, 22 October 1999, sec. A, 1.

3. Paul Boyer, *When Time Shall Be No More: Prophesy Belief in Modern American Culture* (Cambridge: Harvard University Press, 1992), 5. Lindsey's book has also been translated into over fifty languages. According to Randall Balmer, the *New York Times* declared Lindsey the bestselling author of the seventies. *Blessed Assurance*, 53.

4. Boyer, *When Time Shall Be No More*, 127.

5. Michael Drosnin, *The Bible Code* (New York: Simon & Schuster, 1997).

6. Lorraine Ali, "The Glorious Rise of Christian Pop," *Newsweek*, July 16, 2001, 40.

7. David D. Kirkpatrick, "A Best-Selling Formula in Religious Thrillers," *New York Times*, 11 February 2002, sec. C, 2.

8. Kevin Sack, "Apocalyptic Theology Revitalized by Attacks," *New York Times*, 23 November 2001, sec. A, 33.

9. Fierman and Flynn, "The Greatest Story Ever Sold," 61.

10. Ali, "The Glorious Rise of Christian Pop," 46.

11. For a helpful, quick summary of the mainline approach, see Bruce M. Metzger, *Breaking the Code: Understanding the Book of Revelation* (Nashville: Abingdon, 1993).

12. Special advertising section, "How to Use Christian Film and Video," *Christianity Today*, 28, no. 13 (21 September 1984), 40.

13. John Dart, "Religion: Graham's Studio Ready to Issue First Films since Leaving Burbank," *Los Angeles Times*, 4 July 1992, sec. B, 4.

14. Review of *Time to Run* (Collier, 1973), Cheryle Forbes, "Film Evangelism: A Time to Change," *Christianity Today*, 17, no. 12 (16 March 1973), 17.

15. Like Moon, prophecy theologians understand their object of study as *scientific*. See, for example, John F. Walvoord, *Every Prophecy of the Bible* (Colorado Springs: Chariot Victor, 1999), 12. Boyer explains that nineteenth-century dispensationalists "insisted that their methods paralleled those of the laboratory researcher. By Baconian, inductive techniques, one searched the apocalyptic scriptures, formulated a 'hypothesis' about their meaning, then tested that hypothesis by examining history past and present" (294). See also George Marsden, "Evangelicals, History, and Modernity," in *Evangelicalism in Modern America*, ed. George Marsden (Grand Rapids, MI: Eerdman's Publishing Co., 1984). James H. Moorhead argues in *World without End: Mainstream American Protestant Visions of the Last Things, 1880–1925* (Bloomington: Indiana University Press, 1999) that Protestants have not always agreed about the scientificity of premillenial apocalyptic belief.

16. Collier cited in Mel White, "Does Christian Film Work in the Neighborhood Theater?" *Christianity Today*, 27, no. 15 (7 October 1983), 20.

17. Balmer, *Mine Eyes*, 61.

18. Balmer, *Mine Eyes*, 61–62.

19. Some evangelicals, for example, don't believe in the Rapture, and there are major differences between "premillenialists" and "postmillenialists." For more historical insights on these issues, see George M. Marsden's classic, *Fundamentalism and American Culture*, as well as Moorhead, *World without End;* and Boyer, *When Time Shall Be No More.*

20. See Steven Isaac, review of *Left Behind: The Movie,* at http://www.family.org/pplace/pi/films/A0013507.htm.

21. Andrew Hicks, "Yet Another Year in the Life of a Nerd," March 13, 1997. At http://students.missouri.edu/~ahicks/year3/mar1397.htm.

22. Ibid.

23. Balmer, *Mine Eyes,* 64.

24. Balmer, *Mine Eyes,* 62.

25. Adam Davidson, "The Mean Spirit," *Feed* (8 April 1999); www.feedmag.com/deepread/dr200.shtml (accessed 29 April 2001).

26. Tim LaHaye and Jerry B. Jenkins, *Left Behind* (Wheaton, IL: Tyndale House, 1995), 243.

27. LaHaye and Jenkins, *Left Behind,* 252. Shortly after his negative words for Reagan, Carpathia's speech turns hopeful when he says, "with the end of the Cold War in the 1990s, however, your next president, Mr. Bush, recognized what he called the 'new world order,' which resonated deep within my young heart" (252).

28. Tim LaHaye and Beverly LaHaye, *The Act of Marriage: The Beauty of Sexual Love* (Grand Rapids, MI: Zondervan, 1998).

29. Herman, *The Antigay Agenda,* 187. Like many politically involved evangelicals, LaHaye is an ardent Zionist. Evangelical politicians and activists believe the continued existence of the modern Israeli state is necessary for the fulfillment of Biblical prophecy. As Jerry Falwell has said, "Theologically, any Christian has to support Israel, simply because Jesus said to," cited in Boyer, *When Time Shall Be No More,* 203. Boyer reports that "Tim LaHaye in 1984, illustrating his point that 'the Jews today occupy only a small portion of what God intended for them to enjoy,' superimposed 'God's Original Land Grant to Israel' on a map of the modern Middle East; it showed Israel absorbing all of Lebanon, part of Saudi Arabia, and most of Jordan, Syria, and Iraq" (195).

30. Tim LaHaye, *What Everyone Should Know about Homosexuality* (Wheaton, IL: Tyndale House, 1978). Beverly LaHaye has written a pamphlet published by Concerned Women for America entitled *The Hidden Homosexual Agenda* (1991).

31. Tim LaHaye, *Battle for the Mind* (Old Tappan, NJ: Fleming H. Revell, 1980).

32. Advertisement in Crossings Christian book club mailing for *Mind Siege,* spring 2001 (emphasis in the original).

33. Tim LaHaye, *The Beginning of the End* (Wheaton, IL: Tyndale House, 1972, 9) cited in Boyer, *When Time Shall Be No More,* 315.

34. Pat Robertson, *The New World Order* (Dallas: Word Publishing, 1991).

35. Robertson does not believe in the Rapture and leaves it out of both *The New World Order* and also his prophesy novel, *The End of the Age* (Dallas: Word Publishing, 1995). Robertson's novel includes the explicit religious language that is censored from *The New World Order.*

36. For further explanation of prophecy's political applications, see Kathleen M. Lee, "Waiting for the Rapture: The New Christian Right and Its Impact on U.S. Public Policy," *Humboldt Journal of Social Relations* 16, no. 2 (1991): 65–91.

37. Boyer, *When Time Shall Be No More,* xi.

38. Joe Queenan, "New World Order Nut," *Wall Street Journal,* 31 December 1991, sec. A, 5.

39. In 2002, Lalonde released *Left Behind II: Tribulation Force* on DVD and VHS. Peter

collaborates with his brother Paul as producer and writer on all of the Cloud Ten films. Peter Lalonde is the Cloud Ten spokesman and portrays himself as the primary creative force.

40. Boyer, *When Time Shall Be No More,* 129.

41. "'The Crescendo of peace rhetoric' in the world," wrote Jack Van Impe, "'is but a sign of end-time destruction, the harbinger of history's bloodiest hour.'" Boyer, *When Time Shall Be No More,* 176.

42. Cited in Boyer, *When Time Shall Be No More,* 326.

43. Jakes is an African American televangelist who, unlike Hagee and Van Impe, does not focus on prophecy in his sermons. Jakes is the author of numerous popular Christian self-help books, including *Woman, Thou Art Loosed* (Tulsa: Albury Publishing, 1995), *Lay Aside the Weight: Take Control of It before It Takes Control of You* (Tulsa: Albury Publishing, 1997), and *Maximize the Moment: God's Action Plan for Your Life* (New York: G. P. Putnam's Sons, 1999).

44. LaHaye and Jenkins, *Left Behind,* 194.

45. LaHaye and Jenkins, *Left Behind,* 214.

46. LaHaye and Jenkins, *Left Behind,* 216.

47. This is an interesting inversion. Usually small independent films with a limited market open only in a few select big cities such as New York, Chicago, and Los Angeles. But these cities are not where the most evangelicals are, so *Omega Code* opened in the Southern and Midwestern cities that are usually *least* likely to screen independent films.

48. Martelle and Garvey, "A Film Christians Believe In."

49. David Germain, "Church Moves into Mega-Plex," *Ottawa Citizen,* 21 October 1999, sec. A, 16.

50. Richard Vara, "Box Office Bonanza: Unorthodox Marketing Promotes Movie," *Houston Chronicle,* 23 October 1999, religion sec., 1.

51. Ali, "The Glorious Rise of Christian Pop," 47.

52. On the difficulty of breaking even with small-budget independent films, see James Schamus, "To the Rear of the Back End: The Economics of Independent Cinema," in *Contemporary Hollywood Cinema,* ed. Steve Neale and Murray Smith (New York: Routledge, 1998).

53. The film opened weakly but ended up grossing $20 million, drawing mostly Christian audiences in middle America. Martelle and Garvey, "A Film Christians Believe In."

54. Martelle and Garvey, "A Film Christians Believe In."

55. Scott Collins, "TBN Turns to Film to Spread Faith," *Los Angeles Times,* 16 September 1999, sec. C, 1.

56. Vara, "Box Office Bonanza."

57. "God's Big Break," *Guardian,* 19 October 1999, 17. Crouch also says: "I see these megaplex theaters filled up on weekends. For young people, it's the place to be, and the church parking lots are empty . . . Why not utilize the influence of these huge theaters? I think they're the new street corner churches of the new millennium." Germain, "Church Moves into Mega-Plex."

58. Rick Lyman, "A Sleeper Movie Awakened by a Hungry Audience," *New York Times,* 25 October 1999, sec. E, 1.

59. Michael H. Kleinschrodt, "Anti-Catholic Heavy Hand Breaks Code," *Times-Picayune,* 28 October 1999, sec. E, 9.

60. Lyman, "A Sleeper Movie Awakened by a Hungry Audience."

61. Germain, "Church Moves into Mega-Plex." Providence was founded in 1998 by Norm Miller, chairman of Interstate Battery System of America, in Dallas, Texas. Martelle and Garvey, "A Film Christians Believe In."

62. Germain, "Church Moves into Mega-Plex."

63. Vara, "Box Office Bonanza."

64. HollywoodJesus was begun in 1998 by evangelical David Bruce, shortly after he heard Billy Graham at a 1997 crusade, where he challenged Christians "to use the Internet for good." Matt Donnelly, "The Movie Missionary: David Bruce Uses Film Reviews to Introduce Web Surgers to Jesus," *Christianity Today*, 43, no. 13 (15 November 1999), 92. The site has registered millions of hits and seems to be considered a reputable place to listen and share Christian responses to films. Although all viewers appear to identify as Christians, not all are necessarily evangelical. However, *Omega Code* and *Left Behind* were known to be evangelical films, and most responses were from viewers familiar with prophetic eschatology.

65. See message dated 18 December 1999 by Violet, in review of *Omega Code*, at HollywoodJesus.com.

66. See http://www.hollywoodjesus.com/, *Omega Code* link, Dorene E., message dated 1 November 1999.

67. *Christianity Today* 28, no. 13 (21 September 1984), 46.

68. Ibid.

69. Ibid.

70. Cheryl Forbes, "The Refiner's Fire: Hiding in Harmony," *Christianity Today*, 19, no, 21 (18 July 1975), 14–15.

71. *The Making of Left Behind*, video (her emphasis).

72. Bob Longino, "'Left Behind' Puts Video Ahead; Unusual Move: Film Based on Revelation Will Go to Homes Three Months before Being Released in Theaters," *Atlanta Journal and Constitution*, 31 October 2000, sec. D, 1.

73. Jay Stone, "Christian Video Hit Comes to Theatres: Canadian Film Is Science Fiction Based on Bible," *Ottawa Citizen*, sec. E, 1.

74. Ali, "The Glorious Rise of Christian Pop," 47.

75. See http://www.hollywoodjesus.com/left_behind.htm, comments link, Phil Newman Franklin, message dated 7 February 2001.

76. See http://www.hollywoodjesus.com/left_behind.htm, comments link, Gary Stokes, message dated 2 February 2001.

77. Specifically, you have to say the "Sinner's Prayer." "The prayer is usually formulaic and generally consists of the following elements: confession of sin, recognizing one's need for salvation, acknowledging Jesus as savior, and a profession of one's determination to live a holy life." Balmer, *Encyclopedia of Evangelicalism* (Louisville: Westminster John Knox Press, 2002), 529.

78. See http://www.hollywoodjesus.com/left_behind.htm, comments link, James Whisler, message dated 26 November 2000.

79. See http://www.hollywoodjesus.com/left_behind.htm, comments link, Tanya, message dated 2 February 2001.

80. Justin Wyatt, *High Concept: Movies and Marketing in Hollywood* (Austin: University of Texas Press, 1994).

81. Wyatt, *High Concept*, 112.

82. Video, *The Making of Left Behind*.

83. Chuck Kleinhans, "Independent Features: Hopes and Dreams," in *The New American Cinema*, ed. Jon Lewis (Durham: Duke University Press, 1998), 307–27, quotation on 320.

84. Kleinhans, 322 (emphasis in the original).

85. See http://www.hollywoodjesus.com/left_behind.htm, comments link, Daniel Miramar, message dated 11 February 2001.

CONCLUSION

1. Ann Burlein, *Lift High the Cross: Where White Supremacy and the Christian Right Converge* (Durham: Duke University Press, 2002).

2. David D. Kirkpatrick, "Shaping Cultural Tastes at Big Retail Chains," *New York Times*, May 18, 2003: 1, 31.

3. Ibid.

4. Jensen and Flynn, 46.

5. Martha Sawyer Allen, "Entertaining Salvation: The Billy Graham Evangelistic Association Doesn't Just Preach Anymore," *Star Tribune* [Minneapolis], 2 June 2001, sec. B, 7.

6. Cited in Allen, "Entertaining Salvation."

7. Ibid.

8. Ibid.

BIBLIOGRAPHY

Alexander-Moegerle, Gil. *James Dobson's War on America*. Amherst, New York: Prometheus Books, 1997.

Ali, Lorraine. "The Glorious Rise of Christian Pop." *Newsweek*, 16 July 2001, 38–48.

Allen, Martha Sawyer. "Entertaining Salvation: The Billy Graham Evangelistic Association Doesn't Just Preach Anymore. Now It Makes You Laugh, and Promotes and Places Mainstream Family Entertainment on Television and in Theaters." *Star Tribune* [Minneapolis], 2 June 2001, sec. B, 7.

Ammerman, Nancy Tatom. *Bible Believers: Fundamentalists in the Modern World*. New Brunswick: Rutgers University Press, 1993.

Apostolidis, Paul. *Stations of the Cross: Adorno and Christian Right Radio*. Durham: Duke University Press, 2000.

Armstrong, Ben. *The Electric Church*. Nashville: Thomas Nelson Publishers, 1979.

Ashdown, Simon. "Christian Kidvid Converts More Consumers." *Kidscreen*, 1 July 2001, 36.

Bajaj, Vikas. "Lott, Armey Not Likely to Accept Invitations from Gay Church." *Dallas Morning News*, 20 June 1998, sec. A, 33.

Balmer, Randall. *Blessed Assurance: A History of Evangelicalism in America*. Boston: Beacon Press, 1999.

———. *Encyclopedia of Evangelicalism*. Louisville: Westminster John Knox Press, 2002.

———. *Grant Us Courage: Travels along the Mainline of American Protestantism*. New York: Oxford, 1996.

———. *Mine Eyes Have Seen the Glory: A Journey into the Evangelical Subculture in America*. New York: Oxford University Press, 1993.

Bellah, Robert N. *Beyond Belief: Essays on Religion in a Post-Traditional World*. New York: Harper & Row, 1970.

Bellah, Robert N., Richard Madsen, William M. Sullivan, Ann Swidler, and Steven M. Tipton. *Habits of the Heart: Individualism and Commitment in American Life*. Berkeley: University of California Press, 1985.

Belluck, Pam. "Gay Church Sues TV Station for Rejecting an Infomercial." *New York Times*, 28 October 1998, sec. A, 16.

Bennett, David H. *The Party of Fear: The American Far Right from Nativism to the Militia Movement*. Rev. ed. New York: Vintage, 1995.

Berger, Peter. *The Sacred Canopy*. Garden City, NY: Doubleday, 1967.

Berger, Peter L., Brigitte Berger, and Hansfried Kellner. *The Homeless Mind: Modernization and Consciousness*. New York: Vintage Books, 1973.

Berke, Richard L. "The 1994 Election: The Voters; Religious-Right Candidates Gain as G.O.P. Turnout Rises." *New York Times*, 12 November 1994, sec. 1, 10.

239

Berlet, Chip. *Eyes Right! Challenging the Right Wing Backlash*. Boston: South End Press, 1995.

Boddy, William. "Senator Dodd Goes to Hollywood: Investigating Video Violence." In *The Revolution Wasn't Televised: Sixties Television and Social Conflict*, edited by Lynn Spigel and Michael Curtin, 161–83. New York: Routledge, 1997.

Bond, Katherine G. "Abstinence Education: How Parents Are Making It Happen." *Focus on the Family*, September 1998, 12–13.

Boone O'Neill, Cherry. *Starving for Attention: A Young Woman's Struggle and Triumph over Anorexia Nervosa*. Minneapolis: CompCare, 1991.

Booth, Wayne C. "The Rhetoric of Fundamentalist Conversion Narratives." In *Fundamentalisms Comprehended*, edited by Martin E. Marty and R. Scott Appleby, 367–395. Chicago: University of Chicago Press, 1995.

Boyer, Paul. *When Time Shall Be No More: Prophesy Belief in Modern American Culture*. Cambridge: Harvard University Press, 1992.

Brasher, Brenda E. "Promise Keepers." In *Encyclopedia of Fundamentalism*, edited by Brenda E. Brasher, 392–393. New York: Routledge, 2001.

Bruce, Steve. *Pray TV: Televangelism in America*. New York: Routledge, 1990.

Brumberg, Joan Jacobs. *Fasting Girls: The Emergence of Anorexia Nervosa as a Modern Disease*. Cambridge: Harvard University Press, 1988.

Burlein, Ann. *Lift High the Cross: Where White Supremacy and the Christian Right Converge*. Durham: Duke University Press, 2002.

Califia, Pat. *Public Sex: The Culture of Radical Sex*. San Francisco: Cleiss, 1994.

Carpenter, Joel. *Revive Us Again: The Reawakening of American Fundamentalism*. New York: Oxford University Press, 1997.

Certeau, Michel de. *The Practice of Everyday Life*. Trans. Steven Rendell. Berkeley: University of California Press, 1988.

Clark, Jeramy. *I Gave Dating a Chance: A Biblical Perspective to Balance the Extremes*. Colorado Springs: WaterBrook Press, 2000.

Collins, Scott. "TBN Turns to Film to Spread Faith." *Los Angeles Times*, 16 September 1999, sec. C, 1.

Dart, John. "Religion: Graham's Studio Ready to Issue First Films since Leaving Burbank." *Los Angeles Times*, 4 July 1992, sec. B, 4.

Davidson, Adam. "The Mean Spirit." *Feed*, 8 April 1999, www.feedmag.com/deepread/dr200.shtml.

Dawidoff, Nicholas. "No Sex. No Drugs. But Rock 'n' Roll (Kind of)." *New York Times Magazine*, 5 February 1995, 68.

Dawkins, Richard. *The Blind Watchmaker: Why the Evidence of Evolution Reveals a Universe without Design*. New York: W. W. Norton, 1987.

"Dear Susie." *Brio*, April 1995, 5–6.

Diamond, Sara. *Not by Politics Alone: The Enduring Influence of the Christian Right*. New York: Guilford Press, 1998.

———. *Roads to Dominion: Right-Wing Movements and Political Power in the United States*. New York: Guilford Press, 1995.

———. *Spiritual Warfare: The Politics of the Christian Right*. Boston: South End Press, 1989.

Dobson, James C. "Dr. Dobson Answers Your Questions." *Focus on the Family*, January 1994, 5.

Donnelly, Matt. "The Movie Missionary: David Bruce Uses Film Reviews to Introduce Web Surfers to Jesus." *Christianity Today*, 43, no. 13 (15 November 1999), 92.

Drosnin, Michael. *The Bible Code*. New York: Simon & Schuster, 1997.

Dziemianowicz, Joe. "The Lord's Wares: Merchandising the Man Is Booming Business." *New York Daily News*, 5 August 2001, Lifeline sec., 13.

Eldredge, Niles. *The Triumph of Evolution and the Failure of Creationism.* New York: W. H. Freeman, 2000.

Ersoz, Meryem. "Gimme That Old-Time Religion in a Postmodern Age: Semiotics of Christian Radio." In Kintz and Lesage, 211–225.

Evans Price, Deborah. "Shake-Ups Hit Christian Labels." *Billboard,* 7 March 1999.

Eve, Raymond A., and Francis B. Harrold. *The Creationist Movement in Modern America.* Boston: Twayne Publishers, 1991.

Fierman, Daniel, and Gillian Flynn. "The Greatest Story Ever Sold." *Entertainment Weekly,* 3 December 1999, 55–64.

Fiske, John. *Television Culture.* New York: Methuen, 1987.

Fletcher, Andy. "More Thanksgiving Maggot, Anyone?" *Breakaway,* November 1995, 22–23.

Flake, Carol. *Redemptorama: Culture, Politics, and the New Evangelicalism.* Garden City, NY: Anchor Press, 1984.

Flood, Robert G., and Jerry B. Jenkins. *Teaching the Word, Reaching the World.* Chicago: Moody Press, 1985.

Flory, Richard W. "Conclusion: Toward a Theory of Generation X Religion." In *GenX Religion,* edited by Richard W. Flory and Donald E. Miller, 231–249. New York: Routledge, 2000.

Flory, Richard W., and Donald E. Miller, eds. *GenX Religion.* New York: Routledge, 2000.

Forbes, Bruce David, and Jeffrey H. Mahan, eds. *Religion and Popular Culture in America.* Berkeley: University of California Press, 2000.

Forbes, Cheryle. "Film Evangelism: A Time to Change." *Christianity Today,* 17, no. 12 (16 March 1973), 17.

———. "The Refiner's Fire: Hiding in Harmony." *Christianity Today,* 19, no. 21 (18 July 1975), 14–15.

Foucault, Michel. *The History of Sexuality, Vol. 1: An Introduction.* New York: Vintage Books, 1980.

Frankl, Razelle. *Televangelism: The Marketing of Popular Religion.* Carbondale: Southern Illinois University Press, 1987.

———. "Transformation of Televangelism: Repackaging Christian Family Values." In Kintz and Lesage, 163–189.

Friedman, Richard Elliott. *Who Wrote the Bible?* New York: HarperCollins, 1997.

Gardiner, Steven. "Through the Looking Glass and What the Christian Right Found There." In Kintz and Lesage, 141–158.

Germain, David. "Church Moves into Mega-Plex." *Ottawa Citizen,* 21 October 1999, sec. A, 16.

Gilbert, James. *Redeeming Culture: American Religion in an Age of Science.* Chicago: Chicago University Press, 1997.

Godfrey, Laurie R., ed. *Scientists Confront Creationism.* New York: W. W. Norton, 1983.

"God's Big Break." *The Guardian,* 19 October 1999, 17.

Goodstein, Laurie. "New Christian Take on the Old Dating Ritual." *New York Times,* 9 September 2001, 1, 38.

Gould, Stephen Jay. *Rock of Ages: Science and Religion in the Fullness of Life.* New York: Ballantine, 1999.

Griffith, R. Marie. *Born Again Bodies: Flesh and Spirit in American Christianity.* Berkeley: University of California Press. Forthcoming.

———. *God's Daughters: Evangelical Women and the Power of Submission.* Berkeley: University of California Press, 1997.

"Guy Talk." *Brio,* April 1995, 24.

"Guys Gab about Going Out." *Breakaway,* February 1996, 28.

Guzman, Rafer. "Praying for a Crossover Hit." *Wall Street Journal*, 7 October 1997, sec. A, 20.

Haas, J. W., Jr. "Irwin A. Moon, F. Alton Everest and Will H. Houghton: Early Links btween the Moody Bible Institute and the American Scientific Affiliation." *Perspectives on Science and Christian Faith*, 43, no. 4 (December 1991), 249–258.

Hadden, Jeffrey K. "Religious Broadcasting and the Mobilization of the New Christian Right." In *Fundamentalism and Evangelicalism*, edited by Martin E. Marty, 310–311. Munich and New York: K. G. Saur, 1993.

Hadden, Jeffrey K., and Anson Shupe. *Televangelism: Power and Politics* New York: H. Holt, 1988.

Hall, Stuart. "Encoding/Decoding." In *Culture, Media, Language*, edited by Stuart Hall, Dorothy Hobson, Andrew Lowe, and Paul Willis, 128–39. London: Hutchinson, 1980.

Halley, Janet E. "The Construction of Heterosexuality." In *Fear of a Queer Planet*, edited by Michael Warner, 82–102. Minneapolis: Minnesota University Press, 1993.

Hangen, Tona J. *Redeeming the Dial: Radio, Religion, and Popular Culture in America*. Chapel Hill: University of North Carolina Press, 2002.

Harding, Susan Friend. *The Book of Jerry Falwell: Fundamentalist Language and Politics*. Princeton: Princeton University Press, 2000.

———. "If I Should Die before I Wake: Jerry Falwell's Pro-life Gospel." In *Uncertain Terms: Negotiating Gender in American Culture*, edited by Faye Ginsburg and Anna Lowenhaupt Tsing, 76–97. Boston: Beacon, 1990.

Harrell, David Edwin. *Pat Robertson: A Personal, Religious, and Political Portrait*. San Francisco: Harper & Row, 1987.

Harris, Joshua. *I Kissed Dating Goodbye*. Sisters, OR: Multnomah, 1997.

Hayes, Michael, and Judith Hayes. "The Purity Ring." *Focus on the Family Magazine*, May 2000, 16–17.

Hayward, Alan. *Creation and Evolution*. Minneapolis: Bethany House, 1995.

Hebdige, Dick. *Subculture: The Meaning of Style*. London: Routledge, 1988.

Hendershot, Heather. "Onward Christian Solders?: A Review Essay." *Velvet Light Trap* 46 (fall 2000): 4–11.

———. "Shake, Rattle and Roll: Production and Consumption of Christian Youth Culture." *AfterImage* (February/March 1995): 19–22.

———. *Saturday Morning Censors*. Durham, NC: Duke University Press, 1998.

———. "Teletubby Trouble: How Justified Were Rev. Falwell's Attacks?" *Television Quarterly* 31, no. 1 (spring 2000), 19–25.

Herman, Didi. *The Antigay Agenda: Orthodox Vision and the Christian Right*. Chicago: University of Chicago Press, 1997.

Hexham, Irving. "The Evangelical Response to the New Age." In *Perspectives on the New Age*, edited by James R. Lewis and J. Gordon Melton, 152–163. Albany: State University of New York Press, 1992.

Hogan-Albach, Susan. "High Fidelity Faith: Contemporary Christian Music and Its Accent on Celebrity." *Sojourners Online*, 28, no. 1 (Jan.–Feb. 1999), 50–51, 53.

Hoover, Mab Graff. *God Even Likes My Pantry: Meditations for Munchers*. Grand Rapids, MI: Zondervan, 1983.

Hoover, Stewart. *Mass Media Religion: The Social Sources of the Electronic Church*. Newbury Park, Calif.: Sage, 1988.

Horner, Tom. *Jonathan Loved David: Homosexuality in Biblical Times*. Philadelphia: Westminster, 1978.

"How to Use Christian Film and Video." *Christianity Today*, 28, no. 13 (21 September 1984), 40.

Hunter, James Davison. *American Evangelicalism.* New Brunswick: Rutgers University Press, 1983.

Jakes, T. D. *Lay Aside the Weight: Take Control of It Before It Takes Control of You.* Tulsa: Albury Publishing, 1997.

———. *Maximize the Moment: God's Action Plan for Your Life.* New York: G. P. Putnam's Sons, 1999.

———. *Woman, Thou Art Loosed: Healing the Wounds of the Past.* Tulsa: Albury Publishing, 1995.

James, Allison. "Confections, Concoctions, and Conceptions." In *Popular Culture: Past and Present,* edited by B. Waites, T. Bennett, and G. Martins, 294–307. London: Croom Helm/Open University Press, 1982.

Jeffords, Susan. "The Big Switch: Hollywood Masculinity in the Nineties." In *Film Theory Goes to the Movies,* edited by Jim Collins, Hilary Radner, and Ava Preacher Collins, 196–208. New York: Routledge, 1993.

Jenkins, Henry. "'Going Bonkers!': Children, Play, and Pee-wee." *Camera Obscura* 17 (May 1988): 169–193.

———. "Out of the Closet and into the Universe." In *Science Fiction Audiences: Watching Doctor Who and Star Trek,* edited by Henry Jenkins and John Tulloch, 237–265. New York: Routledge, 1995.

———. *Textual Poachers: Television Fans and Participatory Culture.* New York: Routledge, 1992.

———. "'x Logic': Repositioning Nintendo in Children's Lives." *Quarterly Review of Film and Video* 14, no. 4 (1993): 55–70.

Jensen, Jeff, and Gillian Flynn. "The Next Temptation." *Entertainment Weekly,* 10 December 1999, 43–48.

Jensen, Lori, Richard W. Flory, and Donald E. Miller. "Marked for Jesus: Sacred Tattooing among Evangelical GenXers." In *GenX Religion,* edited by Richard W. Flory and Donald E. Miller, 15–30. New York: Routledge, 2000.

Johnson, Eithne. "The Emergence of Christian Video and the Cultivation of Videovangelism." In Kintz and Lesage, 191–210.

Johnson, Victoria E. "Welcome Home?: CBS, PAX-TV, and 'Heartland' Values in a Neo-Network Era." *Velvet Light Trap* 46 (fall 2000): 40–55.

Kauffman, L. A. "220,000 Jesus Fans Can't Be Wrong: Praise the Lord and Mammon." *Nation,* 26 September 1994, 308.

Kintz, Linda, and Julia Lesage, eds. *Media, Culture, and the Religious Right.* Minneapolis: University of Minnesota Press, 1998.

Kipnis, Laura. "(Male) Desire and (Female) Disgust: Reading *Hustler.*" In *Cultural Studies,* edited by Lawrence Grossberg, Cary Nelson, and Paula Treichler, 373–391. New York: Routledge, 1992.

Kirkpatrick, David D. "A Best-Selling Formula in Religious Thrillers." *New York Times,* 11 February 2002, sec. C, 2.

———. "Shaping Cultural Tastes at Big Retain Chains." *New York Times,* 18 May 2003, sec. A, 1, 31.

Klatch, Rebecca E. *Women of the New Right.* Philadelphia: Temple University Press, 1987.

Kleinhans, Chuck. "Independent Features: Hopes and Dreams." In *The New American Cinema,* edited by Jon Lewis, 307–327. Durham: Duke University Press, 1998.

Kleinschrodt, Michael H. "Anti-Catholic Heavy Hand Breaks Code." *Times-Picayune,* 28 October 1999, sec. E, 9.

Koehler, Manny. "Don't Gag at the Bench Press." *Breakaway,* March 1995, 8.

Kolakowski, Victoria S. "The Concubine and the Eunuch: Queering Up the Breeder's

Bible." In *Our Families, Our Values: Snapshots of Queer Kinship,* edited by Robert E. Goss and Amy Adams Squire Strongheart, 35–49. New York: Harrington Park, 1997.

LaHaye, Tim. *Battle for the Mind.* Old Tappan, NJ: Revell, 1980.

———. *The Beginning of the End.* Wheaton, IL: Tyndale House, 1972.

———. *What Everyone Should Know about Homosexuality.* Wheaton, IL: Tyndale House, 1978.

LaHaye, Tim, and Beverly LaHaye. *The Act of Marriage: The Beauty of Sexual Love.* Grand Rapids, MI: Zondervan, 1998.

LaHaye, Tim, and Jerry B. Jenkins. *Left Behind: A Novel of the Earth's Last Days.* Wheaton, IL: Tyndale House, 1995.

Lamont, Stewart. *Religion Inc.: The Church of Scientology.* London: Harrap, 1986.

Larson, Edward J. *Summer for the Gods: The Scopes Trial and America's Continuing Debate over Science and Religion.* New York: Basic Books, 1997.

Lau, Kimberly J. *New Age Capitalism: Making Money East of Eden.* Philadelphia: University of Pennsylvania Press, 2000.

Lee, Kathleen M. "Waiting for the Rapture: The New Christian Right and Its Impact on U.S. Public Policy." *Humboldt Journal of Social Relations* 16, no. 2 (1991): 65–91.

Lelwica, Michelle M. "Losing Their Way to Salvation: Women, Weight Loss, and the Salvation Myth of Culture Lite." In *Religion and Popular Culture in America,* edited by Bruce David Forbes and Jeffrey H. Mahan, 180–200. Berkeley: University of California Press, 2000.

Lerner, Sharon. "Abstinence Scofflaws." *Village Voice,* 21–27 August 2002, 64.

Lesage, Julia. "Christian Coalition Leadership Training." In Kintz and Lesage, 295–325.

Light, Alan. "About a Salary or Reality? Rap's Recurrent Conflict." *South Atlantic Quarterly* 90, no. 4 (fall 1991): 857–858.

Longino, Bob. "'Left Behind' Puts Video Ahead; Unusual Move: Film Based on Revelation Will Go to Homes Three Months before Being Released in Theaters." *Atlanta Journal and Constitution,* 31 October 2000, sec. D, 1.

Luckmann, Thomas. *The Invisible Religion: The Problem of Religion in Modern Society.* London: Macmillan, 1967.

Lyman, Rick. "A Sleeper Movie Awakened by a Hungry Audience." *New York Times,* 25 October 1999, sec. E, 1.

MacGregor, Jeff. "And the Road Runner Fosters Disrespect for Speed Limits." *New York Times,* 13 February 1999, sec. A, 19.

Marsden, George. "Evangelicals, History, and Modernity." In *Evangelicalism and Modern America,* edited by George Marsden, 94–102. Grand Rapids, MI: W. B. Eerdman's, 1984.

———. *Fundamentalism and American Culture: The Shaping of Twentieth-Century Evangelicalism, 1870–1925.* New York: Oxford University Press, 1980.

———. *Reforming Fundamentalism: Fuller Seminary and the New Evangelicalism.* Grand Rapids, MI: W. B. Eerdmans, 1987.

Martelle, Scott, and Megan Garvey. "A Film Christians Believe In." *Los Angeles Times,* 22 October 1999, sec. A, 1.

Massery, Jim. "Finding Love in All the Right Places: Fathers and Daughters Dance the Night Away." *Focus on the Family,* February 2000, 22.

Mathisen, James A. "I'm Majoring in Sport Ministry: Religion and Sport in Christian Colleges." *Christianity Today,* May–June 1998, 24–28.

Mazer, Sharon. "The Power Team: Muscular Christianity and the Spectacle of Conversion." *Drama Review* 38, no. 4 (winter 1994): 162–188.

McClary, Susan. "Same as It Ever Was: Youth Culture and Music." In *Microphone Fiends: Youth Music and Culture,* edited by Andrew Ross and Tricia Rose, 29–40. New York: Routledge, 1994.

McDannell, Colleen. *Material Christianity: Religion and Popular Culture in America*. New Haven: Yale University Press, 1995.

McLoughlin, William G. Jr. *Billy Graham: Revivalist in a Secular Age*. New York: Ronald Press Co., 1960.

McNeill, John J. *The Church and the Homosexual*. 4th ed. Boston: Beacon Press, 1993.

McNulty, Edward N. *Hazardous to Your Health: AIDS, Steroids and Eating Disorders*. Loveland, CO: Group, 1994.

Medved, Michael. *Hollywood vs. America: Popular Culture and the War on Traditional Values*. New York: HarperCollins, 1992.

Metzger, Bruce M. *Breaking the Code: Understanding the Book of Revelation*. Nashville: Abingdon, 1993.

Miller, Phil. "Christian Thriller Has Fans Flocking to Cinema Aisles." *Scotsman*, 27 October 1999, 11.

Miller, Steve. *The Contemporary Christian Music Debate: Worldly Compromise or Agent of Renewal*. Wheaton, IL: Tyndale House, 1993.

Milner, Sherry. "Bargain Media." In *Roar! The Paper Tiger Television Guide to Media Activism*, edited by Daniel Marcus, 16–18. New York: Paper Tiger Television, 1991.

Montagu, Ashley, ed. *Science and Creationism*. Oxford: Oxford University Press, 1984.

Montgomery, Kathryn. *Target: Prime Time*. New York: Oxford University Press, 1989.

Mookis, Ioannis. "Faultlines: Homophobic Innovation in *Gay Rights/Special Rights*." In Kintz and Lesage, 345–361.

Moore, R. Laurence. *Selling God: American Religion in the Marketplace of Culture*. New York: Oxford University Press, 1994.

Moorhead, James H. *World without End: Mainstream American Protestant Visions of the Last Things, 1880–1925*. Bloomington: Indiana University Press, 1999.

Morgan, David. *Visual Piety: A History and Theory of Popular Religious Images*. Berkeley: University of California Press, 1998.

Niebuhr, Gustav. "Number of Religious Broadcasters Continues to Grow." *New York Times*, 12 February 1996, sec. D, 9.

Numbers, Ronald L. *The Creationists*. New York: Alfred A. Knopf, 1992.

———. "The Creationists." In *Modern American Protestantism and Its World*, Vol. 10, edited by Martin E. Marty, 248–80 New York: K. G. Saur, 1992.

———. *Darwinism Comes to America*. Cambridge: Harvard University Press, 1998.

Oakley, J. Ronald. *God's Country: America in the Fifties*. New York: Dembner Books, 1986.

O'Connor, Joey. "Eating Disorders: Starving for Attention." In *Hot Buttons II: Insight from God's Word on Twelve Burning Issues*, compiled by Rick Bundschuh and edited by Annette Parrish Ventura, 93–105. Ventura, CA: Regal Books, 1987.

O'Donnell, Paul, with Amy Eskind. "God and the Music Biz." *Newsweek*, 30 May 1994, 62–63.

Peretti, Frank E. *This Present Darkness*. Westchester, IL: Crossway Books, 1986.

Perry, Reverend Troy D., with Thomas L. P. Swicegood. *Don't Be Afraid Anymore*. New York: St. Martin's, 1990.

Piazza, Michael S. *Holy Homosexuals*. Dallas: Sources of Hope, 1997.

———. "Politics Prod Lott, Armey to Bash Gays." *Dallas Morning News*, 16 June 1998, sec. A, 11

———. *Rainbow Family Values: Relationship Skills for Lesbian and Gay Couples*. Dallas: Sources of Hope, 1995.

Polkinghorne, John. *Faith, Science and Understanding*. New Haven: Yale University Press, 2000.

Prieto, LaDawn. "An Urban Mosaic in Shangri-La." In *GenX Religion*, edited by Richard W. Flory and Donald E. Miller, 57–73. New York: Routledge, 2000.

Queenan, Joe. "New World Order Nut." *Wall Street Journal*, 31 December 1991, sec. A, 5.

Rabey, Steve. "Of Concerts and Concerns." *Christianity Today*, 19 September 1986, 42.

Ranke-Heinemann, Uta. *Eunuchs for the Kingdom of Heaven*. New York: Doubleday, 1990.

Reed, Ralph, Jr. Introduction to *Contract with the American Family* by the Christian Coalition, ix–xiii. New York: Moorings, 1995.

Rheingold, Howard. *The Virtual Community: Homesteading on the Electronic Frontier*. Rev. ed. Cambridge: MIT Press, 2000.

Roberts, Donald F., and Peter G. Christenson. "Popular Music in Childhood and Adolescence." In *Handbook of Children and Media*, edited by Dorothy G. Singer and Jerome L. Singer, 395–413. Thousand Oaks, CA: Sage, 2001.

Robertson, Pat. *The New World Order*. Dallas: Word Publishing, 1991.

Romanowski, William D. "Contemporary Christian Music: The Business of Music Ministry." In *American Evangelicals and the Mass Media*, edited by Quentin J. Schultze. 143–169. Grand Rapids, MI: Zondervan, 1990.

———. "Evangelicals and Popular Music: The Contemporary Christian Music Industry." In *Religion and Popular Culture in America*, edited by Bruce David Forbes and Jeffrey H. Mahan, 105–24. Berkeley: University of California Press, 2000.

———. *Pop Culture Wars: Religion and the Role of Entertainment in American Life*. Downers Grove, IL: InterVarsity, 1996.

Ruse, Michael. *Can a Darwinian Be a Christian? The Relationship between Science and Religion*. Cambridge: Cambridge University Press, 2000.

Sack, Kevin. "Apocalyptic Theology Revitalized by Attacks." *New York Times*, 23 November 2001, sec. A, 33.

Schamus, James. "To the Rear of the Back End: The Economics of Independent Cinema." In *Contemporary Hollywood Cinema*, edited by Steve Neale and Murray Smith, 91–105. New York: Routledge, 1998.

Schmidt, Leigh Eric. *Consumer Rites: The Buying and Selling of American Holidays*. Princeton: Princeton University Press, 1995.

Schultze, Quentin J., ed. *American Evangelicals and the Mass Media*. Grand Rapids, MI: Zondervan, 1990.

———. "The Two Faces of Fundamentalist Higher Education." In *Fundamentalisms and Society: Reclaiming the Sciences, the Family, and Education*, edited by Martin E. Marty and R. Scott Appleby, 490–535. Chicago: University of Chicago Press, 1993.

Schulze, Laurie, and Frances Guilfoyle. "Facts Don't Hate; They Just Are." In Kintz and Lesage, 327–344.

Sedgwick, Eve Kosofsky. "How to Bring Your Kids Up Gay." In *Fear of a Queer Planet: Queer Politics and Social Theory*, edited by Michael Warner, 69–81. Minneapolis: University of Minnesota Press, 1993.

Seiter, Ellen. *Sold Separately: Parents and Children in Consumer Culture*. New Brunswick: Rutgers, 1993.

———. *Television and New Media Audiences*. New York: Oxford University Press, 1999.

"Selling Food to Children." In *The Children's Culture Reader*, edited by Henry Jenkins, 463–467. New York: New York University Press, 1998.

Shattuc, Jane M. *The Talking Cure: TV, Talk Shows and Women*. New York: Routledge, 1997.

Shellenberger, Susie. *Guys and a Whole Lot More: Advice for Teen Girls on Almost Everything*. Grand Rapids, MI: Fleming H. Revell, 1994.

———. "What Is Sexual Purity?" *Brio*, October 1995, 26.

Shellenberger, Susie, and Greg Johnson. *258 Great Dates While You Wait*. Nashville: Broadman and Holman Publishers, 1995.

Shiflett, Dave. "Lambs with Chops." *Wall Street Journal* 3 November 2000, sec. W, 18.

Silk, Mark. *Spiritual Politics: Religion and America since World War II.* New York: Simon and Schuster, 1988.

Sizer Frankiel, Sandra. *Gospel Hymns and Social Religion: The Rhetoric of Nineteenth-Century Revivalism.* Philadelphia: Temple University Press, 1978.

Smith, Christian. *American Evangelicalism: Embattled and Thriving.* Chicago: University of Chicago Press, 1998

Smithhouser, Bob. "High Voltage." *Brio,* February 1995, 30.

Smoodin, Eric. "Who Was the Sponsor of *Our Mr. Sun?* Frank Capra, the Television Audience, and Science in the 1950s." Paper presented at Society for Cinema Studies conference, Dallas, 1996.

Spigel, Lynn. *Make Room for TV: Television and the Family Ideal in Postwar America.* Chicago: Chicago University Press, 1992.

Stephens, Amy. "Trust Your Kids, Not Condoms." *Focus on the Family,* March 1998, 12–13.

Stone, Jay. "Christian Video Hit Comes to Theatres: Canadian Film Is Science Fiction Based on Bible." *Ottawa Citizen,* sec. E, 1.

Styll, John, ed. *The Best of CCM Interviews, Vol. 1: The Heart of the Matter.* Nashville: Star Song, 1991.

Svetkey, Benjamin. "Is Your TV Set Gay?" *Entertainment Weekly,* 6 October 2000, 24–28.

Sweasey, Peter. *From Queer to Eternity: Spirituality in the Lives of Lesbian, Gay and Bisexual People.* Washington: Cassell, 1997.

Teen Study Bible: New International Version, The. Grand Rapids, MI: Zondervan, 1993.

Tichi, Cecilia. "Consider the Alternative: Alt-Country Musicians Transcend Country Music Stereotypes." *Women's Review of Books* 18, no. 3 (December 2000): 14.

Toumey, Christopher P. *God's Own Scientists: Creationists in a Secular World.* New Brunswick: Rutgers University Press, 1994.

"20 Million Cassettes Later." *Focus on the Family,* March 2000, 19.

Vara, Richard. "Box Office Bonanza: Unorthodox Marketing Promotes Movie." *Houston Chronicle,* 23 October 1999, religion sec., 1.

Voskuil, Dennis N. "The Power of the Air: Evangelicals and the Rise of Religious Broadcasting." In *American Evangelicals and the Mass Media,* edited by Quentin J. Schultze, 69–95. Grand Rapids, MI: Zondervan, 1990.

Walvoord, John F. *Every Prophecy of the Bible.* Colorado Springs: Chariot Victor, 1999.

Ward, Mark. Sr. *Air of Salvation: The Story of Christian Broadcasting.* Grand Rapids, MI: Baker Books, 1994.

Warhol, Robyn R., and Helena Michie. "Twelve-Step Teleology: Narratives of Recovery/Recovery as Narrative." In *Getting a Life: Everyday Uses of Autobiography,* edited by Sidonie Smith and Julia Watson, 327–350. Minneapolis: University of Minnesota Press, 1996.

Watson, Justin. *The Christian Coalition: Dreams of Restoration, Demands for Recognition.* New York: St. Martin's, 1997.

Watt, David Harrington. *A Transforming Faith: Explorations of Twentieth-Century American Evangelicalism.* New Brunswick: Rutgers University Press, 1991.

West, Mona. "The Book of Ruth: An Example of Procreative Strategies for Queers." In *Our Families, Our Values: Snapshots of Queer Kinship,* edited by Robert E. Goss and Amy Adams Squire Strongheart, 51–60. New York: Harrington Park, 1997.

White, Mel. "Does Christian Film Work in the Neighborhood Theater?" *Christianity Today,* 27, no. 15 (7 October 1983), 14–20.

White, Mimi. *Tele-Advising: Therapeutic Discourse in American Television.* Chapel Hill: University of North Carolina Press, 1992.

Wilcox, Clyde. *Onward Christian Soldiers? The Religious Right in American Politics.* 2d ed. Boulder: Westview, 2000.

Wilson, David B., ed. *Did the Devil Make Darwin Do It? Modern Perspectives on the Creation-Evolution Controversy*. Ames: Iowa State University Press, 1996.

Wilson, Nancy. *Our Tribe: Queer Folks, God, Jesus, and the Bible*. San Francisco: Harper, 1995.

Winston, Diane. *Red-Hot and Righteous: The Urban Religion of the Salvation Army*. Cambridge: Harvard University Press, 1999.

Witten, Marsha G. *All Is Forgiven: The Secular Message in American Protestantism*. Princeton: Princeton University Press, 1993.

Wolfenstein, Martha. "Fun Morality: An Analysis of Recent American Child-Training Literature." In *The Children's Culture Reader*, edited by Henry Jenkins, 199–208. New York: New York University Press, 1998.

Wuthnow, Robert. *The Restructuring of American Religion*. Princeton: Princeton University Press, 1988.

Wuthnow, Robert, and Matthew P. Lawson. "Sources of Christian Fundamentalism in the United States." In *Accounting for Fundamentalisms: The Dynamic Character of Movements*, edited by Martin E. Marty and R. Scott Appleby, 18–56. Chicago: University of Chicago Press, 1994.

Wuthnow, Sara. "Working the ACOA Program: A Spiritual Journey." In *"I Come Away Stronger": How Small Groups Are Shaping American Religion*, edited by Robert Wuthnow, 179–204. Grand Rapids, MI: W. B. Eerdmans, 1994.

Wyatt, Justin. *High Concept: Movies and Marketing in Hollywood*. Austin: University of Texas Press, 1994.

"Yo Duffy!" *Breakaway*, February 1996, 16.